One Like Us

One Like Us

A Psychological Interpretation
of Jesus

JACK DOMINIAN

DARTON·LONGMAN+TODD

First published in 1998 by
Darton, Longman and Todd, Ltd
1 Spencer Court
140–142 Wandsworth High Street
London SW18 4JJ

ISBN 0–232–52210–3

A catalogue record for this book is available from the British Library.

Designed by Sandie Boccacci.
Phototypeset in 9/12.75 pt Cheltenham Book by Intype London Ltd.
Printed and bound in Great Britain by
Page Bros, Norwich, Norfolk.

Dedicated to the memory of the late John Todd,
with whom I often discussed this book.

Acknowledgements

I would like to thank the following:

My wife and my daughter, Elise Milne, who spent countless hours preparing the manuscript. Dr K. Wilson of the Queen's Foundation, Birmingham. Mr C. Clulow of the Tavistock Marital Studies Institute. Father J. Wijngaards of Housetops, and other friends, for many helpful suggestions.

I also want to thank SCM Press Ltd for permission to quote from *Jesus Matters* by C. J. den Heyer, trans. J. Bowden, 1996.

The Scripture quotations are from the New Jerusalem Bible Standard Edition, published by Darton, Longman & Todd and Doubleday & Co Inc. (1985).

Contents

Introduction

It was my tutor at Cambridge who reminded me that the examination would be on the text of the Gospels, and my understanding of the person of Jesus. He said that it was the commentaries which were supposed to illuminate the text of the Gospels, not the other way round. On the strength of this observation, he advised me to read the Gospels. I was grateful for his advice. In reading this book by Dr Dominian I realise that he is giving me the same advice. I am grateful to be reminded of it. This is, after all, how we will get to know Jesus.

But it is difficult not to be misled by fashionable conversation about Jesus into mere speculation about him. Who is Jesus? Can we be content to recall that he is referred to with the titles of Messiah, Saviour, Prince of Peace, Son of God? Are the debunkers right when they see him as self-deceived, naïve, immature, an ill-starred witness to an impossible future?

'Not a bit of it', says Dr Dominian. 'Jesus is a real person. He is someone we could meet and know as a human being.' Dr Dominian draws on his intimate knowledge of developmental psychology and lifetime of counselling to make his point. The personal maturity of Jesus, as developmental psychology helps us to see it in the Gospels, comes through his experience of the affection of his family and his experience of living in a world of real people. Jesus is indeed not *a* person but *the* person; the one human person in whom we can see what it is to be whole in theological and psychological terms. Moreover, because he knows God, his Father, and knows himself, Jesus is free to give himself to others in courteous love and enriching presence without fear or anxiety.

I have not read anything else which so clearly presents the humanity of Jesus, yet does so with such complete concern for his divinity. The book points to the wholeness of Jesus. It is on this that the Christian needs to focus, if he or she is to have the opportunity to be a whole human self, and know what it is to love God and enjoy him for ever.

It is perhaps a mark of our sinfulness – our incompleteness as human beings – that we are inclined to be content to be less than we might be. In a world where we tend to deny the wholeness of our humanity by assuming the affective within the intellectual, and by reducing the political to the economic, it is good to have this encouragement to come to terms with what it is to be really human, in the person of Jesus.

However, this is not another merely informative tome to which the author invites us to say, 'That's interesting'. It is clearly the author's intention to disturb our complacency and, by pointing to the human person of Jesus, to help us in our journey towards the wholeness of human life that is faith. I hope it does. Dr Dominian is a wise counsellor.

KENNETH WILSON
Director of Research, The Queen's College, Birmingham
Whitsuntide, 1998

Preface

Rᴇᴀᴅᴇʀs ᴍᴀʏ ᴀsᴋ ᴡʜʏ a psychiatrist decided to write a book on the psychology of Jesus. In this brief introduction I have tried to answer this question by means of an outline of my spiritual and professional journey.

I was born in Greece in 1929 as a cradle Catholic, my father being Roman Catholic and my mother Greek Orthodox. I went to a Roman Catholic School in Athens until I was 12 years old, then to a similar school in Bombay until I was 16, and I finished my schooling in England. I then trained as a doctor, qualifying in 1955.

During the whole of my upbringing I was nurtured in the traditional universal world of Church, which had existed for centuries in the Latin Church. Greek Orthodoxy had no impact on me.

I was accustomed to the Latin Mass, the strict discipline of the Church, aware of the need for obedience and orthodoxy. The Church was at the heart of my faith, and I believed in an unquestioning way.

In the midst of this traditional Catholicism, I had a special awareness of Jesus. In fact, in the midst of one of my childhood illnesses, I had a vision of Jesus. I am not sure of the details and I think my high tempera-ture at the time may have made me delirious. In any case, some 60 years later, I still remember the vivid vision of Jesus which made a direct impact on me. This vision has never left me and, in addition to the Church's impingement on my life, I have had a private passion for Jesus which was separate but very real. With the passage of time I became emotionally less dependent on the Church, and indeed critical of it. I believe this is partly down to personal growth, but also part of the process of maturation of the whole of Western society. This is a combination which I believe has led to an exodus from the Church as millions have outgrown their emotional dependence on it.

In my own case, I became critical of its teaching on sexuality, its hierarchical structure, which addresses its members at an infantile level, and the gap between its institutional reality and the community of love which Jesus set up.

I did not leave the Church. Instead I began a long journey of writing, particularly in the field of marriage and sexuality, which was my contribution to what I think the truth is. My professional training as a psychiatrist has helped me to a better understanding of love, and increasingly my passion for Jesus coincided with this understanding – it is these two realities that I have tried to bring together in this book.

The second Vatican council raised my hopes and I found in its teaching a renewed belief in the type of Church which I visualised. There followed the disappointment after the council, as the love of Pope John XXIII has been followed by a slowing down of the council's accomplishments. In my view, the Church has yet to put into effect the inspiration of the Spirit that moved Vatican II, but the Spirit lives with the Church and much will be accomplished in the fullness of time. In particular, we have to shift from being an institutional Church to become a community of love.

In all this personal struggle, my preoccupation with Jesus remained undiminished, and gradually my professional background gave me insights into the life of Jesus which I longed to turn into a full-length study. This book has been in preparation for over 20 years! I hesitated to tackle such a topic, but in the end I resolved to do so with the result that only the readers can judge. In particular, I hesitated because I have no formal theological training. All I know about theology I have picked up from my reading. My theology was formulated from my psychology. My psychological training started in 1958 at the Maudsley Hospital, London. The training I received was sociobiological – that is to say, mental illness was largely understood through biological and social factors.

After completing my training and becoming a psychiatrist in 1962, I practised as an adult psychiatrist and continue to do so. Shortly after qualifying, I had a personal analysis which lasted seven years. In the course of my analysis I read widely on the subject of dynamic psychology, but I did not train as a psychoanalyst. In my orientation, therefore, I remained an eclectic practitioner of psychiatry, responding to patients according to their needs with medication and/or psychotherapy.

Preface

In the course of my reading of dynamic psychology, I became familiar with the importance of childhood and the theories that illuminate the experience of acquiring love in our first intimate relationship with our parents, and then in our later intimate relationships of marriage and friendships. What I had not realised in the depth of analytical experience, I have touched in the extensive experience with therapy in personality disorders and marital problems.

In a sense, therefore, I have combined in this book a theology without formal theological training and a psychology without a formal analytical training. The result has removed orthodoxy from both, and the specialists in both will notice my limitations. But I have gained intuitive insights which have helped to illuminate Jesus, the object of my adoration.

I am therefore aware that there will be deficits, both theologically and psychologically. But I hope I have grasped the essentials of both and reconciled the two.

J. DOMINIAN
March 1998

I

A Background

1

The Historical Jesus

THE CHRISTIAN WHO ATTENDS church regularly learns from the declared word of God what Jesus said and did 2000 years ago. The man and woman in the pew, at the moment of listening, do not analyse these words in terms of scholarly criticism. The listener does not say, 'These are the words of the pre-Easter Jesus', or 'This is the interpretation of the post-Easter Christ'. They do not perplex themselves with how the words in the New Testament were developed and transformed.

Thus in December 1993, accompanied by much media attention and a major advertising campaign, a new multicoloured edition of the gospels was published. Entitled *The Five Gospels: The Search for the Authentic Words of Jesus*,[1] it was the product of a six-year study of a group of North American scholars, collectively known as the 'Jesus Seminar'. They represented well over 100 specialists, including Catholics, Protestants and others, who came together and, after studying pre-circulated papers, voted to assess the degree of scholarly consensus about the historical authenticity of each of the sayings attributed to Jesus in the New Testament, and in other early Christian documents written before the year 300. They voted in colours: red meant that it was the real Jesus; pink, it sounded like him; grey, it could have been him; and black that this was definitely not him. The seminar was aware that what Jesus said cannot actually be determined by voting – and majorities are sometimes wrong. Nevertheless, the findings represent a consensus of current opinion of experts in North America. They found that only 20 per cent of the sayings attributed to Jesus in the gospels were printed in red or pink, while the other 80 per cent were in grey or black. Thus, according to this study, most of what we hear every Sunday are not the words of Jesus.

Other studies of the New Testament reach similar conclusions, and the faith of the Christian can be shattered by a close look at the analysis of the experts. In fact, there are two worlds in contemporary Christianity. On one hand, there is the world of faith in which Jesus is seen as a whole, as a picture of the New Testament Son of God who came to live, die and rise again for the sins of humankind. He is believed as God and the truth of his divinity, apart from the attestation of the Church, goes back to the sense of wonder he elicits in the life of miracles, healing and teaching portrayed in the New Testament, culminating in the resurrection. There is, on the other hand, the work of the scholars who are studying the origins of the New Testament, the meaning of words. They come to different views about individual sayings and their significance. Although the findings of experts percolate to the wider public through homilies and commentaries, it would be true to say that there is a wide gap between the two worlds.

I mention this at the beginning of this book to show that I am aware of these two worlds, and that I have chosen deliberately the world of faith as the context in which to see the Jesus of my study. This is the Jesus who I and fellow Christians worship every Sunday, whose words I hear in the gospels, who makes an impact on me, with whom I have a relationship and who remains the basis of my faith. I say this in order to anticipate the criticism of those belonging to the other world who will read this book, who will say Jesus never said that and so the conclusions are irrelevant or wrong.

The work of the experts continues and, apart from studying the words of the New Testament, has progressed to trying to reconstruct the historical Jesus. In the words of Marcus J. Borg: 'The historical Jesus is in the news both in the scholarly world and in the much broader world of the public'.[2] The last 15 years have seen a revitalisation of the academic discipline of Jesus scholarship, especially in North America, but also in Britain.[3]

The quest for the historical Jesus went into eclipse soon after the beginning of this century. The reasons for this were twofold. Firstly it was considered theologically irrelevant. This followed Albert Schweitzer's historical analysis – a brilliant portrait of Jesus as a mistaken apocalyptic in the book *The Quest of the Historical Jesus*.[4] According to Schweitzer, Jesus believed in the imminent end of the world, which he hastened to bring about by his own death. This apocalyptic Jesus dominated thought throughout most of this century and made the historical Jesus irrelevant. Secondly, there was a strong conviction that little could be learnt about the historical Jesus. In the nineteenth century it was believed that the words of Jesus would give a clue about his message, his preaching and teaching. In 1921 this century's most influential New Testament scholar published *The History of the Synoptic Tradition*.[5] This study indicated that very little of the preaching and teaching of Jesus as reported in the gospels can be traced back to Jesus himself. This scepticism of Bultmann's form-critical work was further reinforced after World War II by redaction criticism, the study of how the evangelists modified and shaped the traditions they had received to develop them for their own times and convictions. The early Christian communities had a major say in the final formulations of the gospels. Bultmann's belief that little of what Jesus said could be traced back to him and that, in any case, the oral traditions of what Jesus said were adapted to the needs of the early Christian community, coupled with the belief that Jesus was concerned with the end of the world, dampened any enthusiasm for the historical Jesus.

Since the 1970s there has been a resuscitation of studies of the historical Jesus. In the last ten years Jesus scholars have begun to use insights from the history of religions, cultural anthropology and the social sciences. The new questions set by these sciences have provided disciplinary allies and an interdisciplinary quest for the historical Jesus has started.

These new studies of the last 20 years have shown that the old consensus – that Jesus was an eschatological prophet who proclaimed the imminent end of the world – has disappeared, although it lingers on in such a book as *The Religion of Jesus the Jew*,[6] where Professor Vermes argues that Jesus was an enthusiastic herald of the imminent kingdom of God, who did not entertain the idea of founding an organised society intended to endure for ages to come, and who died in despair. This doom-and-gloom apocalyptic interpretation has left recent historical research of Jesus. Modern scholarship has changed the word 'eschatological' from an end-of-the-world meaning to a decisive pointing to the end as entering history – but evolving history, which is the way in which Christians interpret their faith.

A second consensus that is emerging sees Jesus as a teacher, especially a teacher of subversive wisdom. Every culture has its conventional wisdom, the wisdom of what everybody knows. The Pharisees were constantly questioning Jesus about his violations of their norms; these norms – concerning the man/woman, oldest son/younger son,

Jew/Gentile, aristocrat/peasant, rich/poor, righteous/sinner – between them provide identity, status and sanctions. It is this world of conventional wisdom that Jesus subverts in his teaching, offering a much deeper penetration of the truth. In the process he was a profound source of destabilisation. He offered a world-reversal view, an invitation to see things differently.

The third feature is not a consensus but a convergence on the social world of the age. For example, purity issues – the polarity of pure and impure, clean and unclean – were part of the fundamental, political structure of Jesus' first-century social world. This pure and impure polarity correlated with other boundaries – righteous and sinner, Jew and Gentile, male and female, rich and poor – all of which play a prominent part in the gospels. Thus disputes about clean and unclean, which featured prominently as part of the controversies of Jesus and the Pharisees, were not trivial, but were concerned fundamentally with how society was to be constructed. Disagreements about purity were potentially world-shattering.

Thus modern studies locate Jesus' words and deeds rigorously within the social world of his time. M. J. Borg suggests that his mission was much more concerned with that social world.[7] This could be interpreted as saying that Jesus was merely concerned with transforming the social world of his day and says nothing of his messianic mission to be the Son of God and the saviour of the world – but this is a rapidly defensive view against modern scholarship. The Jesus of faith is the Son of God, the second person of the Trinity, but he too had to work within a context, and modern studies are focusing on his social milieu and on a person who was, *par excellence*, a subversive teacher who formed a community around him.

In his book Borg outlines five portraits by modern North American scholars describing the historical Jesus. These are E. P. Sanders' *Jesus and Judaism*,[8] Burton Mack's *A Myth of Innocence: Mark and Christian Origins*,[9] Elisabeth Schüssler Fiorenza's *In Memory of Her*,[10] Marcus J. Borg's *Conflict, Holiness and Politics in the Teachings of Jesus*,[11] Richard Horsley's *Sociology and the Jesus Movement*[12] and John Dominic Crossan's *The Historical Jesus*.[13]

Of all these books Crossan's is probably the best known. He says that the historical Jesus must be understood within his contemporary Judaism, and that this contemporary Judaism was richly creative, diverse and variegated – indeed, his book shows how complex that society was. It is not surprising that there is no popular understanding of that society and that Christianity lives its life in the Christ of faith. If studies of the historical Jesus flourish, then the future will hold a vista of placing the Jesus of faith against an accurate historical background.

Crossan suggests that the historical Jesus was a peasant, Jewish Cynic. His peasant village was close enough to a Graeco–Roman city like Sepphnis so that sight and knowledge of Cynicism was neither inexplicable nor unlikely. Jesus worked among the farms and villages of lower Galilee. His strategy, implicitly for himself and explicitly for his followers, was the combination of free healing and common eating, a religious and economic egalitarianism that negated at one and the same time the hierarchical and patriartrical normalities of Jewish religion and Roman power. Miracle and parable, healing and eating, were calculated to force individuals into immediate physical and spiritual contact with God and immediate physical and spiritual contact with one another. He announced, in other words, the boundless kingdom of God.

The present book fits loosely into the historical study of Jesus. Unlike the books described so far, it returns to the Jesus of faith, mediated by the word of God as experienced in the pew. As such, I am aware of the methodological difficulties in interpreting the New Testament as described in the next chapter. Against a background of the Christ of faith, the saviour of the world, the second person of the Trinity (with all that means to a living faith), and that of a historical Jew who was a subversive teacher working in his social milieu, challenging its norms, I try to interpret psychologically Jesus' inner world. My methodology is to use the insights of modern dynamic psychology, starting from Freud and then moving mainly to British psychologists, to interpret in their theories Jesus' childhood from the writings referring to his adult life. To do this, I use a combination of historical events found in the New Testament and an interpretation of his relationship with his Father and the community around. For this I hypothesise that, despite the different social milieu between our day and first-century Palestine, the truths that these psychological theories contain are universal, and hold for Jesus as they do for us. I explain these psychological theories in detail for, although their ideas have been in circulation for over a century, apart from Freud, the other figures are not well known outside psychological circles.

I am well aware that to use psychological theories, with their uncertainty, against the New Testament texts, with their complexity of origin (particularly the gospel of John), is a hazardous undertaking. I may fall between two stools of pleasing neither psychologists nor theologians – but this is a risk I must take. I remain convinced that Jesus, as a fully human person, had an inner psychological world, which, however difficult, remains to be explored. As Crossan says, all there is is reconstruction. For a believing Christian, both the life of the Word of God and the text of the word of God are like a graded process of historical reconstruction. If you cannot believe in something produced by reconstruction, you may have nothing left to believe in. I do not ask the reader to believe in the reconstruction of the inner world of Jesus described in this book. It is undoubtedly incomplete and defective – but I hope that, by the end of the book, a new image, a new dimension of Jesus, will appear, which will aid living faith in him as being both the Son of God and fully human.

2
The Gospels

THE NEW TESTAMENT was written as a result of the early Church finding itself in liturgy, that is in worshipping and in prayer, and as a result of the requirement to confess the faith, the need for self understanding, controversy within and without the Church, catechesis, instruction – and for other such reasons. Moule describes the gospel of Matthew as a collection of traditions by a Christian group, who may have had a definite viewpoint of their own and a definite defence to maintain against Jewish antagonists.[1] It is a manual, a catechist's book for apologetic, as much as for instruction in religion and morals. Mark's gospel also furnishes material for explanation and defence. Mark presents Jesus as a self-effacing wonder-worker, who did not want to parade his powers as a supremely exalted figure, who interpreted his exaltation in terms of service, suffering and death. Luke is probably addressed to catechumens, people on the fringe looking for instruction. The Synoptic Gospels are the story of Christians explaining what led to their existence, how they came to be. John's gospel presents an enigma. In the words of Moule: 'The fourth gospel is so complex and the circumstances of its composition so obscure that speculation is rife, but clear conclusions virtually impossible'. In this book I rely a great deal on the gospel of John for Jesus' understanding of himself, and I am inclined to look sympathetically on the views that the origin of this gospel is connected with John the apostle, who was the beloved disciple.

Scholarly study of the gospels depends on form criticism, which is essentially the study of the functions of each unit of tradition under consideration. It is generally recognised that the gospels are not biographies, in the modern sense; they were written to describe the life, words, deeds, death and resurrection of Jesus for the purpose of faith. They were the good news – and there is endless speculation about what refers to the pre-Easter Jesus and what to the post-Easter Christ. But whatever the division between the two parts, whatever the adaptations made after the resurrection, there is an essential connection between the two. It is suggested that the events, sayings and deeds of Jesus were handed down orally, built into traditions which were both oral and written, and redaction criticism, (the study of how each evangelist selected and edited his material) seeks to illuminate what we know of the final versions of the gospels. But we must take note of Moule's saying that 'The assured facts are too scanty for most guesses to be really firmly grounded'.

With this complicated exegesis, it is easy to understand how scholars came to doubt that the words we find in the gospels are the words of Jesus himself, except in a few instances. This book is not an exegesis of the gospels. I am not competent in any respect to handle this interpretation of them – but my reliance on the words of the gospel is based on two beliefs. The first is that, even though we cannot rely on these words as emanating directly from Jesus, they approximate his thoughts and intentions, and that the main facts portrayed in the gospels are accurate, particularly the events relating to his death. Secondly, these words are what the ordinary Christian receives and hears in Church, which formulate his or her vision of the Word. They form part of the living faith, the *kerygma*, and they are the nearest approximation to the life of Christ. From them and with them, I draw an interpretation of what his inner life may have been. From the reading of the Scriptures there are certain things of which I am fairly sure – namely that the key to the inner world of Jesus was his relationship with his heavenly Father, and the value from which he drew all his motivation was love. As John says, he was love (1 John 4:8). I draw my interpretation from these two beliefs and, although the importance of the Father is seen in the Synoptic Gospels, it is John who gives us the greatest insights psychologically into that relationship. Also, with my understanding of love as making a crucial contribution to Jesus' life, I look upon his personality primarily in terms of understanding how that love developed – hence the importance of his childhood, if our modern understanding of love is reliable.

In summary, therefore, I am aware that modern scholarship looks very critically at the gospels and is critical of a naïve, superficial interpretation of the reading of Scripture. But ultimately we are dependent on that reading to get the flavour of Jesus, and it is that flavour that stirs both Christian and non-Christian into a view of him – not only as a religious leader, not only as the person who started the Christian faith, but as the most compassionate, loving person who ever existed and who ultimately fuses the divine and love into a unity. He is the human reflection of God and, in so far as we are all striving to divine perfection, we can be helped by an insight into how his personality functioned. As I said in the previous chapter, this book is only possible if we combine the theories of psychology with the difficulties of inter-preting the gospels. Such a combination presents formidable problems, but it is an adventure I feel compelled to try to tackle. The shortcomings are many, but I hope something useful will be salvaged from the effort.

What I am saying in these opening chapters is that, in technical terms, my analysis will be based on the Christ of faith (Jesus as presented to us in the scriptural sources).

As a psychiatrist I take the stories of the Christ of faith with utter seriousness. And this extends to their details. I accept them at face value and analyse them as I would any revelation made to me by my patients. I do so even if I am aware that certain details may owe their origin or their form to the catechetical concerns of the early Christian communities.

My justification for this is twofold.

In the first place, as explained above, despite our modern awareness of the complex process by which the stories about the Christ of faith have been formulated and transmitted to us, I feel confident (along with the rest of the believing Christian community) that these stories present a picture of the historical Jesus that is globally correct.

Secondly, it is precisely this Christ of faith, rather than a speculative historical Jesus, who has moulded the consciousness of Christians throughout the centuries. Granted that the stories of the Christ of faith contain elements filled in through theological elaboration by the early preachers and evangelists, they still deserve detailed psychological analysis. Not unlike legendary or partly fictional characters, such as King Arthur, Robin Hood and Florence Nightingale, who can be validly analysed on account of the influence they have exerted on others. How much more does this apply to the person of the Christ of faith, whose stories have been handed down and meditated on through 2000 years with such devotion and commitment.

It is not my task as a psychiatrist to judge the accuracy or inaccuracy of the first Christian believers as reporters and historians. But, if I may venture a comment, it is refreshing to see that the collective effort of those believers concentrated on substantial priorities such as love. And the wholesome and consistent psychological picture of the Christ of faith that emerges from the gospels, as I will outline in this book, betrays a strong source as its origin. And it bears witness to a high level of perception and maturity among Jesus' early followers.

3
Psychiatry and Psychology

PSYCHIATRY IS AS OLD AS humankind and is concerned with the presence of mental illness. The understanding of the causes of mental illness has varied, ranging from religious, magical reasons to the modern biological and psychological theories. Psychiatric illness pertains to affective disorders such as manic depressive illness, of which depression is by far the most common manifestation. Everybody suffers from moments, or even days, of feeling 'down' but, when depression reaches clinical proportions, there is a lower mood in which the patient feels utterly miserable, their behaviour is narrowed in range, their sleep is disturbed and so is their appetite. Their span of attention and concentration is limited and ultimately they have no desire to live. It is a condition closely associated with suicide.

The next most common condition is an anxiety state. All of us are prone to feel anxious under stress, but the illness of anxiety is really a manifestation of severe anxiety and stress. Other presentations of anxiety are phobias, obsessional disorders, hysteria and psychosomatic illness.

Much rarer, but far more destructive, is schizophrenia – a condition which affects young people, is chronic in nature and is characterised by thought disorder, flat affect (that is, a flattening of the mood), hallucinations (particularly auditory ones), a state of withdrawal and bizarre notions of reality.

Finally, there are illnesses of mental deterioration, called the dementias, in which memory and thought are crippled.

In ordinary language Jesus is frequently portrayed as being 'mad'. There is no evidence whatever, from the Scriptures or historical accounts, that Jesus suffered from any of the conditions listed above. His mental health was intact and, however extraordinary his sayings

13

and actions appear, there is not the slightest hint that they were the product of a psychiatrically disturbed mind, as we currently understand that term. There is, however, evidence in the Scriptures of a man who is described in terms of mental illness:

> They reached the territory of Gerasenes on the other side of the lake, and when he disembarked, a man with an unclean spirit at once came out from the tombs towards him. The man lived in the tombs and no one could secure him any more, even with a chain, because he had often been secured with fetters and chains but had snapped the chains and broken the fetters and no one had the strength to control him. All night and all day, among the tombs and in the mountains, he would howl and gash himself with stones. (Mark 5:1–6)

Here is a picture of a highly disturbed man whom one can recognise as mentally ill. He turns to Jesus for help and there follows the familiar story of the unclean spirits – the equivalent of mental illness – which left him and went into a herd of pigs, which charged down the cliff into the lake where they were drowned. The story of evil spirits sounds strange to our modern ears, but the reality of mental disturbance crosses the passage of time and sounds authentic. The transformation of the maniac is real enough: 'They came to Jesus and saw the demoniac sitting there – the man who had the legion in him – properly dressed and in his full senses' (Mark 5:15).

Not only do we not have any evidence of mental illness in Jesus, but here, as elsewhere, we have the evidence that he had the capacity to heal such illness. Many have suggested that the illnesses which Jesus healed were neurotic in character, rather than genuine mental illness, and that a charismatic effect was the main element in the transformation. The case of the demoniac does not suggest such an instance, but rather the presence of a psychotic illness – that is, an overt mental illness which is not amenable to simple psychological healing – and that Jesus intervened in a real, supernatural way.

Reference to psychological healing introduces the subject of psychology. Unlike psychiatry (which is the study of mental illness), psychology is the study of the personality and its various components, such as intelligence, memory, attention, concentration, etc. Like mental illness, the study of the personality has a long history.

The modern era of the study of the personality was inaugurated by

Freud, to whom the next chapter is devoted. He formulated the view that the human personality is laid down in childhood – in his theories, in the first five years of life – and that we get access to these early memories through psychoanalysis. Freud postulated that many things happen in this talking dialogue between patient and therapist. But one of the principal events is that the patient begins to believe in, and to experience, the therapist as a parental figure through whom the patient relives the early childhood experiences. The therapist, who usually has had an analysis, can distinguish between what belongs to him/her, and what is transferred from the past which refers to childhood events and experiences. We now know that this process of transference takes place in other situations in which there is a close encounter between persons. We tend to see in others not only the characteristics which belong to them, but also the contents of our own past, which we transfer on to them.

My main theoretical tool in this book is this human capacity to see, in adult exchanges, the remnants of the past. I have used the Scriptures as a living reality in which the deeds and sayings of Jesus reflect his own experiences of his own childhood. This method allows us to link the past with the present of the scriptural descriptions, and allows us to reconstruct the childhood of Jesus about which the Scriptures are blank.

Is this methodology valid? As already mentioned, the gospels are not biographical accounts and we have no details of what Jesus actually said, except in a small percentage of his words. But what the Scriptures contain are close approximations of what he said and did and give us a flavour of the direction of his thoughts and feelings. I acknowledge that I am using the actual words to carry as much weight as if they were his actual utterances, but I believe there is a close enough proximity between the original and the version that we have for us to get near the transference from past to present.

We divide the psychological theories of the personality between those which stem from Freud and his successors (dynamic theories of the personality) and those which use biological infrastructures (such as the structure of the brain), as, for example, that described by H. J. Eysenk, in which the personality is divided into extraversion, introversion and neuroticism.[1] In addition to these biological formulations, there are cognitive and learning theories. In this book only the dynamic theories of Freud and his main British successors are included, along

15

with one prominent American psychoanalyst, E. H. Erikson, and they are briefly described in the following chapters. They are chosen as expressing most succinctly the dynamic aspect of the personality, although clearly in the future other approaches will be made.

In addition to the Freudian school of thought and its successors, there has been the contribution of C. G. Jung. Freud was a declared atheist, whereas Jung believed in God and the role that the spiritual played in the human personality. For this reason Jung is much used in Christian psychological writing, but I have had only minimum knowledge of Jungian psychology, so I leave the theorising of Jung and Jesus to those who are more familiar with Jungian theory. I have confined myself to a brief outline of the mainstream Freudian theories and I am aware that these can be criticised. In the subsequent chapters I shall deal with these criticisms, but enough Freudian theory has stood the test of time, and has entered widely into circulation and into Western consciousness, to justify the link between dynamic psychology and Jesus.

II

Psychological Theories

4

Sigmund Freud
(1856–1939)

Freud is the Father of modern dynamic psychology, and his influence has been immense. Childhood has always been seen as the origin of the future person, but he established this link in the strongest possible way. His unique contribution was through psychoanalysis: he invited the patient to lie on a couch and talk freely about the things that mattered to him or her. This process was called free association. The analysts listened to the material that was offered and did two things with it. They first interpreted the contents in accordance with psychoanalytic theory and tried to make sense of the material, and secondly, they checked what the patient had transferred on to the analyst from early parental experiences. This transference material allows us to get a glimpse of what happened in childhood.

From the process of analysis, Freud constructed a theoretical model of how the personality developed. He postulated that the human personality was built on two instincts, namely the sexual and aggressive drives. The originality of Freud's thought was that sexuality for him did not start with the secondary sexual characteristics of puberty, but rather in infancy. He visualised a pleasurable, sensual experience starting in the mouth, called the oral phase, and stimulated by breast feeding. The oral phase is dependent on the sensations elicited by the mucous membranes of the lips and the mouth which give pleasurable experiences. This takes place in the first year of life.

In the second and third years of life, the pleasurable experiences (technically called the libidinal drive) are focused at the other end of the gastro-intestinal tract in the anus, which is lined with the same type of mucous membrane as the mouth and which gives similar pleasurable sensations. In the fourth and fifth year, the boy becomes conscious of the penis, or absence of penis in the girl. Freud then postulated the famous Oedipus complex, whereby a boy wants to possess his mother and is afraid of his father, who poses the risk of cutting off his penis; as he develops, he gives up his sexual wishes towards mother and identifies towards father. Identification plays a crucial role in dynamic psychology – and so does the Oedipus complex, the resolution of which is considered to be at the centre of a healthy personality development. The appropriate female counterpart is the Electra complex in which the girl gives up her libidinal aspirations towards the father and identifies with the mother. The Oedipus and Electra complexes are highly complicated ideas and there is endless discussion as to whether Freud's theories reflect what actually happens. Nevertheless the triangular emotional links postulated have echoes in real life and, whether or not they occur in the manner suggested by Freud, they certainly cannot be ignored. Freudian theory goes on to indicate that the oral, anal and phallic stages of sexual development have to be negotiated and, when they are not passed in a normal healthy way, they leave a trauma which remains alive in the person, but remains buried in the unconscious.

The presence of buried material in the unconscious formed a prominent part of Freudian theory. Indeed, our modern understanding of sexual abuse trauma in childhood reminds us that such emotional disturbance is only too real, leaving a trail of fear, mistrust, sexual apprehension and difficulties with intimacy. Freudian theory postulated that these sexual traumata are buried with defences (see below) and that, in the course of therapy, the defences are uncovered, and the trauma identified, ventilated and resolved.

Continuing with the sexual development, Freudian theory postulated a latent period between the age of six and puberty, during which the sexual drive remains dormant. The process comes alive again with the secondary sexual characteristics of puberty, when the incest taboo puts a barrier between the attraction of the child and parents, and the child now looks outwards to form a relationship outside the home circle with somebody of the opposite sex. The sexual characteristics of infancy join the secondary manifestations of genital sexuality and the two fuse in sexual intercourse.

In Freud's outline of the personality based on sexual and aggressive drives, the unconscious plays a vital role – and this is a feature of Freudian theory that has stood the test of time. Freud laid particular importance on the presence of dreams, and the interpretation of dreams plays a central role in analysis as a pathway to the unconscious. In addition to dreams, Freud postulated other mechanisms of removing material from consciousness. He called them defences. A defence is a psychological mechanism whereby the anxiety engendered from emotional trauma is diverted from consciousness. There is a range of psychological defences. Repression is a process of burying the emotions caused by the trauma, thereby rendering it unconscious – but, while unconscious, the trauma has an energy of its own which aims to reach consciousness. Repression is an unconscious mechanism: it takes place without the intervention of the person's consciousness. It should be contrasted with suppression which is a conscious process, a way of putting something out of one's mind deliberately.

Another common defence mechanism is denial, an unconscious disclaimer of an unacceptable, disagreeable happening. Denial is very frequently used as a way of disclaiming responsibility. Here there can be confusion, because another person may believe that there is conscious culpability and that the denial is a lie or a cover-up. The distinction between unconscious denial and a deliberate conscious avoidance is at the heart of many disputes.

Projection is another defence mechanism: it involves attributing one's own peculiarities to others. Usually we push into others those aspects of ourselves which we do not like. Thus if we are aggressive, it is something we deny – and we see other people as aggressive. Projection is a very common mechanism in which we see in others what we do not want to, or cannot, see in ourselves.

The opposite of projection is identification. Now we adopt qualities of others and accept them as the product of our own effort. We find ourselves claiming the good qualities of others and attributing their characteristics to ourselves.

Substitution, as the name implies, allows us to channel our inner anxieties and tensions into, for example, a physical symptom, such as a headache, a pain, or other form of disability. In dynamic psychology, hysteria is the process whereby an emotional stress is converted into a physical or psychological symptom.

Reaction formation, another defence mechanism, involves the development of a quality or trait opposing some strong unconscious desire, fear or conflict – for example, the extreme puritan reacting against strong sexual urges.

Rationalisation is a very common defence, often used in our everyday life, and, in conjunction with denial, helps us to avoid an unpleasant situation. Ultimately rationalisation is used in order to conceal real motives behind a fence of devised excuses. Thus a dissatisfied husband works late on the grounds that the work is excessive, a frigid wife refuses sex because of some bodily complaint, and the alcoholic has business to conduct near the source of liquor.

Finally, sublimation is the means whereby the energy which flows from our instinctual life is transformed along constructive channels to the higher realms of religion, art, literature and the wide range of socially and spiritually acceptable good works.

The concept of a defence, like the presence of the unconscious, is a part of Freudian theory which has stood the test of time and has entered the consciousness of our psychological identity. Just as the white cells of the blood defend our body against infection, so the defence mechanisms protect us against anxiety.

When Freud had gathered enough material, he proposed a typology of the mental processes. He stipulated that the primitive part of the mind in dynamic terms was formed by the id, which is unconscious and is controlled by the pleasure principle – that is, the end point is pleasurable satisfaction. Pleasure needs to be controlled by the reality principle; this is situated in the ego, the conscious centre in which most of our rational activity is placed. The id pushes for satisfaction, the ego controls this thrust. The third and final element of Freud's mental typology is the super ego, which is a largely unconscious element of the mind, within which reside the forces of prohibition and control, largely established by parents, teachers and other inhibiting sources. An equivalent idea for the super ego is conscience, with its link with guilt.

Thus Freud considered that the human personality, which is built on the dual drives of sex and aggression, is organised in a triple system: the id, seeking pleasurable satisfaction, is balanced by the controlling forces of the super ego, with the ego, the centre of consciousness and reason, mediating between the two. The essential concern for Christianity, developed on Greek thought of reason and intellect, is that the human personality is not a static, rigid concept based on intellect and reason. It is instead a dynamic entity in which feelings, emotions, instincts and drives play an important role. Freud's model makes allowances for this fluid perception of the personality, and it is interesting that Jesus was very much alive to this dynamic force in the human personality. Jesus used the concept of clean and unclean:

> He called the people to him and said, 'Listen and understand. What goes into the mouth does not make anyone unclean: it is what comes out of the mouth that makes someone unclean.' . . . At this, Peter said to him, 'Explain the parable for us.' Jesus replied, 'Even you – don't you yet understand? Can't you see that whatever goes into the mouth passes through the stomach and is discharged into the sewer? But whatever comes out of the mouth comes from the heart, and it is this that makes someone unclean. For from the heart come evil intentions: murder, adultery, fornication, theft, perjury, slander. These are the things that make a person unclean. But eating with unwashed hands does not make anyone unclean.' (Matt. 15:10–20)

This is one of the most powerful evocations of Jesus' understanding of the human personality as being a dynamic entity, and bridges the first-century concepts of personality and our modern Freudian concepts. This understanding from Jesus of the dynamic concept of the personality gives some added verification to the way in which the subject is treated in this book. The gospels, as outlined by the evangelists, are not relying on the intellect for their impact; rather, they capture a world of feelings, love and compassion emanating from Jesus, who goes back to the heart, or the seat of emotions, for the source of the human drive. This strong appeal to feelings makes sense of love being the dominant characteristic for Jesus' emphasis on the supreme importance of compassion, and presumably played a prominent role both in his upbringing and his relationship to his Father and the Spirit.

Returning to Freud, we see that, in his vision of the personality as a dynamic entity, he has developed an original view which remains acceptable, nearly 100 years after its introduction. He thus laid the foundations of much that was subsequently to come in psychiatry and psychology. Modern psychological thinking has cast doubt on his theory that sexual and aggressive drives are the sole basis of the personality – and that part of the theory is no longer entirely acceptable. Modern views tend to attribute the energy of human beings to hormonal and neurotransmitter systems. But the concept of personality as a dynamic, psychosomatic entity, with emotional forces having a fluid entry and oscillating between the unconscious and conscious, is still intact. The control of anxiety by the psychological defences is universally accepted, and so is the importance of infancy for the later development of the personality – a key factor in this book.

There is no doubt that Freud's thought, if not his theories in detail, has revolutionised our thinking about the human personality. From psychoanalysis there has developed psychotherapy, which applies the same principles, and the widespread notion of counselling. It could be said that all the parables of Jesus contain succinct, psychological nuggets of universal application, hence they have stood the test of time.

Which leads again to the question as to whether what Freud propounded in the nineteenth and twentieth centuries applied to Jesus in the first century. I have indicated that a dynamic concept of the personality is evident in the way that Jesus treats the human person. Many of his cures imply a psychosomatic interpretation of disease and the link between spirit, body and psyche is written all over the gospels. Clearly the gospels are neither biographical nor psychological text books, but they give broad hints that the universals which Freud postulated in his view of human beings are not strangers to Jesus' understanding of men and women.

The force that emanated from Jesus, which led to his being able to heal, was not purely psychological – though some would like to interpret his miracles in this way. A supernatural quality was clearly present in his work, but he worked within a concept of the psychodynamic, and this influences me to believe that the theories outlined in this and the subsequent chapters of this section are transferable to his day and time.

5
Melanie Klein
(1882–1960)

MELANIE KLEIN WAS A follower of Freud. She was born in Vienna and was analysed by Ferenze and Abraham, two eminent psychoanalysts. She came to England in 1926 and wrote a great deal which raised fierce controversy. She worked mainly with children, and used their play to gain access to the psyche. She took theory to its earliest stages of development in the psychological dialogue between the baby and the feeding at the breast. In the interaction between the baby and the breast, she postulated the origins of love and hate. The great advance that Klein made was that, working with the two instincts of aggression and sex, she progressed to seeing that these two forces did not operate by themselves but interacted first with mother and then father. The personality of the adult is the fruit of this interaction.

She says: 'The baby does not recognise anyone's existence but his alone (his mother's breast is to him merely a part of himself – just a sensation at first) and he expects all his wants to be fulfilled'.[1] Love is seen as this desire to be fulfilled, to have appetite satiated. It is interesting how this interest in food, which is one of the earliest experiences in all of us, finds a place in the gospels in Jesus' frequent dining, his multiplication of the loaves miracles and his own last meal when he changed bread and wine into his own body and blood. The link between food and life is the incarnational equivalent of the spiritual food of eternal life.

Klein continues: 'He or she wants the breast for love of it, so to speak, for the pleasure of sucking the milk and also to still hunger'. Love was linked by Klein to this satisfaction. 'But what happens if these expectations and wants are not fulfilled? In a certain degree the baby becomes aware of his dependence; he discovers that he cannot supply all his own wants – and he cries and screams. He becomes aggressive.' Klein identified this aggressive feeling with the elementary instinct of aggression and hatred in humankind, and placed its origin in the baby's discontent with the emptiness in its mouth. This emptiness reaches consciousness as hate and aggressive craving.

For the baby, this situation of hunger–aggression is a realisation of non-existence, of something like an overwhelming loss and threatened destruction. It is only with the passage of time that we learn to control our hunger and to delay gratification. Indeed, delay of gratification is a sign of maturity and it gives us a sense of security over our instincts which, in Freudian and Kleinian theories, are always threatening to overwhelm us. Hence, as I shall show in a later chapter, I attach considerable importance to the Jesus' fasting for 40 days in the desert and his ability to reject the overtures of the Devil.

In the mean time, the baby experiences recurrent moments of the pain and associated aggression of hunger. For Klein, satiation was linked with security and safety, hunger with aggression and danger. According to her theories, babies deal with the emotional effects of hunger by using the mechanism of projection which, as we saw in the previous chapter, is a Freudian psychological defence.

Klein places great stress on projection:

> The first and the most fundamental of our insurances or safety measures against feelings of pain, of being attacked or of helplessness, is the device we call projection. All painful and unpleasant sensations or feelings in the mind are by this device automatically relegated outside oneself: one assumes that they belong elsewhere, not in one's self. We disown and repudiate them as emanating from ourselves; in the ungrammatical but psychologically active phrase, we blame them onto someone else.

For Klein projection is the first reaction to pain – and it probably remains the most spontaneous reaction in all of us to any painful feelings throughout our lives. It is a commonplace experience that we blame other people, nations, the government, for all the unpleasant things that are happening to us. Thus the origin of our aggression, according to Klein, lies in the oral stage of our development and is associated with hunger. Just as our ability to delay satisfaction of hunger is linked with maturity, so the control of our anger is a similar sign of maturity. But not all control of anger is a sign of maturity and justified: there is justified aggression in self defence or when we are protecting a value or a principle. Such justified aggression must be distinguished from hatred, when we desire the destruction of the other person. We shall see aspects of aggression in Jesus – for example, in the episode of the expulsion of the money dealers in the Temple. This has traditionally been put forward as a contrast to the picture of a sweet, soft and effeminate Jesus. Yet there is no evidence of this soft-edged picture in the gospels – indeed, the episode in the Temple presents an angry Jesus:

> So they reached Jerusalem and he went into the Temple, and began driving out the men selling and buying there; he upset the tables of the money changers and the seats of the dove sellers. Nor would he allow anyone to carry anything through the Temple. And he taught them and said, 'Does not scripture say: My house will be called a house of prayer for all peoples? But you have turned it into a bandits' den.' (Mark 11:15–17)

This brief description of what Jesus did suggests that mayhem ensued, and he must indeed have been angry. Nevertheless Jesus directed his greater anger towards the Pharisees. In the text of Matthew we discern an unparalleled vehemence:

> 'Alas for you, scribes and Pharisees, you hypocrites! You shut up the kingdom of Heaven in people's faces, neither going in your-selves nor allowing others to go in who want to.
>
> 'Alas for you, scribes and Pharisees, you hypocrites! You travel over sea and land to make a single proselyte, and anyone who becomes one you make twice as fit for hell as you are.
>
> 'Alas for you, blind guides! You say, "If anyone swears by the Temple, it has no force; but anyone who swears by the gold of the Temple is bound." Fools and blind! For which is of greater value, the gold or the Temple that makes the gold sacred? Again, "If anyone swears by the altar it has no force; but anyone who swears by the offering on the altar is bound." You blind men! For which is of greater worth, the offering or the altar that makes the offering sacred? Therefore, someone who swears by the altar is swearing by that and by everything on it. And someone who swears by the Temple is swearing by that and by the One who dwells in

it. And someone who swears by heaven is swearing by the throne of God and by the One who is seated there.

'Alas for you, scribes and Pharisees, you hypocrites! You pay your tithe of mint and dill and cumin and have neglected the weightier matters of the Law – justice, mercy, good faith! These you should have practised, those not neglected. You blind guides, straining out gnats and swallowing camels!' (Matt. 23:13–24)

Here is stinging material which, even allowing for Matthew's own special polemic, shows Jesus in full aggressive mood. His special onslaught on paying tithes but denying justice and mercy go to the heart of Jesus' psyche – the move from the minutiae of the law to compassion being central to his work.

We have seen Jesus in an angry mood at the Temple and against the Pharisees, but in neither case is this anger meant to destroy, which is a feature of hatred. But we do have a rare instance of Jesus' destructive anger, not against persons but against an object – the fig tree. In connection with the withering of the fig tree, we also have another instance of the connection between Jesus and food:

As he was returning to the city in the early morning, he felt hungry. Seeing a fig tree by the road, he went up to it but found nothing on it but leaves. And he said to it, 'May you never bear fruit again,' and instantly the fig tree withered. The disciples were amazed when they saw it and said, 'How is it that the fig tree withered instantly?' Jesus answered, 'In truth I tell you, if you have faith and do not doubt at all, not only will you do what I have done to the fig tree, but even if you say to the mountain, "Be pulled up and thrown into the sea," it will be done.' (Matt. 21:18–22)

The Jerusalem Bible indicates that this is a symbolic episode in which Jesus intends to punish Israel for its fruitlessness. The episode may well convey this meaning, but the human basis of its action is pure, destructive anger. There is no evidence, however, that Jesus held such feelings against persons.

All such instances of anger are postulated by Klein as ultimately being related to states of fullness and emptiness, satiation and hunger. For her, this leads on to a further concept. The means that we use to fill ourselves up or to take in are known by her as the process of introjection, which is the correlate of projection or expulsion. Introjection and projection are prominent mechanisms in Klein's work, and are related to the good feelings which the breast gives through the milk and the expulsion of aggression back into the breast. For the infant, the breast thus represents the whole mother with whom is established a relationship in which she is now 'good' and at another moment 'bad'. These elementary feelings of good and bad remain with us for the rest of our lives, and populate our inner world. In fact, we make constant judgements about people whom we like or dislike. It is clear from the gospels that the scribes and the Pharisees were people whom Jesus disliked and warned his apostles about.

A feeling of satiation is linked with a good meal, but it has a further connotation of an inner sense of security. This process of taking in good things to increase our sense of well-being – which psychologists call internalisation – is basic to human beings. We are constantly seeking for good experiences which give us security and satisfaction. It is part of my fundamental concept of Jesus that his inner world was full and secure and that this sense of security emanated from his relationships with his Father and with his human parents. Indeed, Jesus makes the point of distiguishing between fullness built on human, material things and fullness built on heavenly things – a genuine relationship with our heavenly Father:

> 'Do not store up treasure for yourselves on earth, where moth and woodworm destroy them and thieves can break in and steal. But store up treasures for yourself in heaven, where neither moth nor woodworm destroys them and thieves cannot break in and steal. For wherever your treasure is, there will your heart be too.' (Matt. 6:19–21)

Finally Klein drew a further point from the basic satiation–emptiness experiences of food intake from the breast. As we have seen, she related the pangs of hunger to an aggressive response on the part of the infant. This aggression has many facets but, in the process of crying and screaming, the baby is seeking to overcome the limitations of hunger, to win a battle with mother who is in control, who has the last word. This desire to defeat mother was conceived by Klein in terms of rivalry.

Rivalry in adults is commonly seen and it is a useful trait – but it can go to excess. Some people have to establish their superiority over others at any cost. Indeed, these very people cannot stand competition and surround themselves with inferiors. This proximity to inferiors produces mixed feelings: 'inferiors' are needed to ward off the individual's feelings of insecurity, and yet the individual despises them, considering them as inferior. The need to have near us people whom we see as inferior speaks of a basic insecurity, as if we feel incapable of winning in any future competition.

Jesus had a solid, secure basis to his inner self, and was not afraid to be surrounded by the outcasts of his society, such as tax collectors and prostitutes. Furthermore, he had a remarkably egalitarian relationship with women, who were usually treated as inferiors in his day. His association with the marginalised, his desire to dine with them, was a constant scandal to the Pharisees. Jesus placed himself outside the competitive rivalry situation, not because of fear, but rather because of the fullness of his being.

A Kleinian interpretation of his personality would be that he had had a rich and satisfactory time on the breast:

> It happened that as he was speaking, a woman in the crowd raised her voice and said, 'Blessed the womb that bore you and the breasts that fed you!' But he replied, 'More blessed still are those who hear the word of God and keep it!' (Luke 11:27–8)

Jesus did not deny that he was breast-fed but, in keeping with his mission, he turned the table and directed the woman to God. This concern with God need not distract us from the fact that, in his humanity, he had experienced the natural psychological factors of infancy and that good nutrition played a part in his psychology, if Klein is right in her views.

We have seen that the origins of love and hatred in Kleinian theory start at the beginning of life at the breast. Klein derived these views from analyses of children and, in particular, from interpreting their play. She also saw the persistence of these trends in adults, through psychoanalysis.

The baby sucks at the breast which represents mother, who is the first object of love and hate. She is both desired and hated with all the intensity and strength that is characteristic of the early urges of the baby. In the very beginning, the baby loves the mother when she is satisfying its needs for nourishment, alleviating its feelings of hunger and giving it the sensual pleasure, which it experiences when its mouth is stimulated by sucking at her breast.

But when this stimulation is lacking, it is postulated that the baby experiences rage and has destructive feelings towards the mother. In this situation two crucial psychological features appear. The first is the feeling of guilt in the psyche of the baby. Did Jesus experience guilt feelings? We have to differentiate here between guilt for having done something consciously wrong, which I believe Jesus did not experience, and guilt in the psyche. There is no evidence of Jesus' guilt in the gospels. But while there is no evidence of personal guilt, we must assume that he knew what the experience was like. If he was fully human then, according to Klein, he experienced guilt for having the destructive feelings towards his mother. Thus it is likely that the capacity to experience guilt was part of his human make up, but it was not translated into reality. Nevertheless, it is part of Christian belief that Jesus died for the sins of humanity. I am suggesting that Jesus had the ability to experience guilt but that he did so at one remove, on behalf of humanity. As I said, there is no evidence in the gospels of personal guilt, but the formula I am offering retains Jesus' human capacity to experience guilt, which he does on behalf of men and women, without personally incurring it.

There is ample evidence, however, of Jesus' experience of regret and sadness:

> There was a man named Lazarus of Bethany, the village of Mary and her sister, Martha, and he was ill. It was the same Mary, the sister of the sick man Lazarus, who anointed the Lord with ointment and wiped his feet with her hair. The sisters sent this message to Jesus, 'Lord, the man you love is ill.' . . .
>
> Mary went to Jesus and as soon as she saw him, she threw herself at his feet, saying, 'Lord, if you had been here, my brother would not have died.' At the sight of her tears, and those of the Jews who had come with her, Jesus was greatly distressed, and with a profound sigh he said, 'Where have they put him?' They said, 'Lord, come and see.' Jesus wept; and the Jews said, 'See how much he loved him!' But there were some who remarked, 'He opened the eyes of the blind man. Could he not have prevented this man's death?' Sighing again, Jesus reached the tomb: it was a cave with a stone to close the opening. Jesus said, 'Take the stone away' Martha, the dead man's sister, said to him, 'Lord, by now he will smell; this is the fourth day since he died.' Jesus replied, 'Have

I not told you that if you believe you will see the glory of God?' So they took the stone away. Then Jesus lifted up his eyes and said:

'Father, I thank you for hearing my prayer.

I myself know that you hear me always,

But I speak

For the sake of all these who are standing around me,

so that they may believe it was you who sent me.'

When he had said this, he cried in a loud voice, 'Lazarus, come out!' The dead man came out, his feet and hands bound with strips of material and a cloth over his face. Jesus said to them, 'Unbind him, let him go free.' (John 11:1–4, 32–44)

The full humanity of Jesus is shown, not only in his regret and sadness over the death of Lazarus, but in the fact that his distress was not prevented by the anticipation of the miracle that was to follow. Jesus does not allow his triumph to remove the pain he experienced at a time of death.

The difference between guilt and sorrow is fundamental, and in this section I am trying to show that Jesus' personality fully respected the theological understanding of his full humanity and divinity. He knew and was capable of knowing guilt at one remove, but sadness and regret directly.

The baby, who experiences feelings of guilt at its destructive feelings towards mother, cannot remain long with this sense of desolation. It needs to repair the harm. Side by side with the destructive impulses in the unconscious mind both of the child and the adult, there exists a profound urge to make sacrifices in order to help and to put right loved people who, in fantasy or reality, have been harmed or destroyed. This is a process which Klein called reparation – the ordinary meaning of the word suggests the desire to make up for harm done. In Klein's own words: 'In the depths of the mind, the urge to make people happy is linked up with strong feelings of responsibility and concern for them, which manifests itself in genuine sympathy with other people and in the ability to understand them, as they are and as they feel.' In other words, we must develop the ability to put ourselves in the place of other people or, in technical psychological language, to identify with them. This ability to identify with other people is a strong precondition of love. The capacity to identify with other people, particularly the poor and marginalised, and to love them, was a hallmark of Jesus – and

Kleinian theory suggests that it was developed in this early stage of life.

It is time now to consider the validity of Kleinian theories. At first sight, it seems highly unlikely that such a wide range of psychological traits could be found in the mind of the baby. The validation of such theories is highly difficult and only psychoanalysis claims to have penetrated the psyche at such an early stage. On the other hand, love, anger, pain, anxiety, guilt, reparation, are undoubtedly real and universal entities. They do exist in reality and there is a strong appeal to believing that their origins lie at the beginning of life. Whenever their origins, there is little doubt that we see them in action, and the references to Jesus in this chapter are valid, whatever their source of origin.

Klein's theories put the most fundamental aspects of love and hatred at the earliest phase of our life and, whatever we think about the theoretical mechanisms she has for them, the importance they play in adult life is indisputable. Moreover, as I suggest, Jesus participated in them, and his healthy responses to such feelings was based on his early experiences with his human parents.

6

Donald Winnicott (1896–1971)

W INNICOTT WAS BORN IN 1896 into a comfortably well-off Plymouth family. At 16 he decided to become a doctor, and studied medicine in Cambridge. He became a paediatrician and later was analysed. He concentrated on child psychiatry, to which he made vital contributions. He worked at the same time as Klein and looked at the infant, not in the first few weeks of life, but in the first few months. He emphasised that there was no such thing as an infant alone, the mother played a vital part – and it is the pair that make up the critical entity. He concentrated on what constitutes good mothering in these early stages of development.

He too paid great attention to the need of the baby for food. The baby can be considered helpless and totally reliant on the handling by its mother. The way the baby is held safely gives it a sense of security, and Winnicott sees a continuity between childhood experiences and adult life. All analysts claim that the feelings generated in childhood remain as part of the infrastructure of the psyche in adult life. This is the view on which this book is built – that what happens in the early years shapes adult life and that we see this in the personality and the feelings expressed in the transference situation of interpersonal relationships.

The way in which the baby is held safely gives it a sense of security, and its hunger needs are satisfied by offering the breast with good milk. For Winnicott, matching of hunger with the breast, discomfort with comforting arms and lap, are the elementary rudiments of the 'good enough mother', a phrase of which he was very fond. The absence of such responses gives rise to anxiety, insecurity and discomfort.

Similarly, the evacuation of the bowels in a way that does not leave the baby uncomfortable is the baby's way of matching its gastro-intestinal tract experiences to the mother's sensitive and loving response. For Winnicott, the psyche and the body were in constant dialogue: pain and discomfort in the body gave rise to pain and discomfort in the psyche. This has important implications for the healings of Jesus. In his healings, we see the conquering of evil spirits, which were perfectly understandable in our Lord's time. Today, the healings would be interpreted in terms of both physical transformation and psychological change in the direction of self esteem, and would imply self acceptance in people who reject themselves. But the link between body and psyche exists, and for Winnicott it is the devotion of the mother and her capacity to understand through maternal reverie that forms the basis of mental health. 'His mother stored up all these things in her heart' (Luke 2:52).

Winnicott concentrated on maternal care, and especially on holding. For him, good enough holding protects the baby from physiological insult, takes account of the infant's skin sensitivity – touch, temperature, auditory and visual sensitivity – and also protects from the sense of disintegration at falling and from the infant's lack of knowledge of the existence of anything other than the self. Holding includes the whole routine of care throughout the day and night, and it is not the same with any two infants because it is part of the infant, and no two infants are alike. Such holding follows the minute day-to-day changes belonging to the infant's growth and development, both physical and psychological.

The mental health of the individual is laid down by this maternal care, which, when it goes well, is scarcely noticed. The mother's holding is not merely physical but is also empathetic: there is a meeting-point between the psyche of the infant and that of the mother, and the sensitivity of the growing individual is based on the fine tuning of this encounter.

Given the extraordinary sensitivity of Jesus seen in the gospels, we can assume that the holding and empathy between Jesus as a baby and his mother must have been both excellent and a perfect fit. For Winnicott the 'nursing couple' constitutes a dyad. When things go well this dyad evolves without setback, and the child develops quite naturally.

Winnicott pays attention not only to the maternal constituents but also to the atmosphere. Thus, the baby does not need only to be given the correct feed at the correct time, so much as to be fed by someone feeding her own baby. From subsequent events in the stability of the adult Jesus, we can interpret that he felt loved when he was fed. For a mother to be giving this loving devotion, she must herself be supported and her needs met – and in this sense the role of Joseph is vital. He must have loved Mary and fully supported her in the early years of Jesus' life. We know very little about Joseph, but we have this information in Matthew:

> This is how Jesus Christ came to be born. His mother Mary was betrothed to Joseph; but before they came to live together she was found to be with child through the Holy Spirit. Her husband Joseph, being an upright man and wanting to spare her disgrace, decided to divorce her informally. (Matt. 1:18–19)

The words 'being an upright man and wanting to spare her disgrace' hardly constitute a biographical note. Nevertheless, we can deduce that Joseph was a person who wanted to do the right thing, to stand by Mary. If he wanted to do the right thing when he found that she was pregnant, it is likely that, when he stayed with her through her pregnancy and the care of the child, he would have given her the support that she needed as a wife and mother. The 'good enough mother' of Winnicott presumes a supportive and sensitive husband, and it is likely that Joseph was one. We shall have occasion later on to look at Joseph as a father, but it is not unreasonable to assume that he was a good husband.

In the context of good mothering and handling, the baby emerges as a person whose skin is becoming a limiting membrane to which there is an inside and an outside. Winnicott accepted the duality of the baby's benign and aggressive instincts. Klein posited two phases which the baby goes through: the paranoid in the first three months, and the depressive in the next three months. She believed that the depressive phase is reached when the infant realises that both its love and hatred are directed towards the same object, the mother, and the baby comes to appreciate ambivalence, the concern to protect her from its hate and to make reparation for what damage it imagines its hate has done. For Winnicott the capacity to become depressed came a bit later, at weaning: he felt that concern enters the life of the baby at this time, along with the capacity to feel grief. At whatever stage of development the baby's capacity to feel grief and concern, and to make reparation, occurs, it remains vital – and this cycle carries on in adult life. Grief and concern were crucial experiences of Jesus, and we see that these psychoanalysts place them at this early stage of development where, with the help of the good enough mother, the baby can integrate its experiences of good and bad, and retain this knowledge in the depths of its inner being in order to deal with the vicissitudes of later life.

One of the things that Winnicott wrote about was the capacity to be alone – something which features in Jesus' life (John 6:15). Winnicott discussed the positive aspects of the capacity of being alone, which is one of the most important signs of mature emotional development. He believed that at the heart of being alone is a good experience of being with the mother, and he used the phrase 'ego-relatedness' to describe the meeting-point between the ego of the child and that of the mother – the presence of a loving interaction as opposed to id-relationship, which is a physical encounter. The child who feels good, safe, benign, in the presence of the mother can use this good relatedness to create the psychological energy that permits aloneness without anxiety.

Jesus went and prayed alone; he was alone in a world which did not understand him and yet he persevered. This perseverance speaks of an inner strength, which, according to Winnicott, must have arisen from the many encounters with his mother when, in silence, good feelings were exchanged between them.

Winnicott carried on where Klein left off. He saw the psyche in terms of love and aggression, as she did, based on physical experiences, and the well-being of the infant as of supreme importance. He placed enormous importance on mothering, and for him the good enough mother was the key to the child's healthy development. Of course, there was also the usual Freudian triangular life of the mother, father and child, which, in addition to the sexual drama of Freud, was now seen in terms of the child's psychological and material needs being met by the mother, who is in turn supported by the father. We have here a picture of baby care which is less difficult to grasp, and Winnicott's view, of the interaction between psyche and body in these early months leaving an imprint for life, makes a lot of sense.

7
John Bowlby
(1907–90)

THE ANALYSTS REFERRED TO in the last few chapters made giant contributions, and all of them agree that the satiation of food, infantile sex and physical handling are the main reasons for forming human bonds. This has a surface appeal which has stood the test of time but which has never been completely satisfactory – the explanation of the origins of human love through the satisfaction of these two drives alone, given the giant proportions it can reach, appears incomplete. Furthermore, placing the roots of the personality in infantile sexuality puzzles many people, for whom the elaboration of the psyche in the first five years, built on these instincts, remains an enigma. The unsatisfactory nature of all these theories led John Bowlby, a psychoanalyst himself, to seek an alternative explanation for the origins of love. He was impressed by the work of Lorenz, an ethologist who studied the behaviour of animals and the formation of bonds between parents and their young. Bowlby was greatly influenced by this work.

Basing his views on ethology, he outlined a theory of human attachment as a propensity of human beings to make strong affectional bonds to particular others, which also explains the emotional distress of anxiety, anger, depression, caused by separation and by loss.[1] He distinguished between the 'dependency' of infant on parents because of food needs and between adults because of sexual needs, and a basic attachment of loving affection formed when a person turns to some other preferred individual who is usually seen as stronger or wiser. While especially evident during childhood, attachment behaviour is believed to characterise human beings from cradle to grave, and explains the relationship of Jesus and his entourage.

The newly born infant forms an attachment to its mother by relating visually to her face, auditorily to the sound of her voice and through touch. In this way, a primitive bond of affection is formed. This bond makes the child feel safe. This attachment is associated with crying or calling when left alone, which brings parents rushing to the baby, and also with following and clinging behaviour and strong protest when the baby is left alone or with strangers. With age, the frequency and intensity with which such behaviour is elicited diminishes. But it continues throughout life, particularly when we are distressed, ill or afraid. The arousal of such behaviour when we are frightened is seen by Bowlby as a way in which we need safeguarding when we are threatened. Human beings can feel threatened when they are alone, in the dark, in the presence of a loud noise, or by strange conditions, hunger or fatigue. All these circumstances elicit attachment behaviour – that is, proximity to a safe figure who can terminate the fear and give succour. The universal phenomenon of turning to a familiar figure for comfort when in distress is an experience too well known to need stressing.

Attachment behaviour, forming an affectionate bond, is orientated specifically to a few individuals in order of preference, and may endure for the whole lifetime, providing a profound source of security. It has survival value, and is conceived as a class of bonding behaviour distinct from feeding and sexual orientations.

When a young child has a secure basis – for example, a safe figure, usually the mother – it is free to leave her side and explore its environment. The parental figure acts as a safety centre from which the child can distance itself and to which it can return when frightened or tired. The need for a secure basis is sought universally by human beings in their homes and the families they produce. There is a constant need to return to this continuous source of security. In the light of this interpretation, it is vital to enquire what was the secure basis in the life of Jesus. On a surface reading he had no secure basis as an adult:

> When Jesus saw the crowd all about him he gave orders to leave for the other side. One of the scribes then came up to him and said to him, 'Master, I will follow you wherever you go.' Jesus said, 'Foxes have holes and the birds of the air have nests, but the Son of man has nowhere to lay his head.' (Matt. 8:18–20)

The gospels give us a view of Jesus as a peripatetic person, going from village to village, town to town, and of course to the Temple in Jerusalem. He had no settled residence, and so his sense of security did not come from a fixed home. In the light of this chapter, I conceive his security as an inner one, based on the formation of a secure early attachment to his parents, which we now know to be the foundation of a sound personality.

So far, attachment theory has been defined as the formation of an affectionate bond through vision, sound and touch to a sufficiently constant significant figure, usually the mother, who in turn may be replaced in adult life by other significant figures, such as friends, spouse, relations.

Returning to the mother, attachment behaviour needs a care-giving response. The care-giving response is the equivalent of the holding behaviour of Winnicott. This response means being available and responsive, as and when needed, and also means intervening when the child is in trouble. There is now a wide consensus that the way in which this care response is given determines to a large degree the mental health of the adult individual, his or her capacity to be a loving person and to feel secure. Furthermore, there is a strong causal relationship between a person's experience with parents and the later capacity to make affectionate bonds.

From what we know through the insights given in the gospels, we can safely conjecture that the care-giving response of the parents of Jesus must have been a very good one. There is also strong evidence that, when there is a sound care-giving response, children grow up to be secure and self reliant, to be trusting, co-operative and helpful to others. In all these respects, the picture we get of Jesus in the gospels fits this image, and therefore we are not in the realms of wild guesswork to envisage him in his early years as growing up in a home where there was a good fit between attachment behaviour and caring response.

On the other hand, people who are referred to psychiatrists are often anxious, insecure, depressed men and women. Research shows that many of these individuals have often been subjected to one or more of the following upbringing conditions:

1 One or both parents being absent or persistently unresponsive to the child's care-eliciting behaviour, accompanied by constant rejection.
2 Persistent threats not to love the child, used as a means of control.
3 Threats by parents to abandon the family or to commit suicide.
4 Threats by parents, particularly the mother, to abandon the child.

5 Inducing the child to feel guilty by blaming it for parental illness or death.[2]

It is safe to suppose that Jesus did not experience any of these patterns of parental behaviour.

Attachment behaviour presupposes that, when there is a separation from the attached figure or figures, anxiety, depression, anger, even despair, are experienced by the person who has sustained the loss. In the life of Jesus, we see his preparation of the apostles for his impending death. He empathised with them about their coming loss, and must have felt anxious, depressed and sad himself at his departure. We shall explore his death further, but we can presume that the link between the apostles and Jesus was in the nature of an attachment bond, and that Jesus nurtured them as an ideal care giver.

It is agreed in psychological circles that the way in which we behave towards others bears a close resemblance to the way in which we were treated in our own upbringing. This has usually been observed in detail in the case of damaged upbringing, such as the physical abuse of children. Those who are physically aggressive have frequently been shown to have been physically punished in their own childhood. This is the negative side of the human cycle. Bowlby and others have demonstrated a positive cycle, and it is legitimate to interpret the loving nature of Jesus as having been anticipated by a secure, loving upbringing. Thus the reverence and honour given to Mary theologically has nothing to fear from the psychological exploration of the part she played in the upbringing of Jesus. In the gospels, the life in Nazareth is almost a blank – but with the help of psychology we can begin to fill in the words of Luke: 'He went down with them and came to Nazareth and lived under their authority. His mother stored up all these things in her heart. And Jesus increased in wisdom, in stature and in favour with God and with people' (Luke 2:51–2). From what we know now, we can equate wisdom, stature and favour with security, trust and care.

I have ended the previous psychological chapters with a certain ambivalence. The psychoanalytic theories presented have a certain ring of truth and appeal, and yet are incomplete and require a certain imagination to accept them – which is not to say that they do not contain kernels of truth. But with attachment theory the conclusion is different. Here is a theory which has a wide consensus of approval, has a quality of universality which is very strong and which also speaks for its authenticity loud and clear. It is a theory to which I attach great importance, and which forms a strong foundation for the childhood and life of Jesus. At the time of writing, the theory, nearly 40 years old, has gained strong support and it can safely be put forward as very likely standing the test of time.

8

Erik H. Erikson
(1902–94)

ERIKSON, AN AMERICAN PSYCHOANALYST concerned with children and youth, presented human growth in stages analogous to Freud's psycho-sexual development. So, unlike Bowlby, he stuck to Freud's libido theory – but he expanded the meaning and he developed different concepts of what the child achieves at each stage. He conceived de-velopmental stages right up to old age, but in this chapter I shall confine myself to the first three.

Erikson designated his stages by the prefix 'a sense of', followed by the characteristic which is acquired and its opposite feature. Thus in the first year, the child achieves a sense of basic trust and its opposite feature, a sense of basic mistrust. He writes of basic trust as a pervasive attitude towards oneself and the world derived from experiences of the first year of life. The presence of a basic trust in the personality, which is acquired in the first year, remains throughout life and is, according to him, the cornerstone of a vital personality. In common with Winnicott and Bowlby, Erikson says that the amount of trust derived from the earliest infantile experiences does not depend on absolute quantities of food but on the quality of the relationship with the mother. Thus we see, in the majority of works cited, a continuity of the importance of the maternal response. For Winnicott, it was the handling of the baby by the mother; for Bowlby, it was the caring response to the attachment needs of the child. Since Jesus is certainly presented in the gospels as a vital personality, the trust which he had in himself must have been strong, and he must have had very good mothering indeed to produce such a quality. The importance attached by the Church to the circum-stances surrounding the conception, pregnancy and birth of Jesus, and the role played by Mary, must go beyond her willingness to respond to God according to his will; according to my thesis, it also relates to the quality of her nurturing in his infancy. It is no figment of the imagination to propose that the handling of Jesus by his mother was the appropriate one to bring out the fullness of his human potential. Indeed, as far as basic trust is concerned, we see in the gospels a mutual trust between Jesus and his heavenly Father on which the whole meaning of his life depended. In the same way, his judgement and trust came into operation in his choice of apostles, to whom he entrusted the building up of the community of the Church. The picture we get from the gospels is of a sureness and certainty in his actions, particularly in his dealings with the Pharisees, which speaks of a very high degree of trust in himself.

But he also knew the opposite characteristic, namely basic mistrust. Jesus was no blind believer in people. We have seen his pronounced criticism of the Pharisees and scribes for their hypocrisy, and in John's gospel there is a most perceptive passage describing his inner world of trust and mistrust:

> During his stay in Jerusalem for the feast of the Passover many believed in his name when they saw the signs that he did, but Jesus knew all people and did not trust himself to them; he never needed evidence about anyone; he could tell what someone had within. (John 2:23–5)

The Evangelist says that Jesus knew all people. We must presuppose, as in all aspects of his personality, that, in addition to the divine influence in his make up, he had a human dimension – and there was a constant meeting between the two. The point made in these psychological chapters is that Jesus' human formation was such as to give him a full human potential of maturity which could respond to the divine dimension in the sense of Genesis: '"Let us make man in our own image, in the likeness of ourselves"' (Gen. 1:26). The mystery of the incarnation is that the fullness of the divine meets the fullness of the human, and these psychological chapters are attempting to give a clue as to how this full humanity was achieved.

Erikson suggests that the earliest sense of identity arises out of the encounter between mother and infant – an encounter which should be one of mutual trustworthiness and recognition.

Another specific feature of Erikson's theories is his suggestion that each stage of development has a special relationship to a basic human institution. In this respect he casts a wider psychosocial net, and relates psychology to society. He is of the opinion that the life-cycle and human institutions have developed together. For him, religion is the institution which, throughout human history, has striven to verify basic trust. To use his own words, 'Trust then, becomes the capacity for faith'.[1] This link between faith and trust is fundamental for Jesus. Again and again, he seeks faith as the basic ingredient for his miracles – or 'signs', as John calls them. In the cure of the daughter of the Canaanite woman, the latter persisted in her request, despite the fact that she was a Canaanite. Jesus said to her: '"Woman, you have great faith. Let your desire be granted." And from that moment her daughter was well again' (Matt. 15:28).

This quality of trust comes out in the great dialogues of John's gospel. Exegetes say clearly that the words in this gospel are very unlikely to be those of Jesus but, as I have suggested at the beginning of this book, John must have been conveying a sense of what he understood about the inner world of Jesus. In his address to the apostles and, in particular, in his reply to the enquiry by Philip, Jesus showed a degree of exasperation with all of them, and then launched into his definite belief about himself and his relationship with the Father:

> Philip said, 'Lord, show us the Father and then we shall be satisfied.' Jesus said to him, 'Have I been with you all this time, Philip, and you still do not know me?
>
> 'Anyone who has seen me has seen the Father,
> so how can you say, "Show us the Father"?
> Do you not believe
> that I am in the Father and the Father is in me?'
>
> (John 14:8–10)

What is clear is that, in all these dialogues, the relationship between trust and faith is very close, and that the apostles, despite having Jesus in their midst, despite the evidence of his miracles, had problems in faith even though they had a strong trust. We see this link between faith and trust in the constant references in many passages to people who followed Jesus, now believing in him, now not believing, now following him and now deserting him. To Jesus, this wide range of response from the crowd must have been one of the constant pains he experienced in himself. He wanted them to believe, but he had to tolerate the disappointment of disbelief. This uncertainty is a common human trait. Our age has sought veracity from scientific proof, but in human interpersonal relationships we seek to be trusted and believed because of what we are. Jesus was also trying to persuade through the strength of his personality. In theology, there is an enormous exegetical emphasis on the titles of Jesus which give clues to his identity and his divinity. In this book, the emphasis is on his personality, the integrity of his personality, which gives us the clues as to who he was.

Erikson associated the period of the second and third years of life, the classical Freudian phase of anal libido, with a sense of autonomy. In his own words:

> The overall significance of this second stage of early childhood is the rapid gains in muscular maturation, in verbalisation, in discrimination and the consequent ability to co-ordinate a number of conflicting action patterns characterised by the tendencies of 'holding on' and 'letting go'. In this way the child begins to experience his autonomous will.[2]

These are the years when the toddler will learn to walk, talk, dress, pick up things and drop them. It is this age that brings a conflict of wills between toddler and mother. The mother prohibits, says 'no', but the infant pursues its own autonomous world. It will go to forbidden places, touch things it must not and generally test the patience of its mother. In this battle of wills, much patience is needed on the part of the mother, and yet the time will come when her patience will snap and she will shout and even smack. It is fascinating to ask whether Jesus was ever smacked! Alas we do not know, and I have tried to keep this book within the realms of what we can see in Jesus' childhood from his later behaviour in adulthood.

What is certain is that conflict between mother and child is inevitable, and that discord brings a rebuke from mother, which to the child is a profound shock. This leads to the cycle of conflict after aggressive autonomy, rebuke, guilt, a sense of paradise lost as intimacy with mother appears to be ruptured, and then forgiveness and the return to grace. This well-known human cycle is reckoned by Klein to occur in the first six months of life, with the drama occurring at the breast through the instinct of aggression, guilt and reparation. We cannot be sure what happens at six months, but we understand much more easily what happens in the second and third years of life. Whenever it happens, it is clearly part of the human cycle that we all can recognise. Aggression, conflict, forgiveness and restoration of harmony are certainly visible in the gospels in Peter's question: 'Then Peter went up to him and said, "Lord, how often must I forgive my brother if he wrongs me? As often as seven times?" Jesus answered, "Not seven, I tell you, but seventy seven times"' (Matt. 18:21–22).

In the above context we see the child contravening the boundaries set by the parents. For Bowlby, this is a period when the toddler, with a secure basis in the mother, leaves her side and explores the environment and returns to her when anxious or disturbed. We can see here the range of theories. For Freudians and for Erikson, the starting-point of this age is the libidinal drive of anality. The anal zone lends itself to the stubborn insistence on conflicting impulses, namely retention and elimination, and is seen by Erikson as a battle of autonomy. It is the time when the toddler delineates 'I' and 'you', 'me' and 'mine'. This is the retentive–eliminative stage. In adult life, holding on and giving up play a crucial part in relationships, and Freudians believe that hoarding is an anal characteristic emanating from this stage of development. However absurd this connection may appear to our adult, non-Freudian minds, the fact is that there are personalities who do hoard. The idea of hoarding or storing up is not absent in Jesus:

'Do not store up treasures for yourselves on earth, where moth and woodworm destroy them and thieves can break in and steal. But store up treasures for yourselves in heaven, where neither moth nor woodworm destroy them and thieves cannot break in and steal. For wherever your treasure is, there will your heart be too.' (Matt. 6:19–21)

As against the libidinal, sexual theory of human development, we have seen that Bowlby posed an attachment view whereby food and sex do not play a major role in development. But we have noted how important food is in the gospels, from the miracle of the multiplication of the loaves and fishes to the Last Supper in Jesus' transformation of bread and wine into his body and blood.

For Erikson, this stage of autonomy becomes decisive for the ratio between loving goodwill and hateful self insistence, between co-operation and wilfulness, and between self expression and compulsive self restraint. Erikson summarised the outcome of this stage as 'a sense of self control without loss of self esteem'. On the other hand, from an unavoidable sense of loss of self control or parental over-control comes a propensity for doubt and shame, the opposite characteristics of autonomy.

We see in Jesus a well-developed sense of autonomy from his parents in the episode at the Temple when he was 12 years old (Luke 2:41), and later on, both from his family (Matt. 12:46) and from the Hebraic law in which he was brought up. The only dependence we see in the gospels is on his heavenly Father, and that was a dependency of mutual love:

> 'I have loved you
> just as the Father has loved me.'
> (John 15:9)

We saw that Erikson related basic trust to the institution of religion. What institution does he connect to the safeguard of autonomy? Erikson says:

> Man's basic need for a delineation of his autonomy seems to have an institutional safeguard in the principle of law and order which in every day life as well as in the courts of law apportions to each his privileges and his limitations, his obligations and his rights. It is law that safeguards us from arbitrariness.

There are examples in the gospels in which the courts and judges are referred to, but Jesus emphasised above all the law of love.

In fact, Jesus wielded enormous power. Theologians will say that, as the Son of God, it is right and proper that he should do so. But neither Jesus nor the Father nor the Spirit are arbitrary users of power. There is no sense of dictatorship in the Trinity. Jesus indeed claimed enormous authority: '"All authority in heaven and earth has been given to me"' (Matt. 28:19). Jesus combined authority with autonomy but there is present the influence of love, gentleness and humility (Matt. 11: 28–31). The power of the Pharisees is, on the other hand, criticised – for it is based on outward appearances, show and wealth. These are not criteria of integrity, at the time of Jesus or at any time.

At the next stage of development, the age of four to five years, Erikson says: 'Being firmly convinced that he is a person on his own, the child must now find out what kind of person he may become'. We may speculate that the separation which Jesus experienced later on between his earthly home and his heavenly Father may have begun at this age. The child learns now to move more freely, more exuberantly, and therefore can explore a much wider range of goals. His language develops further, and he can understand and cope with many things. Both language and locomotion allow the child to expand his imagination, and it is here that Jesus' understanding of the possibility of his wider divine purpose may have started. He can, humanly speaking, assume many roles in his imagination – and these may have included that of the Messiah.

Psychology cannot of course penetrate the inner world of the child Jesus that led to his imaginative thinking about being a Messiah – but it can confirm that his human development could sustain such a possibility. In any case, out of the growth of locomotion, verbal fluency and imagination, Erikson writes of the development of a 'sense of initiative' for a realistic sense of 'ambition and purpose'. The child suddenly becomes more himself, more loving, more relaxed, and develops into a more vital self.

The intrusive mode which is the principal feature of this stage is characterised by intrusion into space by powerful locomotion, intrusion into the unknown by strong curiosity, intrusion into people's ears by an aggressive voice, intrusion into bodies by physical attack. Erikson, who retains the Freudian schema in which this is the phallic stage, added that for the child, in fantasy, this is the intrusion of the phallus into the female body. We may or may not accept this last Freudian component, but for the rest we can recognise the young boy or girl who is full of vigour and zest, causing havoc by their energy.

Erikson attributed jealousy and rivalry to this stage, emanating from the competitive spirit of the nature of the child's experience. Jesus was aware of feelings of jealousy, and on the occasion of the request of the mother of Zebedee's sons, he introduced the idea of service against that of power:

> The mother of Zebedee's sons came with her sons to make a request of him, and bowed low; and he said to her, 'What is it you want?' She said to him, 'Promise that these two sons of mine may sit one at your right hand and the other at your left in your kingdom.' Jesus answered, 'You do not know what you are asking. Can you drink the cup that I am going to drink?' They replied, 'We can.' He said to them, 'Very well; you shall drink my cup, but as

for seats at my right hand and my left, these are not mine to grant; they belong to whom they have been allotted by my Father.'

When the other ten heard this they were indignant with the two brothers. But Jesus called them to him and said, 'You know that among the gentiles the rulers lord it over them, and great men make their authority felt. Among you this is not to happen. No, anyone who wants to become great among you must be your servant, and anyone who wants to be first among you must be your slave, just as the Son of man came not to be served but to serve, and to give his life as a ransom for many.' (Matt. 20:20–28)

Erikson puts the emergence of conscience at this stage, as the child hears the inner voice of self observation, self guidance and self control. This is also the time of the development of Freud's super ego.

There is little doubt that Jesus had a supremely well-defined sense of conscience. His sense of justice, the rightness of things, his compassion, the concern for the poor, the demands of the neighbour, the need for forgiveness, reparation – all these showed a highly sensitive conscience which was intimately linked with his awareness of his Father.

The sense of self esteem is put by Erikson in the next stage, but I believe that by now the child appreciates feeling loved by its parents and this awareness of being lovable contributes to the sense of self esteem. Erikson believed that what the initiative stage contributes to later identity development is to free the child's initiative and sense of purpose for adult tasks which promise a fulfilment of its range of capacities. The child now feels, 'I am what I can imagine I will be'. The initiative stage is very important for Jesus. He had to fulfil a role which was unique in the history of humankind. He was questioned by his family who thought he was mad, by the Pharisees who considered him possessed, and, I suspect, was looked upon with bewilderment by the apostles who, although they accepted his credentials, must have often been puzzled by what they saw and experienced. Jesus had to have a sense of clarity about his mission which allowed him to pursue his work, undaunted by the resistance he met. So indeed from an early stage he was convinced that he could be what he imagined he was.

This brings to an end the discussion of Erikson's three stages, which allow us to see the child developing in an awareness with which we can identify, and which lays the foundations for the adult self.

9

Summary of Psychological Theories

THE WORK OF Freud, Klein, Winnicott, Bowlby and Erikson does not exhaust the theories of of dynamic psychology. However, their work is a primary source for the point I want to illustrate – namely that the psychological theories which emanate from them have validity for the adult personality. In this book I am using these theories to show firstly, that, despite different social settings, the principles enunciated have a universal validity; secondly, that there is a continuity of childhood experiences into adulthood; and thirdly, that the interpersonal interaction of feelings and emotions can give us insights into the world of childhood. I have used this third point to link pyschological theory with the events and sayings of Jesus.

These three principles form the methodology of this book. They will help us to have a vision of the humanity of Jesus. They will enable us to see afresh familiar passages and to put new constructions on them. But above all, I hope they will help us to link up with the life of Jesus on earth which goes on for all time – just as we have used psychological theories for universals, so we can use the life of Jesus as a universal for our lives.

In the previous five chapters we have seen, first of all, the great advances of Freud in seeing life as a dynamic entity, with conscious and unconscious interacting, and feelings and emotions playing a vital part. We are so constrained by our education, which emphasises the intellect, that we fail to see life as a dynamic entity. We think of achievement as an intellectual pursuit. This is not to say that cognitive intelligence is not important – it certainly is. Jesus, as depicted in the gospels, has an acute and intelligent mind – but it is not his intelligence that we worship. Rather, the gospels come alive much more as dynamic stories of a caring human being who held all those around him in a spell woven by his compassion and love. His power does emanate from his humanity in the widest sense of that word, and we owe a debt to Freud for enabling us to read the gospels with this dynamism in mind.

Klein takes us further along this route of infantile sexuality and food, where love and security is gained from the battle of oral satisfaction and the ascendancy of love over hatred. We may have doubts about whether all that she claims actually happens in the infant's life. We may have difficulty in conceptualising it – but the pangs of hunger and the biting of the breast are real, and we should not be surprised if they leave a trail of feelings and emotions behind. There is certainly no doubt that food played a part in the ministry of Jesus, and the Eucharist is a miracle of the transformation of food.

Winnicott brings us nearer to a reality which we can understand as the link between psyche and body. The importance he attaches to the handling of the baby as a means of creating love is unquestionable, and the tenderness with which parents handle the baby speaks knowingly of the link between love and touch, which all adults can testify to.

Bowlby brought a whole new dimension to psychological theory with his views on human attachment and the corresponding caring response. Attachment theory is convincing, and we can all test it in our adult relationships and in our interpersonal links. The link between attachment, security and love speaks strongly of authenticity and this theory is the strongest candidate for our understanding of the human personality.

Erikson added a measure of immense enrichment to our knowledge of the child, and hence of the adult. We can understand how trust develops in the first year, we can see the toddler displaying autonomy and the older child initiative.

All these theorists give us an outline of how love in human beings is developed – and it is the development of this love in Jesus that is fascinating. From across the centuries, it is this love, care and compassion that reverberates, finally concluding in the supreme example of love in his death. The resurrection is the cornerstone of the Christian faith, but his life is the endless inspiration and example for us. This was a life of love and these psychological theories give us a means to penetrate its origins. Freud and Klein attribute this love to the satisfaction of instinctual needs. Winnicott stressed the handling of the infant. Bowlby asserted that the roots of human love lie in the attachment bond between child and mother, and later father. All of them stress the response of the mother and then of the father, and it is to the relationship of Jesus to his mother and father that we now turn.

III

Family Relationships

10

Jesus and his Mother

THE RELATIONSHIP OF Jesus to his mother and father was essential for his human development. His parents were not mere providers of nurture; they were active and influential to the person he became. The gospels, less concerned with this, lay their whole emphasis primarily on the adult Jesus and so, both in this chapter and the next (on his relationship to his father), reconstruction is my theme. With both mother and father, this reconstruction is based on the psychological methodology already enunciated.

We begin with the relationship of Jesus and his mother in the womb, when Mary first realised that she had conceived:

> In the sixth month the angel Gabriel was sent by God to a town in Galilee called Nazareth, to a virgin betrothed to a man named Joseph, of the House of David; and the virgin's name was Mary. He went in and said to her, 'Rejoice, you who enjoy God's favour! The Lord is with you.' She was deeply disturbed by these words and asked herself what this greeting could mean. (Luke 1:26–30)

'She was deeply disturbed.' We can imagine Mary's reaction at being confronted by a pregnancy, knowing full well that she had not had sexual intercourse with Joseph – or, for that matter, anybody else. After 2000 years we accept this event unthinkingly, but at its original moment it must have been startling and most perplexing.

We do not know what the relationship of Mary was to Joseph, except that she was betrothed to him. Given the times, it is unlikely that this was a love affair, rather more likely that it was an arrangement. Even so, she knew that she had not had sexual intercourse with him. A virginal conception is not an everyday event, and the time of the annunciation was no exception. So the words of Luke – that Mary was deeply disturbed – are an understatement of her psychological state at receiving the news. The angel continues his address:

> But the angel said to her, 'Mary, do not be afraid; you have won God's favour. Look! You are to conceive in your womb and bear a son, and you must name him Jesus. He will be great and will be called Son of the Most High. The Lord God will give him the throne of his ancestor David; he will rule over the House of Jacob for ever and his reign will have no end.' (Luke 1:30–33)

Mary was not only faced with a totally unexpected pregnancy but she was forewarned of the birth of a person who had the highest credentials. She must have wondered what had made her God's choice. When something unusual happens to any of us, the most natural question is 'Why me?' It would have been surprising if Mary did not ask the same question. I think we can posit that her personality was mature enough to withstand the shock of the surprise. Her question to the angel is not a denial or abdication of the responsibility laid on her; rather she asks: '"But how can this come about, since I have no knowledge of man?"' Mary was very pragmatic in her response. She had had no sexual intercourse, so how was she to become pregnant?

> The angel answered, 'The Holy Spirit will come upon you, and the power of the Most High will cover you with its shadow. And so the child will be holy and will be called Son of God. And I tell you this too: your cousin Elizabeth also, in her old age, has conceived a son, and she whom people called barren is now in her sixth month, for nothing is impossible to God.' (Luke 1:35–7)

Mary was being told that her conception would bring her into direct relationship with the Son of God. She had her whole life to come to terms with this reality. We can imagine a personality that could absorb this momentous happening – that is to say, of being in a state of considering its possibilities while not necessarily fully grasping their meaning. We see evidence of this blind faith in the miracle of Cana: 'His mother said to the servants, "Do whatever he tells you".' (John 2:5). Mary had faith in her son, and this capacity to have faith in him suggests that she had faith in herself. She was familiar with trust in her life. We see this in some people who, whatever they are asked to do, respond in the affirmative because they know intuitively that they have the capacity to perform a wide range of roles.

Did Mary know that she was being asked to be the mother of the Son of God? It is unlikely that the question would have arisen in this specific way. What is certain is that she was aware that she was being placed in a special relationship to God. Her awareness of what she was being asked to do is relevant to her reply. She recognised that God was asking her to do something special which would transform her life. As a woman, a pregnancy and becoming a mother were crucial happenings in her life, central to her being. She was not being asked to cook meals or change her household routine. She was being asked to change her whole life, to become, in our everyday language, a single mother.

Joseph was clearly moved by finding Mary pregnant. He did not expect it. He too had to be informed of the meaning of the event by the angel. Before being enlightened, he was shocked and he wanted to spare Mary any disgrace. This potential disgrace Mary was also facing. And yet her response was: ' "You see before you the Lord's servant, let it happen to me as you have said" ' (Luke 1:38).

Mary's response was no frightened acquiescence nor blind obedience. Both theologically and psychologically, we must see in her affirmative reply a response of her whole being which, without fully appreciating all the implications of what was in store for her, put her personality in readiness in the service of God. This was not a partial 'yes'. In her 'yes' she was accepting full responsibility not only for her pregnancy, but for being in an exceptional relationship to God. In her reply we have one of those special meeting-points between God and humanity. She used her personality to acknowledge the presence of God and the special intervention in her life.

It was the awareness of this intervention that she wanted to share with her cousin Elizabeth. The visitation was certainly a social interaction. Both women were pregnant and had much to share, as pregnant women do. But, as we shall see in Luke, it was also the first public affirmation of her special status. Elizabeth greets Mary thus:

'Of all women you are the most blessed, and blessed is the fruit of your womb. Why should I be honoured with a visit from the mother of my Lord? Look, the moment your greeting reached my ears, the child in my womb leapt for joy. Yes, blessed is she who believed that the promise made her by the Lord would be fulfilled.' (Luke 1:42–5)

Elizabeth confirmed the blessedness of Mary, and the latter must have felt affirmed by her cousin. This affirmation, coupled with the vindi-cation of Joseph and the words of the angel, must have given Mary a peace of mind which could have lasted throughout the pregnancy. We know that the mental state of the mother is important to the foetus. It is possible to imagine a highly anxious and agitated mother who, throughout the pregnancy, was pouring adrenaline into her system and activating her hormones to cope with the shock of the birth. In reconstructing Mary's pregnancy, we can envisage her having a relaxed attitude in certainty and security, as she says in the canticle that follows:

> 'My soul proclaims the greatness of the Lord
> and my spirit rejoices in God my Saviour;
> because he has looked upon the humiliation of his servant.
> Yes, from now onwards all generations will call me blessed,
> For the Almighty has done great things for me.'
>
> (Luke 1:46–9)

These words are put in Mary's mouth by Luke: we cannot imagine Mary going around actually saying them. But we can imagine her state of equanimity, influencing her pregnancy by a state of mind which was at peace in the relationship she had with God, and excited by the coming birth of her child.

And so we come to the birth of Jesus:

> Now it happened that at this time Caesar Augustus issued a decree that a census should be made of the whole inhabited world. This census – the first – took place while Quirinius was governor of Syria, and everyone went to be registered, each to his own town. So Joseph set out from the town of Nazareth in Galilee for Judaea, to David's town called Bethlehem, since he was of David's house and line, in order to be registered together with Mary, his betrothed, who was with child. (Luke 2:1–5)

Mary was advanced in her pregnancy. We can imagine the trauma of travelling long distances in the discomfort of that age. We have no evidence of Mary complaining, but this does not mean that she did not suffer. Indeed, we know that she was at the foot of the cross at Jesus' crucifixion and must have suffered intensely. But we have not reached yet her relationship with Jesus as an adult. Now it was time to give birth:

> Now it happened that, while they were there, the time came for her to have her child, and she gave birth to a son, her first-born. She wrapped him in swaddling clothes and laid him in a manger because there was no room for them in the living-space. (Luke 2:6–8)

There are no grounds for believing that Mary was spared the pangs of childbirth. She very likely experienced birth contractions and the pain of labour. Her hymen was probably ruptured at the birth because the essentials of her virginity were not solely physical, and the birth had to respect the course of its human nature. The joy after the labour pains safeguarded the bonding with her child, and the vital moments of holding the baby in her arms. In this respect it is very relevant to suggest that, in all probability, Joseph was with her at the time of the birth, also initiating his paternal bond with Jesus. The circumstances of the birth suggest poverty – here we see that, from the very beginning of his life, Jesus was familiar with the conditions of poverty.

At his birth Jesus was acknowledged by both his mother and father, who were witnesses to his arrival. But just as the pregnancy was affirmed by Elizabeth, so the birth of Jesus was affirmed by the shepherds. The shepherds had been alerted by the angel of the Lord:

> 'Do not be afraid. Look, I bring you news of great joy, a joy to be shared by the whole people. Today in the town of David a Saviour has been born to you; he is Christ the Lord. And here is a sign for you: you will find a baby wrapped in swaddling clothes and lying in a manger.' (Luke 2:10–12)

The birth of Jesus prompted Luke to make the event of global significance. The whole people are involved, and the shepherds are their representatives. Just as in his adult life Jesus had a special relationship with the marginalised and the poor, so at the beginning of his life it is the shepherds who are given to us as the representatives of humankind to greet and acknowledge him. The whole scene of the manger and the shepherds is reminiscent of the Beatitudes. '"How blessed are you who are poor: the kingdom of God is yours"' (Luke 6:20). Going back to Mary's Magnificat we find: '"He has pulled down princes from their thrones and raised high the lowly"' (Luke 1:52). And so it happened that the shepherds visited Mary and the baby:

> The shepherds said to one another, 'Let us go to Bethlehem and see this event which the Lord has made known to us.' So they hurried away and found Mary and Joseph, and the baby lying in the manger. When they saw the child they repeated what they had been told about him, and everyone who heard it was astonished at what the shepherds said to them. As for Mary, she treasured all these things and pondered them in her heart. (Luke 2:15–19)

There are two points in this passage which need comment. First, that the shepherds repeated what they had heard – that this baby was Christ the Lord. I do not suppose that, despite the uniqueness of every baby, baby Jesus looked different from any other. And yet those who heard the news of the shepherds were astonished. They had every right to be. The whole setting of the manger and the poverty of the circumstance mitigated against the proclamation, which declared that this was the awaited Messiah. The words astonished, and similar terms – used later on in the gospels for the reactions of the crowds to Jesus' deeds – show that something special surrounded the presence of Jesus, which did not escape people's attention. It is this special quality of awe that we find in the pages of the gospel. It is not fear in the presence of the spectacular, but the extension of the human psyche to its utter limits – a natural reaction when the human meets the divine. This meeting is often indirect – but we are left in no doubt, in the passages of the gospel, that it is most powerful.

The second point to comment upon are the words, 'As for Mary, she treasured all these things and pondered them in her heart'. For Mary, there was no lightning insight, no mystical revelation. Instead, there was a receptivity of the wonder of what was proclaimed interacting with her psyche. We can propose a process of growth, or what Jungians would call individuation. Mary remained sensitive to all that she experienced, and this psychologically reacted with her personality. Theologians might want to see an interaction between the Old Testament and the events surrounding Jesus which proclaimed his messianic identity. I do not deny that this could have happened. Here I am suggesting that Mary interacted in her psyche with the growing child, and was slowly shaped by what she saw and felt about him – and, as with the apostles and the crowd later in his life, it was the vitality of his personality that, at the human level, influenced her reaction.

I see the childhood of Jesus as an interaction between Mary and Jesus in which Jesus developed his individuality, to which Mary responded by safeguarding its essentials. She did not only give birth to the baby, but her selection by God as a unique personality safeguarded her whole mothering from impeding the growth of Jesus. In a moment I shall explain what I mean by this.

After the birth of Jesus, there follows his circumcision – at which ceremony the name of Jesus was given to him. Luke follows the event of the circumcision with the story of the presentation in the Temple at Jerusalem. Jerusalem was central to Jesus' mission, and his presentation there as a baby anticipates the role of the same site at the culmination of his life.

The sacrifice that was offered at the purification was a pair of turtle doves or two young pigeons. Both these were offerings given by the poor, emphasising again the circumstances of poverty surrounding Jesus' birth. Luke goes on to describe an incident involving a man called Simeon who had been told that he would not die until he had seen Christ the Lord. Prompted by the Spirit, Simeon came to the Temple. There he took Jesus in his arms and said:

> 'Now, Master, you are letting your servant go in peace,
> as you promised;
> for my eyes have seen the salvation
> which you have made ready in the sight of the nations;
> a light of revelation for the gentiles
> And glory for your people Israel.'

As the child's mother and father were wondering at these things that were being said about him, Simeon blessed them and said to Mary his mother, 'Look, he is destined for the fall and for the rise of many in Israel, destined to be a sign that is opposed – and a sword will pierce your soul too – so that the secret thoughts of many may be laid bare.' (Luke 2:29–35)

The parents wondered at what Simeon said. Jesus was presented to them as a light of the Gentiles and a glory of Israel but, in the following passage, as a sign of contradiction, as a result of whom Mary was to be pierced by a sword. At the human level these were perplexing revelations which the parents stored in their psyche. They were certainly prepared for special events in the life of their son and knew that his uniqueness was linked with his relationship with God. They became aware that they were guardians of this uniqueness. How was this uniqueness transacted? In Luke's words, we discover a theological summary: 'When they had done everything the Law of Lord required, they went back to Galilee, to their own town of Nazareth. And as the child grew to maturity, he was filled with wisdom; and God's favour was with him' (Luke 2:39–40).

This passage does not tell us very much and this is where I make use of reconstruction, according to the earlier psychological chapters. I am suggesting that Jesus' mother and father performed their ordinary tasks, at least, as Winnicott would say, in a 'good enough' manner; but also, as I wish to propose, in fostering the fullness of his human capacity.

We know nothing about the childhood of Jesus other than the episode in the Temple, to which I will refer below. But we know a great deal about the adult Jesus. We see in the adult Jesus a human being of mature and balanced characteristics, with a loving and compassionate nature, who could capture wisdom in pithy one-liners and memorable parables, who suffered, lived, died and, in the faith of Christianity, we believe that he rose from the dead. His resurrection is, in theological terms, the signature of his divinity; in human terms, it is the stamp of his perfection. Such a man needed an appropriate childhood and the sort of mothering that carried the tasks of motherhood to their fullest capacity. At this point I shall be accused of some idealisation. My defence is that, if his adult life has managed to impress the world 2000 years on, it is not unreasonable to assume that his childhood had the appropriate characteristics to produce it. So I am suggesting that his feeding at the breast was full and satisfactory.

Deviating for a moment, we may see in Jesus' reply to his parents in the Temple (Luke 2:49) a slight distancing of himself from his mother. We shall see the same distancing in later passages. I am not suggesting that Jesus did not love his mother or that he had ambivalent feelings towards her: in John's gospel we see his devotion to her from the cross. What I am suggesting here are two things. First, Jesus was not a family man in the narrow sense of that word: his family was the whole world. Secondly, Jesus was not a mother's boy: he stood on his own as a person in his own right, and it is a tribute to his mother that she offered a mothering which allowed him to realise his autonomy. Going beyond feeding at the breast, we have to bear in mind how Jesus was handled as a child, physically and psychologically. We do not know about this directly, but I am suggesting that there was a handling which gave Jesus a comfortable connection between his body and his psyche. Later in his life he showed a sensitivity to the link between body and spirit:

> When he returned to Capernaum, some time later word went round that he was in the house; and so many people collected that there was no room left, even in front of the door. He was preaching the word to them when some people came bringing him a paralytic carried by four men... Seeing their faith, Jesus said to the paralytic, 'My child, your sins are forgiven.' Now some scribes were sitting there, and they thought to themselves, 'How can this man talk like that? He is being blasphemous. Who but God can forgive sins?' And at once, Jesus, inwardly aware that this was what they were thinking, said to them, 'Why do you have these thoughts in your hearts? Which of these is easier: to say to the paralytic "Your sins are forgiven" or to say, "Get up, pick up your stretcher and walk"? But to prove that the Son of man has authority to forgive sins on earth' – he said to the paralytic – 'I order you: get up, pick up your stretcher, and go off home.' And the man got up, and at once picked up his stretcher and walked out in front of everyone, so that they were all astonished and praised God saying, 'We have never seen anything like this.' (Mark 2:1–12)

This passage is important, not only for the miracle, not only for the theological point about Jesus' capacity to forgive sins or his remarkable awareness of what the scribes were thinking, but for the psychosomatic way of the healing. Jesus connects the inner world of sin, psyche and body, which suggests an inner link in Jesus himself – not between sin, psyche and body, but psyche and body. This in turn suggests that, in his childhood, the link between his body and the quality of his handling by his mother was delicate, sensitive and smooth. In the miracle, Jesus showed that he understood the connection, as he did in other psychosomatic miracles. By 'psychosomatic', I am not suggesting that emotions were the only cause of the paralysis, but that there was a link between body and brain which truly represented a miraculous cure.

Beyond psychosomatic interaction (as suggested by Winnicott), there is the further point that, in his childhood, Jesus was handled in such a way that his awareness of pain in his body was coupled with the conviction and hope that it could be overcome. I am suggesting that he was not left with pangs of hunger that were not met, and so he developed an optimistic attitude to stress. There are so many people who, in the presence of pain or distress, feel overwhelmed. Jesus showed optimism in his approach to disease, which he felt could be conquered, and to his own suffering, which he was convinced would not overwhelm him – and ultimately, he was also optimistic in his awareness that death is not the end. Such perfect optimism is very likely to have had its origin in the way in which he was helped to handle his own pain. Optimism rather than pessimism was the trait of the adult Jesus, who is shown in the pages of the gospels to be convinced that good will prevail over evil. Theologians may say that this is a divine insight – and so it is. But the divine, in the incarnation, needs fertile human soil in which it can take root, and I am suggesting that his optimism had its origins in the way in which he was helped to overcome inclemency as a child.

Delicate handling in childhood also creates a sensitive personality. I use the word 'sensitive' here not in the sense of easily offended, but meaning empathetic, having the capacity to feel the inner world of others. We see this sensitivity in the following passage from Mark:

> The apostles rejoined Jesus and told him all they had done and taught. And he said to them, 'Come away to some lonely place all by yourselves and rest for a while'; for there were so many coming and going that there was no time for them even to eat. So they went off in the boat to a lonely place where they could be by themselves. But people saw them going, and many recognised them; and from every town they all hurried to the place on foot and reached it before them. So as he stepped ashore he saw a large crowd; and he took pity on them. (Mark 6:30–34)

There followed the multiplication of the loaves and fishes, but what I want to concentrate on was Jesus' concern for his apostles and the crowd on whom he took pity. This concern was in evidence throughout his ministry, and shows a sensitivity which very likely had its origins in his own handling by his mother. An insensitive mother is hardly likely to have produced such a delicate awareness of the needs of others.

Winnicott writes of ego-relatedness as a sensitive interaction between two conscious selves, mother and child, giving the security for inner self reliance which allows people to remain alone without being lonely. As I have mentioned before, we see Jesus being alone – and we shall have occasion to look at this specifically in his 40 days in the desert. But here I want to widen the idea that this ego contact between child and mother – which means a psychological interaction between adult and child – gives calm, tranquillity and sensitivity. Our awareness of the wider setting between Jesus and his mother gives us a background to an adult Jesus who could be calm aboard the ship in the presence of the storm in which the apostles were terrified of sinking; who showed a sense of tranquillity when the woman caught in adultery was brought to him, surrounded by a group of people eager to punish her and catch him out, to which he responded by writing on the ground. His delicate sensitivity is also revealed in his ambivalent relationship with Peter, whom he elevates to the leadership of the apostles, and yet whom he has to rebuke on more than one occasion. In general, Jesus' sensitivity gave him an an acute awareness of the world around, allowing him constantly to be one step ahead of others, friends and enemies alike.

We move on from Winnicott to Bowlby, whose work on attachment is the current cornerstone of understanding growth in childhood. We saw in Chapter 7 that the child forms an affectionate attachment or bond with mother through the faculties of vision, sound and touch. To the outgoing needs of the child, we need the care-giving response of the mother. The interaction between attachment and the appropriate care-giving response gives rise to a mature, secure, self reliant, trusting, co-operative, helpful and loving person. All these characteristics can be applied to Jesus. He was mature in his relationship with the apostles, with those he cured, with women, with friends and enemies alike. He showed a combination of security and self reliance which was remarkable. His messianic mission – nothing short of transforming the world – meant enormous opposition, and yet he stood his ground and did not engage in a physical battle to overcome his enemies. He put his whole mission in the hands of his apostles and all those who followed him, showing extraordinary trust in them – and events proved that he was right in his trust. He had infinite patience with his apostles, having to co-operate with them to achieve his mission. His capacity to be loving knew no bounds.

Bowlby's attachment theory suggests that the mother (or her equivalent) forms a secure basis from which the child can go away and explore its environment, returning to her when it is threatened. We do not need to reconstruct this psychological ability. We have, in Luke's episode of Jesus in the Temple, a superb example of the boy Jesus exploring his environment and his autonomy. We shall come across the whole of this story later on as a crucial text for Jesus' relationship with his heavenly Father – but in the mean time, I use part of it as an example of his self-reliant exploration of the world:

> Every year his parents used to go to Jerusalem for the feast of the Passover. When he was twelve years old, they went up for the feast as usual. When the days of the feast were over and they set off home, the boy Jesus stayed behind in Jerusalem without his parents knowing it. (Luke 2:41–3)

This passage shows the secure self assurance of the boy Jesus, enabling him to stay behind and explore his environment, as well as showing his autonomy and his gentle rebuke to his mother: ' "Why were you looking for me? Did you not know that I must be in my Father's house?" But they did not understand what he meant' (Luke 2:49). Jesus' secure basis was internal, he carried it within himself. He in turn became the secure basis for his apostles and those who turned to him. In due course, he was to become the secure basis for his Church, which has survived to this very day.

In the last sentence in the story (Luke 2:50), we see that his parents did not understand him. Do we find the same gap between Jesus and his mother's understanding of his mission? This is a delicate and difficult topic. I have already suggested that she was sensitively aware of her task of mothering him in such a way as to facilitate his work. Whether she understood the exact nature of this work, beyond the fact that it was God's will, whether she comprehended that he was the Messiah, is another matter. Luke suggests that, at the annunciation, the angel made clear to Mary who her son was going to be. She knew that he was going to be an exceptional person; she may even have known that her son was the Messiah – but could her humanity grasp the full implications of the arrival of the Messiah? Mary, I believe, lived her life in the certainty of her special mission, but she found in the actual manifestations an ever-growing sense of wonder. It is in this way that we can understand the following passage: 'He went home again, and once more such a crowd collected that they could not even have a meal. When his relations heard of this, they set out to take charge of him; they said, "He is out of his mind" ' (Mark 3:20–21).

This passage suggests that his relatives thought he was mad. A contradictory picture emerges here – one which vacillates between a mother who, in her heart, nurtured the mystery of the origins of her son and the special signs surrounding him, and his behaviour, which appeared bizarre and was certainly unconventional. Even if she could reconcile the two, she must have had a difficult task persuading her relatives. Mark follows this passage with another:

> Now his mother and his brothers arrived and, standing outside, sent a message asking for him. A crowd was sitting round him at the time the message was passed to him, 'Look, your mother and brothers and sisters are outside asking for you.' He replied, 'Who are my mother and my brothers?' And looking at those sitting in a circle around him, he said, 'Here are my mother and my brothers. Anyone who does the will of God, that person is my brother and sister and mother.' (Mark 3:31–5)

On the face of this passage, Jesus spurned his mother and relatives. But it seems to me that here, as in the episode in the Temple, Jesus acknowledged the priority of his heavenly Father over his relationship with his earthly parents. This does not mean that he did not care for his mother – but that their agendas were different. It is in this vein that we must also see the episode in John of the miracle in Cana. Here there was a wedding feast where Jesus, his disciples and his mother were present. The wine ran out and his mother said to him: '"They have no wine"'. It would be characteristic of his mother to be concerned that there was no more wine. Jesus was cool in his reply: '"Woman, what do you want from me?"' The Jerusalem Bible says that this was an unusual address from son to mother – we could even interpret it as rude. He continued: '"My hour has not yet come." His mother said to the servants, "Do whatever he tells you"' (John 2:4–6).

Jesus might have been irritated at being pushed to manifest his powers before he had decided to do so. We also see his mother's awareness of these powers – which seems to answer the dilemma of her insight into who he was. This episode suggests that she knew very well, and Jesus goes on to perform his first miracle. Here, the relationship between Jesus and his mother illustrates a typical human show of independence on the part of the son, with subsequent compliance.

Finally, we see the care and love that Jesus had for his mother when, from the cross, he placed her in the care of his beloved disciple. Here, in the midst of his own profound sufferings, Jesus remembers his mother and links his love for her with the love of his special disciple.

This moment of pure love did not arrive just at this late hour in his life – it is very likely to have been within him throughout his years.

Jesus' relationship with his mother was special. In giving her assent to the angel, she gave up her own intentions for her life in order to serve God in the conception, birth, upbringing and care of her son. This was a life of sacrifice, adapting herself to the original style of Jesus (which cannot have been easy) – and then suffering the pain of his crucifixion and his death. Humanly speaking there is no evidence that she could foretell his resurrection. His death was real to him and real to her. Her heart indeed was pierced by a sword. But we have no reason to believe that she doubted for one moment her destiny or her determination to see her responsibility fully discharged. She trusted her son's mission – and I have suggested that her special role was to deliver, in the way described in this book, the fullness of this mothering. The results of the hidden world of Jesus' childhood are seen in his adulthood, and the completion of Mary's task is seen in what he achieved. He changed the face of the world, and she was the instrument that made this possible. Jesus needed his mother. We have in him no magic wonder-boy or man by-passing human exigencies. He hungered, thirsted, cried, needed comforting, and, in the quality of his mother's response, he discovered the means to answer hunger, thirst and suffering in the lives of others. Jesus found in his mother what he needed – and she did not let him down.

11
Jesus and his Father

IF WE KNOW LITTLE ABOUT the actual relationship of Jesus with his mother, having to reconstruct it from the fragments in our possession, we know next to nothing about his relationship with Joseph, his father. So in writing this chapter I have relied on a psychological interpretation: that Jesus' relationship with his heavenly Father (of which we have extensive knowledge from John's gospel) is based on his experience with his earthly father. The intimacy and warmth with which Jesus describes his relationship with his heavenly Father could not have come about if he had not experienced something similar with his earthly father. This interpretation lends itself to the common-sense view, often psychologically validated, that the child is father of the man. I simply cannot visualise the closeness of Jesus with Yahweh, if he had not first experienced something similar on earth.

A question may be asked here concerning the extent to which we can rely on John's gospel for an authentic version of Jesus' inner world. Exegetes in recent years have thrown great doubt on John's discourses. I belong to the school of thought which believes that, although the actual words that John uses are his own, he nevertheless describes a true interpretation of Jesus' relationship with his heavenly Father. François Dreyfus, professor at the École Biblique of Jerusalem, in a book called *Did Jesus Know He was God?*, asserts in the most definite manner that John's gospel is indeed a true representation of John's late consideration that Jesus was really the Son of God.[1] Dreyfus maintains that this was the view of the patristic and medieval period, and it is only latterly that it has been questioned. Apart from theological considerations, I have always been attracted to John's gospel as a vivid account of an expression of a relationship of love between Father and Son.

Now we turn to Joseph in the gospels. We know that he was betrothed to Mary, the mother of Jesus, and that he was described as an upright man, sensitive in character, a person with a conscience, with a deep religious inclination and with a belief in an inner world whose inspirations (dreams) he could trust. For, when the angel illuminated his mind, he did not stubbornly maintain his intention to divorce Mary. He accepted the deeper religious interpretation.

> He had made up his mind to do this when suddenly the angel of the Lord appeared to him in a dream and said, 'Joseph son of David, do not be afraid to take Mary home as your wife, because she has conceived what is in her by the Holy Spirit. She will give birth to a son and you must name him Jesus, because he is the one who is to save his people from their sins.' (Matt. 1:20–22)

We see Joseph accompanying Mary to Bethlehem where, as I have suggested in the previous chapter, he was probably present at the birth of Jesus. He participated in the visitation of the shepherds and also of the Magi. He must have been aware, from these unique circumstances, that he was involved in the birth of an extraordinary person.

Next we find Joseph involved in the flight to Egypt:

> After they [the Magi] had left, suddenly the angel of the Lord appeared to Joseph in a dream and said, 'Get up, take the child and his mother with you, and escape into Egypt, and stay there until I tell you, because Herod intends to search for the child and do away with him.' So Joseph got up and, taking the child and his mother with him, left that night for Egypt, where they stayed until Herod was dead. (Matt. 2:13–15)

Joseph had the responsibility of looking after Jesus and Mary as a refugee family. Getting a job and supporting them was probably relatively easy because he could use his skills as a carpenter.

After this episode Joseph disappears from the pages of the gospels – apart from an indirect appearance when his family thought that Jesus was out of his mind (Mark 3:21). If we left it where the gospels do, this would be the end of this chapter. But, as I have suggested above, Joseph must have been an excellent model of fatherhood for Jesus to have had such a marvellous conception of his heavenly Father. Theology will tell us that the knowledge of his heavenly Father was direct – but I would insist that it had to have a human infrastructure, a human preparation, to respect the full humanity of Jesus. And so we can move from one to the other. The description in John's gospel of Jesus' relationship to his heavenly Father is extensive – and we shall leave part of this description to the next chapter when I concentrate on that relationship. Here we shall confine ourselves to some salient points concerning Jesus and his earthly father – especially concentrating on John 5:19–47, which the Jerusalem Bible declares to be one of the fullest explanations in John of the relationship between Son and Father.

There is no doubt that the relationship of Jesus and Yahweh was one primarily of love. Jesus felt loved by his heavenly Father: '"For the Father loves the Son"' (John 5:20 – also stated in John 3:35). This powerful experience of Yahweh by Jesus must have been anticipated by his experience of love from Joseph. As a child, Jesus must have felt wanted, recognised and appreciated by Joseph – wanted as a son, recognised for his unique characteristics and appreciated for them. In particular, he must have felt he belonged to Joseph who was taking care of him. While feeling grateful for being taken care of, he must have learned the ingredients of taking care of others, which was such a singular mark of his ministry. We have in the story of the prodigal son a touchingly tender encounter of a father with a son, and it is likely that Jesus learnt the quality of this tenderness from his experience of Joseph.

In Joseph's love of Jesus, we can posit that Jesus identified with his earthly father. We can suppose a Freudian explanation for this in a satisfactory completion of the Oedipus complex. If we do not abide by the Freudian libido theory, we can formulate Bowlby's attachment view (which I favour), that Jesus formed a secure and satisfying bond with his earthly father – or we can dismiss psychological theories and go for the plain common-sense view that Jesus took after his father. Jesus was born in a patriarchal society where the father was of considerable importance, and the relationship between father and son of paramount significance. I am suggesting, in the light of the above, that Jesus' relationship with his earthly father was a good one.

In the opening passage of John 5:19, Jesus says:

'In all truth I tell you,
By himself the Son can do nothing.'

Theologically, this leads to dependence on his heavenly Father – but psychologically, we may get a glimpse that Joseph enabled his son to do things and to be like him:

'He can do only what he sees the Father doing:
And whatever the Father does the Son does too.'

(John 5:19)

It is no attack on theology to suggest that Joseph enabled Jesus to be capable of achieving things which allowed him to feel that he could discharge the wishes of his heavenly Father. We see in life many people who do not feel good enough, their self esteem is not strong enough to enable them to achieve. We shall have occasion to look at the self esteem of Jesus elsewhere – but here I am simply making the point that Jesus understood himself as having a mission to discharge, or, in psychological terms, a task to be accomplished. He felt able to accomplish this through the facilitating powers which he had acquired from Joseph, even though theologically it was his divine power that made it possible. Joseph was an enabler of Jesus.

Apart from the fact that Joseph loved Jesus, what else can we say about him? We find in the same discourse the sentence: ' "For the Father judges no one" ' (John 5:22). Theologically, this judgement refers to power over life and death, and Jesus is considered to be the supreme judge of the last day. Psychologically, we can interpret the sentence as suggesting a non-judgemental attitude. Again, the next sentence reads: ' "He has entrusted all judgement to the Son." '

Jesus assesses, judges people by their faith, their trust in him from the point of view of giving and withholding consent to him. This assessment is merciful and non-judgemental. We are given, psychologically, an impression of the absence of severity – Jesus' attitude in the gospel is one of tenderness and clemency. This non-judgemental approach – an attitude of merciful justice which is the heavenly Father's hallmark – is one which I suggest Joseph prepared Jesus for.

Jesus believes in the Father – his whole attitude is trust in him. I have described Erikson's theories on the acquisition of the sense of trust (Chapter 8), and here I am suggesting that Jesus had trust in Joseph. In fact, a relationship of trust between Joseph and Jesus is a prerequisite for the relationship between the Father and his Son. Not only does Jesus trust the Father but he also honours him:

'Whoever refuses honour to the Son
Refuses honour to the Father who sent him.'

(John 5:23)

Jesus is here talking about the honour that is due to the Father. He tells his audience that, by refusing honour to him, they refuse honour to their God. But the whole concept of honour about which Jesus is talking had to be learnt as an experience – and who better to learn it from than Joseph? In a patriarchal society, honour and reverence were given to the father of the family. Jesus understood and experienced this. Jesus believed in his Father. This is implied in the phrase, ' "[who] believes in the one who sent me" ' (John 5:24). To have belief as Jesus did means two things. First, he himself must have felt believed as a child – faith was shown in him as a person. And secondly he had belief and trust in Joseph – which suggests that Joseph had characteristics of consistency and reliability. Jesus' understanding of faith must have originated from his father, and from his mother.

Trust, faith, love, are all characteristics of a vibrant life. Jesus must have been aware of such a life in his relationship with Joseph. He is aware of this vital life in his heavenly Father:

'For as the Father has life in himself:
So he has granted the Son also to have life in himself.'

(John 5:26)

Because Jesus experienced a sense of vibrant vitality at the hands of Joseph, he was equipped to appreciate the quality of life which he shared with his Father. When we look at the picture of Jesus in John's gospel, we see a sense of fullness of being which accurately describes the life of the Father – and the quality of life that Jesus must have experienced with Joseph.

Was Jesus an obedient child? We have seen in the previous chapter that he stayed behind in the Temple when his family left Jerusalem to journey home. He certainly had the capacity to be autonomous – his whole life was lived in a spirit of independent thought and action. But we find in the next passage an attitude of compliance:

'Because I seek to do not my own will
But the will of him who sent me.'

(John 5:30)

If we continue the model of John 5, imagining the relationship of Joseph and Jesus as modelling that of Jesus and his Father, we can assume a child who was obedient – not in the sense of infantile dependence, but in a progressive growth of assent to Joseph as something correct and right. We can presume no blind, infantile obedience out of fear – this is a point of paramount importance: Jesus' obedience to his heavenly Father was not motivated out of fear, but out of love. Christianity has not always understood this distinction, and at times has based the relationship of faith in God on fear. Reality consists of nothing of the sort.

So we can suggest that Joseph was no autocratic, authoritarian father-figure. His ways, we can deduce, were gentle, inducing in Jesus a trait which allowed him later on in his life to say:

> 'Come to me, all you who labour and are overburdened, and I will give you rest. Shoulder my yoke and learn from me, for I am gentle and humble in heart, and you will find rest for your souls. Yes, my yoke is easy and my burden light.' (Matt. 11:28–30)

Powerful as Jesus was, yet he was gentle – and this gentleness very probably originated in the relationship of Joseph, Jesus and Mary.

A sense of loving obedience did not preclude Jesus from fulfilling the obligations of a son. He did not pick and choose what he did:

> 'My food
> is to do the will of the one who sent me,
> and to complete his work.'
>   (John 4:34)

Jesus knew that he had a task to perform, and he did it willingly. I am suggesting that he learnt from Joseph that life is no endless child's playtime. It has a serious task-performing agenda.

We shall explore other aspects of the relationship between Jesus and his heavenly Father in the next chapter, but here I am indicating that just as John can say:

> No one has ever seen God;
> It is only the Son, who is close to the Father's heart,
> who has made him known
>   (John 1:18)

– so the relationship between Jesus and his Father is indicative of the relationship between Jesus and Joseph and in this way, we get a glimpse of Joseph.

In the last two chapters, I have laid the parental foundations of Jesus' personality which centre on his capacity to love. In the next chapter, I shall concentrate on his relationship with his heavenly Father.

12

Jesus and his Heavenly Father

In MARK'S GOSPEL, in the episode of the agony in the garden, we read of Jesus calling his heavenly Father 'Abba' (Mark 14:36). Now 'Abba' is the Aramaic word that we might translate as 'Daddy' – it is a term of intense familiarity. One of the crucial psychological aspects of Jesus is the developmental separation from his earthly father which enabled him to identify with his heavenly Father. John's gospel makes it clear that Jesus was the pre-existent Son of God. It is vital to know at what point of his development Jesus was humanly capable of grasping this truth. This is a critical meeting-point between his humanity and his divinity.

I have thought for a long time that this passage of Luke is vital for answering this question.

> Every year his parents used to go to Jerusalem for the feast of the Passover. When he was twelve years old, they went up for the feast as usual. When the days of the feast were over and they set off home, the boy Jesus stayed behind in Jerusalem without his parents knowing it. They assumed he was somewhere in the party, and it was only after a day's journey that they went to look for him among their relations and acquaintances. When they failed to find him, they went back to Jerusalem looking for him everywhere.
>
> It happened that three days later, they found him in the Temple, sitting among the teachers, listening to them, and asking them questions; and all those who heard him were astounded at his intelligence and his replies. They were overcome when they saw him, and his mother said to him, 'My child, why have you done this to us? See how worried your father and I have been, looking for you'. He replied, 'Why were you looking for me? Did you not

know that I must be in my Father's house?' [or 'be busy with my Father's affairs'] But they did not understand what he meant. (Luke 2:41–50)

This is a favourite passage illustrating adolescent rebellion – but it is infinitely more important for the fact that, by the age of twelve, Jesus could distinguish between his earthly father and his heavenly Father, with the knowledge that he was the Son. We must presume that Jesus developed this self understanding slowly. It did not come to him suddenly as a bolt from the sky.

His religious upbringing must have made him familiar with the Jewish understanding of Yahweh and, by the psychological mechanism of internalisation, he made this knowledge his own. The further specific understanding that he was the Son of this Yahweh is not something that psychology can elucidate. It calls for direct insight from God his Father. All we know is that, by the age of twelve (and probably much earlier), he had made the separation from Joseph and had reconciled the two parts of his identity, while being clear which was the primary one. It is interesting that his parents, Luke says, did not understand his reply.

Jesus understood – and we move on to John's gospel for further clarification of the relationship between Son and Father. I have already cited Dreyfus' book on the subject of John's gospel[1] – a view which meets with considerable approval from Johannine scholar Raymond E. Brown, in *An Introduction to New Testament Christology*.[2] The words that John puts in Jesus' mouth are important not because they are the exact words spoken by Jesus but because they refer to significant aspects of the relationship between Son and Father. Jesus knows that he comes from the Father: '"I have come in the name of my Father"' (John 5:43) – and that his Father approves of him: '"For on him the Father, God himself, has set his seal"' (John 6:27). This origination from the Father is insisted upon again:

'No one can come to me
Unless drawn by the Father who sent me.'
(John 6:44)

Not only does Jesus specify that he knows he has come from the Father, but he also designates a whole range of intimacy with him:

'You do not know him,
but I know him
because I have my being from him
and it was he who sent me.'

(John 7:29.)

'Just as the Father knows me
and I know the Father.'

(John 10:15)

This intimacy is intense:

'The Father and I are one'

(John 10:30)

'The Father is in me and I am in the Father'

(John 10:38)

'And yet I am not alone,
because the Father is with me.'

(John 16:32)

As will be shown in Chapters 17–19 on love, John's understanding of God is that he is love, and therefore we are not surprised that love between the Father and Son features prominently in the relationship – 'The Father loves me' (John 10:16) – and this love is reciprocal:

'But the world must recognise that I love the Father
and that I act just as the Father commanded.'

(John 14:31)

Not only is the love between Father and Son reciprocal but – to return to a vital point made before – the Son responds to the Father's wishes out of love, not blind obedience. In the Roman Catholic Church, where obedience to authority has assumed such importance, the obedience of Jesus to the Father is given as an example of the ideal Christian attitude to authority. In this there is a mistaken psychological interpretation, confusing a childlike obedience to authority with Jesus' behaviour. Jesus' obedience was not one of submission to a higher authority: he and the Father were one. The binding force is love. This issue is further extended when Jesus says:

'I am not possessed;
But I honour my Father.'
(John 8:49)

It is not fear that Jesus has for his Father, but love and honour.

Jesus is struggling hard to make his disciples understand the equality between his Father and himself – that what happens to him has direct application to what happens to the Father, because the two are one: '"Anyone who hates me hates my Father"' (John 15:23).

The Son has not been sent to this world only as a witness to his Father; he has also been enabled by the Father to do divine things – of which the miracles were an important part. In a later chapter, we shall explore Jesus' search for his identity. Here, we merely note that he believes that his Father testifies on his behalf by the deeds he performs:

'But my testimony is greater than John's:
the deeds my Father has given me to perform,
these same deeds of mine
testify that the Father has sent me.'
(John 5:36)

Jesus' conviction in his power comes out clearly in another passage: 'Jesus knew that the Father had put everything into his hands, and that he had come from God and was returning to God' (John 13:3).

In the next quotation, Jesus' awareness of his power comes in his prayer to the Father. He starts by saying, 'Father, the hour has come' – and much later he says:

'All I have is yours
and all you have is mine.'
(John 17:10)

This relationship of the Son to the Father has tremendous repercussions, in that Jesus knows, from the fruit of his relationship with his Father, that he can act as God. We know that Jesus did not misuse this power. He did not act to attract attention or seek acclamation (although he got both), but to demonstrate his relationship with his Father and to assert his mission. But he harboured no doubts about his capabilities:

'If you ask me for anything in my name,
I will do it.'
(John 14:14)

His powers are not trivial. He can raise the dead:

> 'Thus, as the Father raises the dead and gives them life,
> So the Son gives life to anyone he chooses.'
>
> (John 5:21)

In raising the dead (for example, Lazarus), doing other miracles (such as the multiplication of loaves and fishes), and caring for the sick, Jesus reveals the intimate connection between these actions and the motivation of love. The intimate relationship with his Father did not only give him power – but he used the energy of love which was both his and the Father's nature. This point will be developed throughout the book. The Son is not only able to do extraordinary things which have divine origins, but, through his oneness with his Father, he also understands the Father's mind and does his will:

> 'Because I have come from heaven,
> not to do my own will,
> but to do the will of him who sent me . . .
> It is my Father's will
> that whoever sees the Son and believes in him
> should have eternal life,
> and that I should raise that person up on the last day.'
>
> (John 6:38, 40)

The gospel of John is an attestation of the relationship of the Son and the Father, and of their equality. It is recognised by exegetes that Jesus revealed himself slowly – first to the crowd, then to the disciples as a whole, then to the special three (Peter, James and his brother John), and finally to the beloved disciple mentioned in John's gospel. Some believe that the beloved disciple was an eye-witness to the gospel that bears his name. All this can be found in the appropriate commentaries and books on Christology.

In this book, we are concerned with the psychology of a person who was fully human and fully divine. How did Jesus reconcile the two? Psychology is vital in understanding this accommodation. In Chapter 11, I have reconstructed Jesus' relationship with his earthly father, and in Chapter 10, I discussed his relationship with his mother. From these two chapters, I conclude that a loving relationship with his human parents prepared Jesus for an understanding both of love and of relationship, of being recognised, wanted, appreciated and belonging. All this enabled him to have an infrastructure for his relationship with his heavenly Father. The task of his earthly parents was to prepare the background, to put no obstacles in his way, and to allow the special divine awareness of his identity to take root – even though they themselves simply did not understand his relationship with his heavenly Father, as the Temple episode shows. The mystery of the incarnation (see Chapter 30) is the accommodation of human nature to divine being. Psychologically, Jesus' upbringing was such that it put no obstacles in the way of his divine insights – that is why it is necessary to treat his childhood from a psychological point of view in such detail. I finish this chapter with the principal idea of this book: that, psychologically, the life of Jesus can be understood in terms of his relationship with his heavenly Father, experienced in a life of love, ending in the supreme manifestation of this in his passion and death, and being fulfilled in his resurrection.

IV

Significant People and Events

13

John the Baptist and the Baptism
of Jesus

So FAR, WE HAVE LOOKED at the possible development of Jesus according
to our available psychological theories: his relationship with his mother
Mary, the reconstruction of life with his father Joseph, and his relationship with his heavenly Father, whom he called by the intimate name of
'Abba'. In the next three chapters we shall look at prominent events in
Jesus' life, and at people who impinged on him and his reaction to
them.

We start with John the Baptist, who appears in all four gospels. He
is the last prophet in the Old Testament style, and a precursor of Jesus.
John's gospel, like all the others, proclaims the true role of John:

> A man came, sent by God.
> His name was John.
> He came as a witness,
> to bear witness to the light,
> so that everyone might believe through him.
> He was not the light,
> he was to bear witness to the light.
>
> (John 1:6–8).

In Luke and Matthew, more details are given of his work:

> The word of God came to John the son of Zechariah, in the desert.
> He went through the whole Jordan area proclaiming a baptism of
> repentance for the forgiveness of sins, as it is written in the book
> of the sayings of Isaiah the prophet:

A voice of one that cries in the desert:
Prepare a way for the Lord,
make his path straight!
Let every valley be filled in,
every mountain and hill be levelled,
winding ways be straightened
and rough roads made smooth,
and all humanity will see the salvation of God.

(Luke 3:2–6).

John lived in the desert and baptised in the Jordan. The baptism which he conferred was a baptism of repentance for the forgiveness of sins. It was a preparation for receiving Jesus.

John had a primitive ferocity and did not spare his words:

He said, therefore, to the crowds who came to be baptised by him, 'Brood of vipers, who warned you to flee from the coming retribution? Produce fruit in keeping with repentance, and do not start telling yourselves "We have Abraham as our father," because, I tell you, God can raise children for Abraham from these stones. Yes, even now the axe is being laid to the root of the trees, so that any tree failing to produce good fruit will be cut down and thrown on the fire.' (Luke 3:7–9).

'Brood of vipers' is strong language and John did not mince his words or his intentions. The Jews who came to be baptised claimed descent from Abraham – but their lives left a great deal to be desired. In this message he was anticipating Jesus.

So the people asked John what they had to do to be saved:

He answered, 'Anyone who has two tunics must share with the one who has none, and anyone with something to eat must do the same.' There were tax collectors, too, who came for baptism, and these said to him, 'Master, what must we do?' He said to them, 'Exact no more than the appointed rate.' Some soldiers asked him in their turn, 'What about us? What must we do?' He said to them, 'No intimidation! No extortion! Be content with your pay!' (Luke 3:10–14).

In this passage we get a glimpse of life in Jesus' time. The people were poor, and mostly lived off the land which was controlled by a few landlords. Poverty was rife. John addressed himself to the subject of poverty – and just dealings even by tax collectors and soldiers. John could afford to take such a stand. He believed in and lived an ascetic life: 'This man John wore a garment made of camel-hair with a leather loin-cloth round his waist, and his food was locusts and wild honey' (Matt. 3:4).

John and his disciples baptised in the river Jordan. This was not baptism as we understand it now – a sacrament of initiation. The Jerusalem Bible writes of this baptism thus:

> The rite of immersion, symbolic of purification or of renewal, was familiar to ancient religions and to Judaism (baptism of proselytes, Essene purifications). John's baptism, though suggested by these practices, is distinct from them for three main reasons: it is directed to moral, not ritual, purification; it takes place once only and for this reason appears as a ceremony of initiation; it has an eschatological value in so far as it enrols its recipients among the numbers of those who professedly and actively prepare themselves for the imminent coming of the Messiah and who are, therefore, the Messianic community in anticipation. Jesus alone, and not John, will baptise 'in the Holy Spirit'. John's baptism continued to be administered by the disciples of Jesus until it was absorbed by the new rite which he had instituted.[1]

It is clear that Jesus did not need to be baptised on any of these three counts. He had no need for moral purification; no need for a ceremony of initiation – it was he who was initiating the kingdom of God; and as far as eschatology is concerned, Jesus was inaugurating the eschatological age. In other words, he already carried within himself the transforming powers of this baptism, and there was no need for them to be given to him. Jesus knew all this. John the Baptist also was aware of these realities, so we see his hesitation:

> Then Jesus appeared: he came from Galilee to the Jordan to be baptised by John. John tried to dissuade him, with the words, 'It is I who need baptism from you, and yet you come to me.' But Jesus replied, 'Leave it like this for the time being; it is fitting that we should, in this way, do all that uprightness demands.' Then John gave in to him. (Matt. 3:13–15).

Jesus' reply at the beginning of his work shows him experiencing himself as any other Jew of his age and time might do. Jesus had the difficult task of behaving like any other Jew, and yet initiating change by bringing about the kingdom of God. This was psychologically a profoundly complex deed. He wanted to attest to all that had gone before – and at the same time proclaim that God, who was the creator, was in him and wanted the next phase in the revelation to be initiated. Jesus had to perform a double act, to be continuous with the old and yet start a new era. We have a fundamental example of this in his fulfilment of the Law which was the bedrock of Jewish religious life:

> 'Do not imagine that I have come to abolish the Law or the Pro-
> phets. I have come not to abolish but to complete them. In truth I
> tell you, till heaven and earth disappear, not one dot, not one little
> stroke, is to disappear from the Law until all its purpose is
> achieved.' (Matt. 5:17–19)

The Law is to be obeyed – that is, Jesus claimed continuity with the past. At the same time he developed it:

> 'You have heard how it was said, You shall not commit adultery.
> But I say this to you, if a man looks at a woman lustfully, he has
> already committed adultery with her in his heart . . .
>
> 'Again, you have heard how it was said to our ancestors, You
> must not break your oath, but must fulfil your oaths to the Lord.
> But I say this to you, do not swear at all, either by heaven, since
> that is God's throne, or by earth, since that is his footstool; or by
> Jerusalem since that is the city of the great King . . .
>
> 'You have heard how it was said: Eye for eye and tooth for tooth.
> But I say this to you: offer no resistance to the wicked. On the
> contrary, if anyone hits you on the right cheek, offer him the other
> as well.' (Matt. 5:27–8, 33–5, 38–9)

In these passages, Jesus proclaimed a higher standard of love. From the human point of view, he depended in making these assertions on an inner authority or clarity which was psychological in nature. This inner certainty was another meeting-point between the awareness of what God his Father wanted to proclaim and his human readiness to receive this message and affirm it.

The dilemma experienced by Jesus was how to be man and yet at the same time reveal that he was God. At his baptism there was a resolution of this dilemma. Jesus, in keeping with being Jewish, submitted to being baptised by John. This was showing his humanity – but at the same moment, something else happened:

> And when Jesus had been baptised he at once came up from the water, and suddenly the heavens opened and he saw the spirit of God descending like a dove and coming down on him. And suddenly there was a voice from heaven, 'This is my Son, the Beloved; my favour rests on him.' (Matt. 3:16–17)

At the moment of his acceptance of his humanity, the divinity of Jesus is confirmed. He is the beloved Son of his Father. The Jerusalem Bible says: 'The spirit which hovered over the waters of the first creation (Genesis 1:2) now appears at the beginning of the new creation'.[2] This is an important meeting-point between man and God. But psychologically, it has another importance. We have seen that, in the development of the child, parental affirmation is essential for love of self. The physical, social, emotional and mental growth of the child is not only experienced but also feels good because it is affirmed by the parents and therefore becomes a good experience. Affirmation does not stop in childhood. Adults also need to be affirmed, to be reassured that what they are doing is sound and good. Jesus needed this affirmation as much as any other human being. During most of his public ministry, he was giving out to others. His baptism was a moment when, at the beginning of his work, he received a private and public affirmation. In John's gospel, as we have seen, Jesus claimed to be loved by the Father. Here in the Synoptic Gospels he is affirmed – as he is affirmed again at his transfiguration:

> Six days later, Jesus took with him Peter and James and his brother John and led them up a high mountain by themselves. There in their presence he was transfigured: his face shone like the sun and his clothes became as dazzling as light. And suddenly Moses and Elijah appeared to them; they were talking to him. Then Peter spoke to Jesus. 'Lord,' he said, 'it is wonderful for us to be here; if you want me to, I will make three shelters here, one for you, one for Moses and one for Elijah.' He was still speaking when suddenly a bright cloud covered them with shadow, and suddenly from the cloud there came a voice which said, 'This is my Son, the Beloved; he enjoys my favour. Listen to him.' When they heard this, the disciples fell on their faces, overcome with fear. But Jesus came up

and touched them, saying, 'Stand up, do not be afraid.' And when
they raised their eyes they saw no one but Jesus. (Matt. 17:1–8)

These moments of affirmation suggest that Jesus needed them. His life
was no proclamation of triumphant divinity. He was human, carrying
out the difficult task of revealing the face of God. I suspect that this
posed real demands which he was pleased to accept – but for which
he was also ready to receive some support.

John the Baptist was aware of his mission to be a witness for Jesus.
He proclaims:

'This is the one of whom I said:
He who comes after me
has passed ahead of me
because he existed before me.'
(John 1:15)

John knew what his mission was and that he was inferior to Jesus:

'I baptise you in water for repentance, but the one who comes after
me is more powerful than I, and I am not fit to carry his sandals;
he will baptise you with the Holy Spirit and fire.' (Matt. 3:11)

Although John knew Jesus' work, he did not know whether the rumours
he had heard about Jesus and what he was doing were true. In the
mean time, John had been put into prison by Herod – so he sent his
disciples to ask who Jesus was: '"Are you the one who is to come, or
are we to expect someone else?"' (Matt. 11:3). In his reply Jesus, as
always, does not answer directly but indirectly – yet with full knowledge
that what he was accomplishing was clearly the work of God, with the
power of God:

'Go back and tell John what you hear and see; the blind see again,
and the lame walk, those suffering from virulent skin-diseases
[leprosy] are cleansed, and the deaf hear, the dead are raised to
life and the good news is proclaimed to the poor; and blessed is
anyone who does not find me a cause of falling.' (Matt. 11:4–6)

Although Jesus' answer was indirect, he made a good case for being
the Messiah. In fact, when necessary, Jesus was not afraid to point to the
manifold powers he possessed and the results he was achieving.

Jesus had a very high opinion of John the Baptist – indeed, he allowed him to baptise him. How high he held him in his esteem we see from the words that follow:

> As the men were leaving, Jesus began to talk to the people about John. 'What did you go out in the desert to see? A reed swaying in the breeze? No? Then what did you go out to see? A man wearing fine clothes? Look, those who wear fine clothes are to be found in palaces. Then what did you go out for? To see a prophet?' (Matt. 11:7–10)

Jesus paints a picture of a solid, strong man who lived in poverty and preached a message of repentance. There is a contrast between John, who lived in the desert, ate locusts and wild honey and was sparsely dressed, and Jesus, who lived in towns and in Jerusalem and was frequently entertained at banquets. Yet despite their differences, Jesus appreciated John:

> 'Yes, I tell you, and much more than a prophet; he is the one of whom scripture says:
>> Look, I am going to send my messenger in front of you
>> to prepare your way before you.
>> In truth I tell you, of all the children born to women, there has never been anyone greater than John the Baptist, yet the least in the kingdom of Heaven is greater than he.' (Matt. 11:10–12)

Jesus cannot show greater approval of John, and yet he makes it clear that the humblest member of the kingdom he is inaugurating is greater. In this passage the old and the new meet. It is a moment of the subtlety with which Jesus affirms the Old Testament and yet claims to initiate a new era. John was the epitome of the old, and Jesus was the proclamation of the new. Both the old and the new had, however, a price to pay – and that was death.

Herod had broken the law by marrying his brother's wife, Herodias – and John did not hesitate to condemn them, thereby incurring the wrath of Herodias who wanted him killed. Herod, however, respected John and was afraid of him. It is interesting that John was severe in matters of sexual laxity, and was not afraid to declare the truth, even at the risk of his life. In this respect he was, like Jesus, prepared to die for the truth.

Herod was clearly easily aroused by his sexual passions. On his birthday he gave a banquet. The daughter of Herodias danced and she delighted Herod, who promised to give her whatever she asked. Having asked her mother, she then requested John's head. Herod was caught in a classic sexual dilemma: he either had to fulfil his promise and please the girl, or break his word. Herod gave in and John was executed.

John not only lighted the way for Jesus, but he also suffered martyrdom for the cause of righteousness. When Jesus heard about his death, not only must he have been sad, but he very likely had intimations of his own death. Both John and himself were introducing the path of righteousness, and both paid the supreme price. Despite John's death, Jesus persevered with his mission.

Having acknowledged John's status, been baptised by him, used John's disciples to make a powerful declaration of his identity, Jesus must have felt bereft of any active support after John's death. He had to rely on his disciples and his friends, but, above all, on his inner support which came from his heavenly Father.

14

The Temptation in the Desert

AFTER JESUS' BAPTISM, he was led into the desert where he fasted for 40 days and nights. In a moment we shall see what this fasting implied. But first we need to look at this solitary excursion into the desert. Some people do undertake challenging tasks alone: people venture to the poles, they sail single-handed across the oceans. But the capacity to remain alone for a long time is a challenging one. Most of us need company. We are social animals.

We have seen that Winnicott postulated a good ego-relationship with the mother as a necessary background to the ability to be alone. By 'ego-relationship' he meant an intimate and safe interaction between child and mother which gave the child the sense of safety and security to be alone without fear. Bowlby postulated that the child could leave the mother's side and explore the environment safely. Both theorists suggest that a good, safe relationship with mother allows the building of a self that is strong enough to live with its own resources and not be dependent on the company of others. We must postulate that Jesus had the human background that allowed him to be alone, and that he was also aware of being in the presence of his heavenly Father, who was a source of support for him. His closeness meant that he was not dependent on others for survival. Jesus demonstrated a balance between closeness to others (his disciples and friends), and being on his own. He was capable of both, unlike some men and women who find it very difficult to be alone. His aloneness was an intimate communion with his heavenly Father. His closeness to the disciples and his friends was one of love. There was no assumption of social roles, except that of teacher. But, as we have seen in his teaching, he had to take a stand, to proclaim the dawn of a new era with its message of love. In order to do this, he upset the scribes and the Pharisees. He proclaimed new standards. In this he was alone and, unlike the desert experience, this aloneness was not physical but inner and psychological. He proclaimed the new because he trusted himself that what he was claiming was authentic.

In the desert he had to undergo a test, a temptation. Jesus, we are told, was totally human except that he did not sin – but he was not protected from temptation. Temptation is the option to choose something that is desirable but forbidden. In the case of the first temptation, what was desirable was food. We know that Jesus enjoyed food: he attended banquets, was conscious of the need of food for the crowds that followed him, for whom he multiplied the loaves and the fishes, and he graced food with the transformation of bread and wine into his own body at the Last Supper. In the desert he fasted for 40 days and nights, as did Moses. The biblical allusions suggest that Jesus was seen as the new Moses. But, psychologically, we have to look at how he conquered the temptation:

> And the tester came and said to him, 'If you are Son of God, tell these stones to turn into loaves.' But he replied, 'Scripture says:
>> human beings live not on bread alone
>> but on every word that comes from the mouth of God.'
> (Matt. 4:3–4).

Jesus could have turned stones into bread. The miracles we see him doing later on suggest he had that power – but he refused to use it. He insisted that food is not only external but internal also. He feeds on the word of God. That is all very well, but how does he overcome his hunger? Spiritual food is one thing: but what about human hunger? Forty days is a long time. Here we have to turn to the theories of Freud and Klein. For both of them, the oral stage of development was important for the child. Both speculate that the child needs a satisfactory oral experience to alleviate not only hunger but the turbulence of human growth. Both claim that the satisfactory negotiation of the oral stage enables the child to build up a security against hunger, which can meet real hunger with the strength to overcome its pull. There are men and women who find hunger such a powerful need that they will pinch from the kitchen to satiate their hunger before the meal is set on the table. These men and women live for food.

We see a Jesus who, however much he liked food, was in charge of its need – and not the other way round. Food was not in charge of him.

This suggests to me that his oral phase was successfully negotiated, placing him in a position to appreciate the value of food but not to crave it.

Those who see the temptations in the desert as a lofty spiritual vision may find this preoccupation with food slightly trite, but we have to consider the full humanity of Jesus, and hunger is a powerful appetite which we see him conquering. Beyond conquering hunger in its own right, Jesus was also showing that his ability to conquer was a feature of his strength of character. His claim to be the Son of God is not dependent on his miraculous ability to turn stones into bread; instead, we see the wholeness of his personality through the strength of his character – as shown in the next temptation:

> The devil then took him to the holy city and set him on the parapet of the Temple. 'If you are the Son of God,' he said, 'throw yourself down; for scripture says:
>
>> He has given his angels orders about you,
>>
>> and they will carry you in their arms
>>
>> in case you trip over a stone.'
>
>> (Matt. 4:5–6)

Here the Devil puts a subtle temptation to Jesus. He is saying, more or less, 'If you are the Son of God, then prove it: jump from the parapet'.

This picture of Jesus jumping from the parapet reminds us of Superman who flies through the air safely. In all his ministry, Jesus avoided demonstrating his identity by clever tricks. His miracles were not challenges to God: they were not moments of defiance: he was not out to prove a point. Although he trusted his Father, he was not going to put him to the test. His mission was to inaugurate love, not to shock people into submission. So Jesus replies:

> 'Scripture also says:
>
> Do not put the Lord your God to the test.'
>
>> (Matt. 4:7)

Jesus did not want a triumphalist entry into the bosom of humanity. When he wanted to be triumphant he rode on a donkey. He was not great through triumphs, but through humility and service.

Having failed to tempt him through food and super power, the Devil tried the temptation of power. In the society in which Jesus grew up, where poverty, passivity and impotence were the order of the day, power was greatly attractive. It was a short cut to overcome all the limitations of the period:

> Next, taking him to a very high mountain, the devil showed him all the kingdoms of the world and their splendour. And he said to him, 'I will give you all these, if you fall at my feet and do me homage.' (Matt. 4:8–9)

Men and women often do many despicable things to gain power. Power gives the feeling of being God-like. There is the power of authority, of money, of sex – and all these were being offered to Jesus. Why did he decline them? We must not only hold on to the spiritual power that he had: the spiritual, as we keep seeing, meets the human. We must accept that, at the human level, Jesus had such a fullness of being that he did not need external power. He had all the authority he needed within himself, presumably from his mature upbringing.

It is difficult to convey the sense of fullness of being, other than through the word 'mature'. Jesus was mature – that is, he had within himself all that he needed to be a normal human being. He was not incomplete in any way psychologically. The temptations in the desert show us this fullness. So Jesus replied:

> 'Away with you, Satan! For scripture says:
> The Lord your God is the one to whom you must do homage,
> him alone you must serve'.
>   (Matt. 4:10).

Jesus knew what his priorities were: his life was dedicated to God his Father. He assumed his humanity to show people the way, but he was not confused about his direction. The temptations are also a reminder of how human beings are constantly tempted – tempted instinctively with material things (food, money, sex), tempted for ever with the desire to be dazzled. The thirst for the beyond, the transcendental, is corrupted by the desire to take short cuts to it – hence the attraction of magic, the occult, the futuristic. All these are a way of satisfying the hunger for wonder. And, finally, we are tempted by power. Men and women want heaven on earth, and they are always looking for easy answers to their quests. Instincts, wonder and power are a triad which never ceases to fascinate humankind.

Jesus is shown in the desert episode to have an authentic awareness of God. No cheap human substitutes will do. In order to prevail with the authentic, he not only needed his divine powers, but also the certitude of a powerful human framework which could withstand temptation. In the desert he was alone with the wild beasts, as Mark says, and he battled with the Devil. The Devil is portrayed in the gospels as a real person. How Jesus experienced him we do not know, but experience him he certainly did – and he conquered him. 'Then the devil left him, and suddenly angels appeared and looked after him' (Matt. 4:11). The appearance of angels sounds strange to us. We are not familiar with angels in our scientific age, and the whole theme of the desert, the Devil and the angels appears strange to us. It is so strange that *The New Jerome Biblical Commentary* calls the details a 'narrative midrash' or a later interpolation, added to the real episode in the desert. In keeping with the methodology of this book, however, I have accepted all the details as authentic. The details show a picture of Jesus as having a strong inner world to defend himself against easy solutions to human challenges. This picture is in keeping with what we see in the rest of the gospels of a man strong enough to withstand the temptations of life.

15

Jesus and his Apostles

HAVING BEEN BAPTISED, and having successfully negotiated the temptations in the desert, Jesus was ready for his ministry. For this he needed disciples:

> These are the names of the twelve apostles: first, Simon who is known as Peter, and his brother Andrew; James the son of Zebedee, and his brother John; Philip and Bartholomew; Thomas, and Matthew the tax collector; James the son of Alphaeus, and Thaddaeus; Simon the Zealot and Judas Iscariot, who was also his betrayer. (Matt. 10:2–4)

The relationship between Jesus and the twelve was a close one. In terms of the psychological theories presented in earlier chapters, Jesus was the parental figure, the secure basis, and they were attached to him. It is assumed that there was an affectionate bond between him and the disciples. They were close, and not only marvelled at his deeds and teachings but felt affection for him.

They, in turn, were to be the salt of the earth and the light of the world (Matthew 5:13–14). The conditions for following Jesus were stringent:

> Then Jesus said to his disciples, 'If anyone wants to be a follower of mine, let him renounce himself and take up his cross and follow me. Anyone who wants to save his life will lose it; but anyone who loses his life for my sake will find it.' (Matt. 16:24–5)

These were heavy demands, and we wonder what made the disciples accept them. Why were they spellbound by Jesus? His authority, deeds, charisma, clearly played a part – but Peter gives us the definitive answer. In the face of desertions by some of his followers in John's gospel, Jesus says to the twelve:

'What about you, do you want to go away too?' Simon Peter answered, 'Lord, to whom shall we go? You have the message of eternal life, and we believe; we have come to know that you are the Holy One of God.' (John 6:67–9)

The journey of that faith was a long and arduous one. Despite his continuous presence with them, the disciples were slow to believe, and they were castigated repeatedly for their lack of faith – for example: 'The disciples, having crossed to the other side, had forgotten to take any food. Jesus said to them, "Keep your eyes open, and be on your guard against the yeast of the Pharisees and Sadducees"' (Matt. 16:5–6). But the disciples did not understand what he meant: 'And they said among themselves, "It is because we have not brought any bread"' (Matt. 16:7). Jesus was referring to the false doctrines of the Pharisees and Sadducees; the disciples were concerned with food.

As in various places in the gospels, Jesus knew their misunderstanding. He had a capacity to interpret clearly and to understand the deeper layers of what was being said, so he replies:

'You have so little faith, why are you talking among yourselves about having no bread? Do you still not understand? Do you not remember the five loaves for the five thousand and the number of baskets you collected? Or the seven loaves for the four thousand and the number of baskets you collected? How could you fail to understand that I was not talking about bread? What I said was: Beware of the yeast of the Pharisees and the Sadducees.' Then they understood that he was telling them to be on their guard, not against yeast for making bread, but against the teaching of the Pharisees and the Sadducees. (Matt. 16:8–12)

Jesus had to exercise a great deal of patience with his apostles. They were impressed by what they saw, but the subtleties of Jesus' teaching, the inauguration of the kingdom of God, evaded their grasp. The lack of faith went hand in hand with a poor understanding of Jesus' mentality.

We have another example of this on the occasion of the teaching about the clean and the unclean. Cleanliness was a strong point of the religious teaching of the Pharisees, who were shocked by Jesus' liberal attitude. In John's gospel we find that it was his claim to be the Son of God which perturbed the Pharisees; in the Synoptic Gospels, it was his violation of the purity laws and the sabbath regulations which upset them. Collectively, they had grounds for doubting that this was a man who came from God. Jesus could accept that the Pharisees did not understand – but he found it much harder to take when his own disciples were obdurate: 'He called the people to him and said, "Listen and understand. What goes into the mouth does not make anyone unclean; it is what comes out of the mouth that makes someone unclean"' (Matt. 15:10–11). Jesus is famous for these pithy remarks – along with the parables, they were some of the hallmarks of his teaching.

> Then the disciples came to him and said, 'Do you know that the Pharisees were shocked when they heard what you said?' He replied, 'Any plant my heavenly Father has not planted will be pulled by the roots. Leave them alone. They are blind leaders of the blind; and if one blind person leads another, both will fall into the pit.'
>
> At this, Peter said to him, 'Explain the parable for us.' Jesus replied, 'Even you – don't you yet understand?' (Matt. 15:12–16)

The desperation in this remark of Jesus' reveals the struggle he had to teach even his apostles. It brings into focus another psychological feature of his personality, namely the tenacity, the perseverance, which arose from his inner security that he was right – and this illustrates his love of self, that is to say, his acknowledgement that his inner world was good. So the persistent difficulties he had in convincing the crowd and even his disciples, of whom he expected a better grasp, did not distract him from carrying on. And so the explanation follows:

> 'Can't you see that whatever goes into the mouth passes through the stomach and is discharged into the sewer? But whatever comes out of the mouth comes from the heart, and it is this that makes someone unclean. From the heart come evil intentions: murder, adultery, fornication, theft, perjury, slander. These are the things that make a person unclean. But eating with unwashed hands does not make anyone unclean.' (Matt. 15:17–20)

Put in this way, the explanation is sensible and shows the shallowness of the purity laws of the Pharisees. In fact, the Pharisees' hallmark was hypocrisy and Jesus did not spare them.

Apart from the important explanation of the parable, we have had occasion to use the same story to show that Jesus visualised the human personality not in static, but in dynamic terms, as Freud did. The heart is seen as a centre for feelings, coupled with the motivation for action. It is the combination of these that drives people to evil deeds. Jesus did not emphasise the intellect, but feelings, especially feelings of love. This pursuit of loving feelings comes into the exchange between himself and the disciples, seen in the first miracle of loaves. Jesus had been, as usual, followed by the crowd and his feelings of compassion came to the fore: 'So as he stepped ashore he saw a large crowd; and he took pity on them and healed the sick' (Matt. 14:14). However, he did more than heal the sick. He was concerned for the welfare of the crowd, in contradistinction to the disciples:

> When evening came, the disciples went to him and said, 'This is a lonely place, and time has slipped by; so send the people away, and they can go to the villages to buy themselves some food.' Jesus replied, 'There is no need for them to go: give them something to eat yourselves.' But they answered, 'All we have with us is five loaves and two fish.' (Matt. 14:15–19)

And the scene was set for the first miracle of the multiplication of loaves and fishes. This miracle not only shows the divine powers of Jesus but is set against a background of human need – namely, food and human compassion. The disciples did not think that such a miracle was possible. They did not operate within Jesus' framework of compassion. Repeatedly they wanted to protect Jesus from the crowd and from young children. They did not appreciate his care and warmth.

In the second miracle of the loaves, Jesus called his disciples and said:

> 'I feel sorry for all these people; they have been with me for three days now and have nothing to eat. I do not want to send them off hungry, or they might collapse on the way.' The disciples said to him, 'Where in a deserted place could we get sufficient bread for such a large crowd to have enough to eat?' Jesus said to them, 'How many loaves have you?' They said, 'Seven and a few small fish.' (Matt. 15:32–4)

And the second miracle of multiplication took place.

These are good examples of the contrast between the pragmatic attitude of the disciples and Jesus' compassion. It shows that, even among his disciples, Jesus was lonely and isolated. They were acting like bodyguards who wanted to protect him from being molested; he saw in the crowd the occasion for loving them. We see this love in the following passage:

> Jesus made a tour through all the towns and villages, teaching in their synagogues, proclaiming the goodness of the kingdom and curing all kinds of disease and all kinds of illness.
>
> And when he saw the crowds he felt sorry for them because they were harassed and dejected, like sheep without a shepherd. Then he said to his disciples, 'The harvest is rich but the labourers are few, so ask the Lord of the harvest to send out labourers to his harvest.' (Matt. 9:35–7)

The crowds were the poor labourers and peasants of the area and they lived in tough conditions, just making ends meet. Their religious taskmasters were the Pharisees and the scribes, who imposed impossible conditions on them. Jesus wanted to liberate them from the harsh conditions of their lives, both physically and spiritually. Jesus could not do everything himself, so he commissioned the disciples to go away as missionaries, and we have in Matthew a lengthy passage outlining this work:

> 'Do not make your way to gentile territory, and do not enter any Samaritan town; go instead to the lost sheep of the House of Israel. And as you go, proclaim that the kingdom of Heaven is close at hand. Cure the sick, raise the dead, cleanse those suffering from virulent skin-diseases, drive out devils. You received without charge, give without charge. Provide yourself with no gold or silver, not even with coppers for your purses, with no haversack for the journey or spare tunic or footwear or a staff, for the labourer deserves his keep.' (Matt. 10:5–10)

The apostles were to be as generous as Jesus was, and were not to protect themselves with financial resources. They accepted these instructions. We have seen before that their faith was slow to develop, but in undertaking this missionary work, they put their trust in Jesus. He continued to instruct them:

> 'Whatever town or village you go into, seek someone worthy and stay with him until you leave. As you enter his house, salute it, and if the house deserves it, may your peace come upon it; if

it does not, may your peace come back to you. And if anyone does not welcome you or listen to what you say, as you walk out of the house or town shake the dust from your feet. In truth I tell you, on the Day of Judgement it will be more bearable for Sodom and Gomorrah than for that town. Look, I am sending you out like sheep among the wolves; so be cunning as snakes yet innocent as doves.'
(Matt. 10: 11–16)

In sending his disciples out to be missionaries, we can imagine Jesus as a ball to which a piece of elastic is attached: the ball is the secure basis of Jesus; the elastic is the disciples who are stretched to the periphery. Jesus was preparing the disciples for the time after the ascension when he left them to carry out his work. This was a preliminary run. He warned them to be as cunning as snakes and yet as innocent as doves. This gives us a glimpse of how Jesus himself operated. In his dialogues with the Pharisees, he was cunning; in his dealings with the sick, the poor, the marginalised, he was an innocent who loved them. He would not give the Pharisees any leeway or benefit of doubt – but for the woman taken in adultery, for the prostitutes and tax collectors, he made all possible. In a reminder of modern psychological insights, he penetrated the hearts of those who deviated and saw their fundamental goodness – and made short work of those who wanted to trick him with cunning. But there was a price to be paid:

'Be prepared for people to hand you over to sanhedrins and scourge you in their synagogues. You will be brought before governors and kings for my sake, as evidence for them and to the gentiles. But when you are handed over, do not worry about how to speak or what to say; what you are to say will be given to you when the time comes, because it is not you who will be speaking; the Spirit of your Father will be speaking in you.' (Matt. 10:17–20)

Jesus was here addressing the disciples concerning the journey he was sending them on – but the passage may also be anticipating the lot of the apostles when Jesus had departed from this earth. This work was to lead them into difficulties – as it continues to do throughout the world today, where Christians (some of them missionaries) are persecuted and killed. The direct link between the work of the missionaries and Jesus is evident in the conclusion of the instruction:

'Anyone who welcomes you welcomes me; and anyone who welcomes me welcomes the one who sent me. Anyone who welcomes the prophet because he is a prophet will have a prophet's reward; and anyone who welcomes an upright person because he is upright will have the reward of an upright person. If anyone gives so much as a cup of cold water to one of these little ones because he is a disciple, then in truth I tell you, he will most certainly not go without his reward.' (Matt. 10:40–42)

The disciples, who gave up their families and their work to follow Jesus in conditions of hardship, wondered what the reward of all this sacrifice would be:

Then Peter answered and said, 'Look, we have left everything and followed you. What are we to have, then?' Jesus said to them, 'In truth I tell you, when everything is made new again and the Son of man is seated on his throne of glory, you yourselves will sit on twelve thrones to judge the twelve tribes of Israel. And everyone who has left houses, brothers, sisters, father, mother, children or land for the sake of my name will receive a hundred times as much, and also inherit eternal life. Many who are first will be last and the last first.' (Matt. 19:27–30)

The disciples were saturated with the teaching of Jesus about the kingdom of heaven, but they still did not comprehend its nature. They were imbued with the sense of hierarchy and so we are not surprised when they ask Jesus:

'Who is the greatest in the kingdom of Heaven?' So he called a little child to him whom he set among them. Then he said, 'In truth I tell you, unless you change and become like little children you will never enter the kingdom of Heaven. And so, the one who makes himself as little as this little child is the greatest in the kingdom of Heaven.' (Matt. 18:1–4)

The disciples, accustomed to hierarchies, the sense of the powerful, to kings ruling, must have been surprised by the choice of a little child. Psychologically, Jesus' choice of a child confirms the significance of childhood as a preparation for adulthood. This is another instance of Jesus turning things topsy turvy. He has just said the first will be last and the last will be first. Now he puts the child first, with its complete lack of status in that society. In due course he will teach that love, which is the kingdom, is proclaimed in service.

We have seen previously (in Chapter 8) how the mother of Zebedee's sons came with a request that her two sons should sit on the right and left hand in the kingdom. We have also seen that the rest at the disciples were indignant of this request of envy. Jesus used the opportunity to teach leadership with service:

> Jesus called them to him and said, 'You know that among the gentiles the rulers lord it over them, and great men make their authority felt. Among you this is not to happen. No; anyone who wants to become great among you must be your servant, and anyone who wants to be first among you must be your slave, just as the Son of man came not to be served but to serve and to give his life as a ransom for many.' (Matt. 20:25–8)

Among the many things Jesus did because of his commitment to love was to change the order of precedence. One of the keys of love is service. Authority is not about power but about service. It is clear by now that Jesus' authority did not depend on a display of power. His authority was psychological and spiritual. It was the voice of his Father clothed in humanity, which had the certainty of security within himself, matching the divine certainty of the Father. This certainly was not based on a pyramid of ascendancy; rather, it was based on service. For any Christian organisation, the temptation to use hierarchical power as the basis for the authority is very great – and repeatedly Churches have succumbed. This dialogue between Jesus and his disciples is never obsolete.

We have looked at the choosing of the disciples, at their teaching and at all that they received from Jesus. What did they give him in return? Clearly they formed the basis of the expansion of the kingdom of heaven. They were the instruments of Jesus' work. Later on, with one exception, they were the founders of the Christian community.

But what about a more personal encounter? I have tried to indicate that the link between Jesus and the apostles was not impersonal. This was not a modern company with a managing director and various deputies. The link between Jesus and his apostles was an affectionate bond. They were friends. John's gospel makes this clear:

'You are my friends,
If you do what I command you.
I shall no longer call you servants,
because the servant does not know
the master's business;
I call you friends,
because I have made known to you
everything I have learnt from my Father.'

(John 15:14–15)

Within this community of friends, Jesus proclaimed a pre-eminence for Peter, about whom more below, a group of three (Peter, James and his brother John), the beloved apostle, and, of course, the disciple who betrayed him, Judas. We have to use our imagination to recreate the relationship between Jesus and his disciples. With Peter, there was a continuous battle of love and anger about which the gospels give us numerous details. The group of three, we must assume, came nearer to understanding and appreciating who Jesus was. Being understood must have been of supreme importance to Jesus. All of us crave to be understood, so that our inner world is clear. We do not want to be understood if we first have to explain ourselves. I think it is only natural that Jesus wanted to be understood in this way.

Beyond understanding comes belief and trust. Jesus wanted to be believed and trusted as he was believed and trusted by his heavenly Father. I am assuming that the group of three, Peter, James and his brother John, did understand and believe in him. These three were present at the transfiguration when Jesus showed his identity and was affirmed by his Father. It was a privilege to be present on this occasion. In a sense, their belief was rewarded. This inner circle of disciples must have been privy to Jesus' inner world and shared with him his glory, hopes, disappointments and expectations. In contemporary terms, he must have used them as a means of support, to talk to them and share with them his inner world.

Then we turn to the beloved disciple. Some believe that this was John, the author of the gospel by that name. But whatever his identity, this was the disciple whom Jesus loved. In a sense, Jesus loved all the disciples – but we are given to understand that there was a special relationship between him and this disciple. What is this special relationship between people who love one another? The loved one has a high

108

significance. Their physical appearance attracts us and there is physical contact. (We find this physical proximity in the Last Supper, when the beloved disciple was leaning back close to Jesus' chest.) Their emotional make-up is favourable to us. We can disclose ourselves to the beloved in depth. We can be responded to in depth; we feel secure, wanted and recognised. There is an exclusive understanding. We feel safe in their presence. In the marriage relationship there is also an erotic, sexual dimension. People have suggested that Jesus did not marry because he was a homosexual. We have not the slightest evidence for this – although I am sure that Jesus would have loved and been compassionate to homosexuals, as he was to all the marginalised groups he met.

Jesus, as a human being, needed both friendship and love. He was loved by his heavenly Father, but his human development prepared him for human love and he had the human hunger for that love. Essentially, personal love is a special relationship in which we feel secure, wanted, appreciated, and in which there is a reciprocal, mutual exchange of affection. We can postulate that this is precisely the relationship between Jesus and the beloved disciple, and that it did not pertain in the same way to his relationship with any other disciple.

Being Jesus, he would have experienced the special relationship with care, in order not to arouse envy in the others – but it would possibly have been expressed in his being able to unload his worries, exchange views and seek the opinion of the beloved apostle. In brief, he could rely on him. Certainly Jesus felt that the beloved disciple was wholly reliable, for he placed his own mother in the care of that disciple.

Perhaps we can best understand the love between Jesus and the beloved disciple as equivalent to the love between a mother and a child: total devotion, total commitment, total care. That is the mutuality between Jesus and the beloved disciple.

Jesus had a different relationship with Peter. He makes him the rock on which he builds the foundation of his Church:

> 'You are Peter and on this rock I will build my community. And the gates of the underworld can never overpower it. I will give you the keys of the kingdom of Heaven: whatever you bind on earth will be bound in heaven; whatever you loose on earth will be loosed in heaven.' (Matt. 16:18–20)

Thus Jesus gave Peter, the fisherman, a place of pre-eminence among the disciples.

What sort of person was Peter? We find in the pages of the gospels a personality that was impetuous, fierce in his commitment, eager to embrace and imitate his master, whom he loved, but also idealised. Thus, when he sees Jesus walking on water, he wants to imitate him but has not the resources of faith to succeed:

> And at once he made the disciples get into the boat and go on ahead to the other side while he sent the crowds away. After sending the crowds away he went up into the hills by himself to pray. When evening came, he was there alone, while the boat, by now some furlongs from the land, was hard pressed by rough waves, for there was a head-wind. In the fourth watch of the night he came towards them, walking on the sea, and when the disciples saw him walking on the sea they were terrified. 'It is a ghost,' they said, and cried out in fear. But at once Jesus called out to them, 'Courage! It's me! Don't be afraid.' It was Peter who answered. 'Lord,' he said, 'if it is you, tell me to come to you across the water.' Jesus said, 'Come.' Then Peter got out of the boat and started walking towards Jesus across the water, but then noticing the wind, he took fright and began to sink. 'Lord,' he cried, 'save me!' Jesus put out his hand at once and held him. 'You have so little faith,' he said, 'why did you doubt?' And as they got into the boat the wind dropped. The men in the boat bowed down before him and said, 'Truly, you are the Son of God.' (Matt. 14:22–33)

It was typical of Peter that he thought he could walk on the water as his master did, and yet also characteristic that, although he had the will, his nerve failed and he was afraid.

Jesus appreciated this fervent commitment on the part of Peter. He rewarded him by taking him with him on the occasion of his transfiguration. The relationship between Jesus and Peter was one of admiration on the part of the latter and patient correction by the former. We see this when Peter opposed the declared intention of Jesus to die:

> From then onwards Jesus began to make it clear to his disciples that he was destined to go to Jerusalem and suffer grievously at the hands of the elders and the chief priests and scribes and to be put to death and to be raised on the third day. Then, taking him

110

aside, Peter started to rebuke him. 'Heaven preserve you, Lord,' he said, 'this must not happen to you.' But he turned and said to Peter, 'Get behind me, Satan! You are an obstacle in my path, because you are thinking not as God thinks but as human beings do.' (Matt. 16:21–3)

Peter was shocked on hearing the fate that Jesus outlined for himself. He wanted to protect him from such an outcome, and he tells him not to allow himself to suffer and die. Jesus, however, knew better – and, despite Peter's good intentions, he rebuked him.

Peter continued his zealous service and obsessional loyalty to Jesus. We see him refuse to have his feet washed, an episode we shall consider in Chapter 25. We also see him making loud boasts of loyalty, which he soon betrays again during the passion of his master.

Despite his many weaknesses, Peter had grasped the identity of Jesus and was fully committed to him. He is the prototype of the Christian whose faith is both strong and weak at the same time. If the chosen leader of the apostles could vacillate so strongly, then everyone who tries to follow Jesus has room for reassurance. Peter, despite his vacillations, grasped who his master was:

> When Jesus came to the region of Caesarea Philippi he put this question to his disciples, 'Who do people say the Son of man is?' And they said, 'Some say John the Baptist, some Elijah, and others Jeremiah or one of the prophets.' 'But you,' he said, 'who do you say I am?' Then Simon Peter spoke up and said, 'You are the Christ, the Son of the living God.' Jesus replied, 'Simon, son of Jonah, you are a blessed man! Because it was no human agency that revealed this to you, but my Father in heaven.' (Matt. 16:13–19)

Peter acknowledged that Jesus was the Messiah and also the Son of God. This latter revelation is clear in the gospel of John – but here, it was Peter who made this declaration. With his divine instinct Jesus knew who he himself was – he had been aware of this from at least the age of twelve and perhaps earlier. But, in his human dimension, he needed human reassurance – and Peter provided this. Thus Peter played a leading role in the life of Jesus. Jesus felt safe enough with Peter, despite his vicissitudes, to place the leadership and care of his community in Peter's hands. History reminds us that Peter did not let him down.

111

16

Jesus and the Pharisees

JESUS DIRECTED SOME OF HIS most critical remarks at the Pharisees, an orthodox sect of Jews. In fact, in his confrontation with the Pharisees, Jesus sharpened his own authority and identity. It is in his dialogues with them that he showed the superiority of integrity against hypocrisy, the use of the sabbath for the service of humankind, moral authenticity as against visible cleanliness, and the importance of interiority as against external appearance.

In Matthew 6, Jesus attacked the Pharisees as hypocrites in three areas: almsgiving, prayer and fasting. The reference in the text to hypocrites appertains in particular to the Pharisees. First Jesus tackles almsgiving:

> 'Be careful not to parade your uprightness [good works] in public to attract attention; otherwise you will lose all reward from your Father in heaven. So when you give alms, do not have it trumpeted before you; this is what the hypocrites do in the synagogues and in the streets to win human admiration. In truth I tell you, they have had their reward. But when you give alms, your left hand must not know what your right is doing; your almsgiving must be secret, and your Father who sees all that is done in secret will reward you.' (Matt. 6:1–4)

Here Jesus speaks with the intimate authority of knowing what is in the mind of God the Father, and he says with authority how almsgiving should be done. It is not a question of attracting attention to oneself, but of genuinely caring for the poor.

Similarly with prayer:

> 'And when you pray, do not imitate the hypocrites: they love to

say their prayers standing up in the synagogues and at the street corners for people to see them. In truth I tell you, they have had their reward. But when you pray, go to your private room, shut yourself in, and so pray to your Father who is in that secret place, and your Father who sees all that is done in secret will reward you.' (Matt. 6:5–6)

The phrase 'In truth I tell you' gives expression to a solemn authority which Jesus appropriates to himself. He was able in all these passages to go beyond human show to the heart of the matter.

And the third admonition refers to fasting:

'When you are fasting, do not put on a gloomy look as the hypocrites do: they go about looking unsightly to let people know they are fasting. In truth I tell you, they have had their reward. But when you fast, put scent on your head and wash your face, so that no one will know you are fasting except your Father who sees all that is done in secret; and your Father who sees all that is done in secret will reward you.' (Matt. 6:16–18)

Again, Jesus speaks with authority and tells the disciples how they are to fast: it is the inner intention that matters, not the outer manifestation.

Jesus attacked the showmanship of the Pharisees as contrary to the spirit of God, and he told his disciples to listen to the Pharisees but not to do as they do:

'They tie up heavy burdens and lay them on people's shoulders, but will they lift a finger to move them? Not they! Everything they do is to attract attention, like wearing broader headbands and longer tassels, like wanting to take the place of honour at banquets and the front seats in the synagogues, being greeted respectfully in the market squares and having people call them Rabbi.' (Matt. 23:4–7)

After this paragraph Jesus indicted the scribes and the Pharisees in a seven-fold condemnation, each of which starts with, 'Alas for you, scribes and Pharisees, you hypocrites!' (Matthew 23:13–30). Going beyond external integrity, Jesus tackled the question of washing before eating. The Pharisees and the scribes complained to him because his disciples ate without washing their hands. Cleansing rituals were very important for the Jews at the time of Jesus. Once again, he was showing his unique authority by ignoring them. Even his disciples wanted to know why he behaved in this way. Jesus explained that what was important wasn't what went into the mouth, but whatever came out of the mouth – including evil words and deeds. Eating with unwashed hands does not make anyone unclean (Matthew 15:18–20). Today these charges appear trivial – but then, Jesus' criticism of these purity laws was a central attack on the way the community lived its life. Jesus was showing a unique power. He was also pointing to an important psychological truth, namely that what matters is the inner world and not external appearances. Washing hands was also a hygienic measure which was important. But important as hygiene was, the inner intentions of people were even more important and, as in the case of almsgiving, fasting and praying, it was the encounter between the inner self and God that mattered.

Jesus would not have proclaimed such an approach if he had not himself known its significance from his relationship with his Father. He taught what he had tested personally. It was this inner certainty which gave him the strength to overcome the customs of centuries and, apparently, the testimony of those that mattered in the community. Of course, he knew that in challenging the everyday customs he was inviting disapproval. The Pharisees wanted to know the source of his authority to proclaim this disturbing teaching, which led him to say 'In truth I tell you'. Psychologically, Jesus must have felt a unique strength, and he was using the Pharisees as a means of defining who he was.

Another sacred custom in Jesus' day was the sabbath. It was not permitted to do work on the sabbath or to heal. Jesus broke both these rules: 'At that time Jesus went through the cornfields one Sabbath day. His disciples were hungry and began to pick ears of corn and eat them. The Pharisees noticed it and said to him, "Look, your disciples are doing something that is forbidden on the Sabbath"' (Matt. 12:1–2). Jesus went on to give the example of David and his followers who were hungry, who went into the house of God and ate the loaves of the offering which was forbidden and also the Temple priests' bread on the sabbath, and then he went on in a magisterial way to say: '"Now here, I tell you, is something greater than the Temple. And if you had understood the meaning of the words: Mercy is what pleases me, not sacrifice, you would not have condemned the blameless. For the Son of man is master of the Sabbath"' (Matt. 12:6–8).

In John's gospel, Jesus cured the sick man at the pool of Bethesda on the Sabbath: 'It was because he did things like this on the Sabbath that the Jews began to harass Jesus. His answer to them was, "My Father still goes on working, and I am at work too"' (John 5:16–17). In Matthew we have a passage with similar intent:

> He moved on from there and went to their synagogue; now a man was there with a withered hand. They asked him, 'Is it permitted to cure somebody on the Sabbath day?' hoping for something to charge him with. But he said to them, 'If anyone of you here had only one sheep and it fell down a hole on the Sabbath day, would he not get hold of it and lift it out? Now a man is far more important than a sheep, so it follows that it is permitted on the Sabbath day to do good.' Then he said to the man, 'Stretch out your hand.' He stretched it out and his hand was restored, as sound as the other one. At this the Pharisees went out and began to plot against him, discussing how to destroy him. (Matt. 12:9–14)

This combined assault on purity and on the sabbath made Jesus unacceptable to the Pharisees, and yet he persevered. In the process he was teaching that the inner was more important than the outer, and that humankind, created in the image of God, deserves the best, even if it meant breaking the rule of the sabbath. Jesus was not afraid to alter things to bring out more clearly the message of his Father, and he did this because the kingdom of God had been inaugurated by him. He knew that he was the bearer of ultimate truth and he did not hesitate to proclaim it in word and deed.

The Pharisees were aware that Jesus was healing and that he was performing miracles. They never denied it. The question was, by whose power did he do these things. There were only two possibilities – God or the Devil:

> Then they brought to him a blind and dumb demoniac; and he cured him, so that the dumb man could speak and see. All the people were astounded and said, 'Can this be the son of David?' But when the Pharisees heard this, they said, 'This man drives out devils only through Beelzebul, the chief of the devils.' (Matt. 12:22–4)

In a neat way Jesus turned the tables against them:

> Knowing what was in their minds he said to them, 'Every kingdom

115

divided against itself is heading for ruin; and no town, no household divided against itself can last. Now if Satan drives out Satan,
he is divided against himself; so how can his kingdom last? And if
it is through Beelzebul that I drive devils out, through whom do
your own experts drive them out? They shall be your judges, then.
But if it is through the Spirit of God that I drive out devils, then be
sure that the kingdom of God has caught you unawares.' (Matt.
12:25–8)

Jesus not only taught in words, not only worked miracles, but he was
not lost for intelligent responses to the Pharisees: instead of working
by the power of the Devil, Jesus' miracles were a sign of the arrival of
the kingdom of God.

The arrival of the kingdom of God was the dawn of an era of justice,
peace and equality. This era was inaugurated by many manifestations
but, most important of all, by the presence of Jesus himself. In this era
Jesus would not draw distinctions, he would not pick and choose. The
Pharisees ostracised people, but Jesus would not do that. He mingled
and ate with everybody:

Now while he was at table in the house it happened that a number
of tax collectors and sinners came to sit at the table with Jesus
and his disciples. When the Pharisees saw this, they said to his
disciples, 'Why does your master eat with tax collectors and
sinners?' When he heard this he replied, 'It is not the healthy who
need the doctor, but the sick. Go and learn the meaning of the
words: Mercy is what pleases me not sacrifice. And indeed I came
to call not the upright, but sinners.' (Matt. 9:10–13)

The Pharisees were shocked to see Jesus eating with tax collectors,
prostitutes, sinners. They could not understand how a man who claimed
to be of God could associate with such people. Jesus partly defined
himself by shocking: he befriended the sinners and the marginalised,
and in this way introduced an era of mercy unparalleled hitherto. Mercy
was his distinguishing mark, and so was compassion, which manifested
itself in his healing. Mercy and compassion were superior to ritual, laws
and the prohibitions of the sabbath. The Pharisees, who were controlled
by the details of the Law, could not understand such an approach. The
magnitude of his kindness baffled them and created anxiety. They were
manifestly uncomfortable at what they saw. At all times the good person

makes others feel uncomfortable. The Pharisees saw their purity rules flouted; their clear delineations of the good and the bad made indistinguishable; their rationalisations of whence Jesus drew his power mocked.

It is understandable that they were confused – and more than confused, they were profoundly disturbed. They did not know how to handle Jesus – and in a situation like this, when they could not stop the changes he was introducing, they gradually came to the view that they had to eliminate him. And so the gospels tell us that they began to plot against him.

Jesus knew that what he was doing was dangerous. He could not change things so dramatically without incurring opposition. What is interesting is the inner strength which he summoned within himself to carry out these changes. This strength came from his intimate understanding of his Father – while, humanly speaking, he was continuously defining himself as over and against the Pharisees. But he had to bide his time. The manner of his manifestation was indirect. He manifested himself by transforming the laws of his time and by teaching that the kingdom he was inaugurating was one of mercy and compassion. His disciples heard and saw what he did, but it is clear that they were slow to understand.

The disciples informed Jesus that the Pharisees were shocked at his attack on the purity laws (Matthew 15:10–13). The gospels do not tell us, but it is probable that the disciples were shocked also. Jesus' teaching was so radical that they asked for an explanation, which he gave to them. Thus we see Jesus taking on the opposition of the Pharisees and using them as targets to proclaim the kingdom of God. In this opposition, the Pharisees brought out of Jesus the core of his self awareness and, through them, he was teaching the disciples how reality should be. What is uniquely demonstrated in this encounter between Jesus and the Pharisees is the tug of war between the Establishment and the kingdom. Jesus was becoming aware that this fight would cost him his life, but he did not waver for one moment. It was not a question of obedience to death, but of love of his Father which made him sacrifice himself. In this sacrifice, the Pharisees became the enemy that made love shine out of Jesus.

V

Love

17

The Centrality of Love

G OSPEL WRITERS HAVE BEEN called 'the servants of the Gospel', and their
task was to emphasise emphatically that, as Dodd says,

> the divinely guided history of Israel had reached its climax of
> fulfilment. A new era has dawned, a community has come into
> existence – in effect a new Israel – in which there is forgiveness for
> the past, spiritual power for the present and hope for the future.
> It has its creative centre in the Messiah whom God has sent, and
> this is no other than Jesus of Nazareth, recently crucified and now
> risen from the dead.[1]

The whole theme of the gospels is that a new era has dawned through
the death and resurrection of Jesus Christ. This was an age in which
there was 'the inauguration of a new set of relations between God
and man'.[2] Nothing is more central in this relationship between God and
humanity than that the kingdom of God has arrived. Thus a hope had
become a reality.

In the letters of Paul, John's first epistle and the four gospels, the
central theme of the unique events of the life, death and resurrection
of Jesus Christ is seen as the manifestation of love. In 1 John 4 we have
the shortest declaration of the centrality of love in the New Testament:
'God is love' (1 John 4:8). This statement could be interpreted as a
metaphysical declaration – but it is more than that. In his book *The
Love Command in the New Testament*, V. P. Furnish sees this statement
as meaning that God's loving is not just one of his activities – along
with creating, ruling, judging, forgiving, etc. – but that 'all his activity
is loving activity'.[3]

The Pauline letters are generally accepted as being the earliest extant
documents of the New Testament, but they express Paul's own theology,

whereas the gospels, on which I have primarily based this book, give a lively picture of the kind of thing that Jesus did, the kind of attitude which his actions revealed, the kind of relations in which he stood with various types of people he encountered, and the causes of friction between him and the religious leaders. Above all, the gospels show the kind of things to which he drew people's attention. Exegetes disagree about the limited occasions when it is thought that Jesus is quoted verbatim in the gospels. But nobody disagrees with the notion that the gospels record the thoughts, ideas and events related to the person of Christ. So what do the gospels say about Jesus and love?

There is general agreement that the earliest gospel is Mark. This gospel contains nothing about Jesus' childhood – indeed, it starts with his baptism. Unlike Matthew, it is not a polemic against Judaism. What has Mark to say about Jesus and love?

> One of the scribes who had listened to them debating appreciated that Jesus had given a good answer and put a further question to him, 'Which is the first of all the commandments?' Jesus replied, 'This is the first: Listen, Israel, the Lord our God is the one, only Lord, and you must love the Lord your God with all your heart, with all your soul, with all your mind and with all your strength. The second is this: You must love your neighbour as yourself. There is no commandment greater than these.' (Mark 12:28–31)

In this passage, Jesus refers to the Old Testament. In Deuteronomy 6:5 we have the sentence: 'You shall love Yahweh your God with all your heart, with all your soul, with all your strength'. And in Leviticus 19:18 we find the commandment: 'You must love your neighbour as yourself'. Thus Jesus referred to the Old Testament, declaring that these two commandments are the greatest. In the rest of the passage the scribe agrees with Jesus who, in turn, tells him that he is not far from the kingdom of God. Clearly, then, the kingdom of God which Jesus came to bring about has love as its priority.

In Matthew, the great commandment comes later, in the last week of Jesus' life in Jerusalem. This gospel portrays a more virulent and antagonistic attitude towards the Pharisees and we find this in the passage that is similar to Mark's but yet different. Now the Pharisees asked him a similar question, but in order to trap him:

> But when the Pharisees learned that he had silenced the Sadducees

they got together and, to put him to the test, one of them put a further question, 'Master, which is the greatest commandment of the Law?' Jesus said to him, 'You must love the Lord your God with all your heart, with all your soul, and with all your mind. This is the greatest and the first commandment. The second resembles it: You must love your neighbour as yourself. On these two commandments hang the whole Law, and the Prophets too.' (Matt. 22:34–40)

As in Mark, love of God and love of neighbour are the principles on which all the commandments rest.

At the heart of love is reconciliation, and at the centre of reconciliation is forgiveness – so we would expect the gospels to emphasise forgiveness. In Matthew, we have a truly magisterial passage:

'You have heard how it was said: You must love your neighbour and hate your enemy. But I say this to you, love your enemies and pray for those who persecute you; so that you may be children of your Father in heaven, for he causes his sun to rise on the bad as well as the good, and sends down rain to fall on the upright and the wicked alike. For if you love those who love you, what reward will you get? Do not even the tax collectors do as much? And if you save your greetings for your brothers, are you doing anything exceptional? Do not even the gentiles do as much? You must therefore set no bounds to your love, just as your heavenly Father sets none to his.' (Matt. 5:43–8)

It should be noted that the words 'hate your enemy' are not found in the formulation of the Law, but are a measure of the contrast that Jesus wants to introduce in order to show the importance of forgiveness and love of enemies.

So far Matthew has reiterated the great commandment and emphasised the love of forgiveness; but the dramatic exposition of the Christian's responsibility to love comes in chapter 25 when the scene of the Last Judgement is described:

'When the Son of man comes in his glory, escorted by all the angels, then he will take his seat on his throne of glory. All nations will be assembled before him and he will separate people one from another as the shepherd separates sheep from goats. He will place the sheep on his right hand and the goats on his left. Then the King

123

will say to those on his right hand, "Come, you whom my Father
has blessed, take as your heritage the kingdom prepared for you
since the foundation of the world. For I was hungry and you gave
me food, I was thirsty and you gave me drink, I was a stranger and
you made me welcome, lacking clothes and you clothed me, sick
and you visited me, in prison and you came to see me." Then the
upright will say to him in reply, "Lord, when did we see you hungry
and feed you, or thirsty and gave you drink? When did we see you
a stranger and make you welcome, lacking clothes and clothe
you? When did we find you sick or in prison and go to see you?"
And the King will answer, "In truth I tell you, in so far as you did
this to one of the least of these brothers of mine, you did it to
me."' (Matt. 25:31–40)

And this passage is followed in precisely the same, but negative, terms
to those who had ignored the needy – and thus ignored the king.

This passage introduces a practical element of love. It asks us to feed
the hungry, to quench thirst, to befriend, to clothe, to visit the sick
and the imprisoned – all traditional works of mercy. These are the
familiar poor. Even in our materially well-off society, pockets of poverty
remain – but poverty is rampant in the vast majority of the world. And
there are also the new poor, the emotionally deprived, who have to be
fed and clothed with continuous affection; those imprisoned inside the
walls of depression, anxiety, hopelessness, despair, who live with suic-
idal feelings uppermost in their mind; those who feel rejected; those
who are handicapped, physically and psychologically, by being addicted
to alcohol, drugs or promiscuity. Thus there is no end to the new poor
in whom we meet Christ.

In Luke's gospel we also have the teaching of Jesus in the double
commandment of loving God and loving neighbour:

And now a lawyer stood up and, to test him, asked, 'Master, what
must I do to inherit eternal life?' He said to him, 'What is written
in the Law? What is your reading of it?' He replied, 'You must love
the Lord your God with all your heart, with all your soul, with all
your strength, and with all your mind, and your neighbour as
yourself.' Jesus said to him, 'You have answered right, do this and
life is yours.' But the man was anxious to justify himself and said
to Jesus, 'And who is my neighbour?' (Luke 10:25–8)

And Luke goes on to give us the memorable illustration of the parable of the good Samaritan (Luke 10:30–37).

What stands out in the gospel of Luke is the portrayal of Jesus' ministry from first to last as preaching the gospel to the poor. At the beginning of the Galilean ministry, Jesus goes to a synagogue and he stands up to read. (Incidentally, this is the only passage in the gospels where we are told that Jesus could read.) They handed him a scroll of the prophet Isaiah and he read:

> The spirit of the Lord is on me,
> for he has anointed me
> to bring the good news to the afflicted.
> He has sent me to proclaim liberty to captives,
> sight to the blind,
> to let the oppressed go free,
> to proclaim a year of favour from the Lord.
>
> (Luke 4:17–19)

Quite clearly, apart from indicating Jesus' messianic identity, this is a proclamation of love.

Finally, we get to the gospel of John and to John's first epistle. At the heart of John's gospel is love – the love of the Father for the Son, the Son for the Father (described in Chapter 12) and of the Son for us. In John's gospel we learn that:

> 'The Father loves the Son and
> has entrusted everything to his hands.'
>
> (John 3:35)

> 'For the Father loves the Son
> and shows him everything he himself does.'
>
> (John 5:20)

> 'The Father loves me,
> because I lay down my life
> in order to take it up again.
> No one takes it from me;
> I lay it down of my own free will.'
>
> (John 10:17–18)

Here, in addition to the love of the Father for the Son, we see the reciprocation – death freely chosen by Jesus. The death of Jesus was not obedience run wild. It was a freely chosen act, undergone with full consent, out of Jesus' commitment of loving obedience to the Father. It was an act of supreme love.

Intimately related to this mutual love is Jesus' love for us. In John's gospel his love is displayed to the disciples through the act of washing their feet (13:1–16). In more intimate terms, John puts the word 'love' in Jesus' mouth:

> 'I have loved you
> just as the Father has loved me.
> Remain in my love.
> If you keep my commandments
> you will remain in my love.'
>
> (John 15:9–10)

And in a succinct definition of Jesus' wish for this, he says:

> 'This is my commandment:
> love one another,
> as I have loved you.'
>
> (John 15:12)

We notice here that the word 'commandments' in the plural becomes 'commandment' in the singular, demonstrating that all the commandments, which Jesus came to fulfil unconditionally, are contained in the one commandment to love.

We are in return bidden to love Jesus: '"If you love me you will keep my commandments"' (John 14:15); and

> 'Whoever holds to my commandments and keeps them
> is the one who loves me.'
>
> (John 14:21)

Finally we are asked to love one another:

> 'I give you a new commandment:
> love one another;
> you must love one another
> just as I have loved you.
> It is by your love for one another

that everyone will recognise you
as my disciples.'
(John 13:34–35)

The adjective 'new' is used nowhere else in this gospel – nor is the commandment 'new' in one sense, because it is present in the Mosaic law. According to the Jerusalem Bible, this precept of love is 'new' because Jesus set such a high standard by telling his followers to love one another as he himself loved them, and because love is to be the distinguishing mark of the 'new era', which the death of Jesus inaugurates and proclaims to the world.[4] In John's terms, Jesus has replaced, in his love, darkness with light and death with life. This gospel's idea of love can be summarised by saying that it is love that unites the Father to the Son, and unites the Son to his own who are in this world:

'May they all be one,
just as, Father, you are in me and I am in you,
so that they also may be in us,
so that the world may believe it was you who sent me.
I have given them the glory you gave to me,
that they may be one as we are one.
With me in them and you in me,
may they be so perfected in unity
that the world will recognise that it is you who sent me
and that you have loved them as you loved me.'
(John 17:21–3)

When we come to the first epistle of John, we find the same theme of the supreme importance of love – and probably the most revealing sentence of the Scriptures, that God is love:

My dear friends,
let us love each other,
since love is from God
and everyone who loves is called a child of God and knows God.
Whoever fails to love does not know God.
because God is love.
(1 John 4:7–8)

It is worth pausing here at the statement that God is love. It is a monumental pronouncement which gives pre-eminence to the psycho-

127

logical emphasis on the roots of learning love in childhood. It is there, in our childhood, that we first learn to recognise God, through the love our parents give us. And as discussed above, the love that Jesus experienced at the hands of his parents prepared him to register and acknowledge the love of his Father. John goes on:

> Love consists in this:
> it is not we who loved God,
> but God loved us and sent his Son
> to expiate our sins.
> My dear friends,
> if God loved us so much,
> we too should love one another.
> No one has ever seen God,
> but as long as we love one another
> God remains in us.
> and his love comes to perfection in us.
>
> (1 John 4:10–12)

John then goes on to proclaim his own personal testimony in a unique way – what he is writing about is not second-hand:

> We ourselves have seen and testify
> that the Father sent his Son
> as Saviour of the world.
>
> (1 John 4:14)

This is a personal testimony, and the conviction with which it is felt comes across in the writing of the gospel and the epistle, which have a ringing tone of authenticity:

> God is love
> and whoever remains in love remains in God
> and God in him.
> Love comes to its perfection in us
> when we can face the Day of Judgement fearlessly,
> because even in this world
> we have become as he is.
> In love there is no room for fear,
> but perfect love drives out fear,
> because fear implies punishment

and whoever is afraid has not come to perfection in love.

(1 John 4:16–18)

This passage is of vital psychological importance for Christianity. Time and again in its history, Christianity has used fear to bring people to God – indeed, it is innate to fundamentalist approaches. Fear is connected with punishment, and is also believed in by all those whose approach is authoritarian. The line of demarcation between the use of authority and an authoritarian approach is thin – and all Churches that rely heavily on authority have to be careful about this distinction. As far as I can see, Jesus never sought conversion to faith through fear:

> Let us love, then,
> because he first loved us.
> Anyone who says 'I love God'
> and hates his brother,
> is a liar,
> since whoever does not love the brother whom he can see
> cannot love God whom he has not seen.

(John 4:19–20)

We are initiated into love by God's creative love, manifested in the incarnation. We are loved first and, because God has loved us so much, we should love one another. We needed to be loved first, in order for us to love later. Indeed, that is precisely how Jesus experiences love: the Father loves him and he loves us, and the way in which both Jesus and we experience that love and learn to love is through our upbringing. Our childhood is our first experience of love, and all later love in relationship, friendship and marriage depends on this for its accomplishment. One of psychology's greatest contributions is to illuminate this process.

18

Love of Self

Since God is love, we can say with certainty that love is a mystery. Psychology is attempting to illuminate this mystery. Love of self is commonly understood as taking care of ourselves comprehensively – but psychology has illuminated this concept further and this chapter is concerned with this contribution.

At the heart of love is the process by which we possess ourselves. We cannot be loving – that is, be available to others or to ourselves – if we do not own ourselves – that is, feel that we are the possessors of our beings and that we can dispose of ourselves as we consider fit.

This process starts by our learning to posses ourselves, and this in turn means gaining access to our childhood development and incorporating it into our being. Our development is physical, intellectual, social, emotional and spiritual. Here we shall only be concerned with the emotional, of which the outline has been given in Chapters 4–9 on psychological theory.

The child is born after being nine months in the womb. After birth it forms an attachment to its mother. This attachment is an affectionate bond which is the child's first experience of love, the first experience of an interpersonal encounter, which lays the foundations of all subsequent attachments of personal love. It is within the framework of this relationship, and of subsequent attachments with the father and other key figures (such as brothers, sisters and relations), that the child develops its personality. This development is a process of gradual separation between itself and the parents and, within this process, the child acquires its human and individual characteristics. We have seen that some of these characteristics are laid down in the first few months of life. In the first year in particular, the sense of trust is acquired by the way in which the child's body is handled. This gives the child a sense of safety in the presence of the parents, particularly the mother, who offer a sense of external security. Their presence is also important for the differentiation between 'me' and 'non-me'. Thus the idea of mother, someone other than oneself, is established early on.

As the child progresses to the second and third years of life, it becomes less fused with the parents, and through this separation it acquires its own sense of autonomy. Now it learns to walk and talk, dress and feed itself, and the acquisition of these skills gives it an early sense of love of its self. It takes pleasure in experiencing its capacities. For Freudians this is sexual in the broadest sense of that word. The child's value is now situated in its body and its achievements, and these acquisitions are normally affirmed and encouraged by the parents. Love of self grows by affirmed development. The strength given by this affirmation allows the child increasingly to deal with frustration. Thus it learns to control its own instincts and behaviour.

As we have seen, we have no knowledge of Jesus' development at this stage. We have presumed that it was normal and that his parents affirmed him. We have reflected on the closeness between his earthly father and his heavenly Father, and considered that adult events were anticipated in his childhood – and we have biblical evidence of the affirmation of Jesus. His baptism and his transfiguration are two clear incidents in the adult life of Jesus when he was affirmed by the Father. We saw in John's gospel the extensive affirmation felt by Jesus from his Father. The Synoptic Gospels describe a similar experience, but differently expressed. What I want to emphasise is that the foundations of this affirmation, experienced by Jesus in his adult life, lay in the approval he felt when he was growing up.

By the end of the third year, the child has internalised the mother and is able to leave her for a short time. It will have learnt to keep her memory inside its psyche in her physical absence, and thus feel safe.

At about this time (although Klein puts it much earlier), the child also experiences two other feelings, namely envy and jealousy. Envy is an experience of wanting what the other possesses. For a child, envy is normal, in that it feels small, helpless and inadequate, and wants to possess all the resources of the parents. But as it grows older, this feeling recedes as it acquires all the characteristics that the adult has, and there is no inequality left.

Jealousy is not a twosome but a threesome experience. In jealousy we experience competition between ourselves and third parties who appear more endowed than ourselves. This endowment threatens to take away from us those people (such as a husband, boyfriend, friend) who are precious, or the things we value. Jealousy makes us feel insecure as third parties are forever threatening to displace us from our relationships and possessions.

Both envy and jealousy are threats to love of self. In the one case, we want something we feel we do not have; and in the other, we fear the loss of something we have. I am presuming that both experiences were known to Jesus, even though they did not apply to his own disposition.

With the advent of the fifth and sixth years, the child goes to school. Primary schools existed at the time of Jesus, but we do not know whether he attended one. Nevertheless, he must have been introduced to adult work – and with adult industry, feelings of inferiority can be experienced depending on the competence shown at work. Work experiences can cause one kind of inferiority feelings; another kind is caused when a child feels unloved and unwanted by its parents. Both are blows to love of self, which does not feel good enough.

School, or equivalent adult education, is the time when the child continues to grow physically and cognitively, learning the arts of reading, writing and arithmetic. We know that Jesus could read and write. In this way an ever-developing awareness of self as an independent person becomes possible.

Then comes puberty, which adds the genital/sexual dimension, and the young person is ready to relate sexually to the opposite or same sex. By the end of the second decade, young persons go through the crisis of finding out who they are. Gradually, in adolescence, children take responsibility for themselves, accept their independence and act on the basis of their own initiative.

The acquisition of selfhood in the course of development is part of what I mean by possession of self. We begin life as helpless babies, we do not possess one iota of ourselves, we live by kind permission of adults – our parents, relatives, friends and society. Little by little, we begin to separate from all these adults, particularly our parents, and begin to own our bodies, minds and feelings. By the time we are in our twenties, we are adults, and in full possession of our selves, ready to make free choices. However, this is not always the case. How many people live under the shadow of a parental figure, a mother or father, who continues to influence decisively their inner world? We can be geographically separate from our family, but they can continue to cast a powerful influence on the way we think and feel. This applies also to all other figures of authority in our life. This is not to say that family and authority influences should be set aside – but it implies that we have to separate our own thoughts and feelings from those of others, so that what we offer is genuinely the product of the possession of ourselves; otherwise we live by kind permission of others. This separation from others which makes us independent allows us truly to offer ourselves to others. We no longer offer the mother, father, brother, sister, favourite teacher – but our authentic selves, for which we assume responsibility. Genuine love expressed in this way is the product of our owned being, coupled with responsible and free choice.

We have seen that by the age of 12, Jesus had possessed himself sufficiently to separate himself from his parents and reorientate his life towards his heavenly Father. This process of possessing ourselves proceeds throughout our life. We acquire our inner world slowly, and by degrees learn to identify what is truly ours from what belongs to others. What is more, in addition to the gradual separation, we begin to add later in life our own original increments to our personality, so that we build a genuine combination of what belongs to us, both from the old and the new.

This is the difficult task that Jesus had to accomplish. In inaugurating a new era, the dawn of the kingdom of God, he had to preserve the Law and at the same time develop it. In doing so, he had to go slowly, or else his audience, including his disciples, would not understand what he was doing. He could not assume overtly the mantle of the Messiah, or claim to be God without stretching those who were listening to him. His battle with the Pharisees was constantly at this level – how to reveal who he was and yet not to scandalise them with his identity. He failed with most of the Pharisees – a failure which cost him his life – and the disciples only grasped the reality fully after the resurrection and Pentecost. During his life he had to grapple with the continuity of the old and discontinuity, the arrival of the new. Not surprisingly, his audiences were perplexed, for while Israel looked forward to a Messiah, the omens of his origins were not good and they believed him with difficulty.

In John's gospel, we see the Jews complaining to each other about him: 'They were saying, "Surely this is Jesus son of Joseph, whose father and mother we know. How can he now say, 'I have come down

from heaven?'"' (John 6:42). His origins and the fact that he came from
Galilee were against him.

To return to love of self: having first possessed ourselves, what we
possess must feel good. Love requires the freely donated sense of
ourselves, but what is given must be of value, positive and creative. If
what we have to offer is anger, hostility, destructiveness, jealousy, envy,
hate, resentment, confusion, then what we are offering is not love.

What we offer depends on what we feel about ourselves. If we feel
good and lovable, then what we have to offer will be transmitted in a
loving way. We cannot be loving if we hate ourselves, if we feel dubious
about our worth and value, if we doubt ourselves. Under those circumstances, what we offer is a sense of worthlessness, doubt and
uncertainty. Here we have to distinguish between the humility of the
image of ourselves and the worth of our contribution. This is a subtle
distinction which is often confused. Humility is a clear awareness of
our limitations, the openness to learning, correction and change, the
desire to serve rather than to pontificate, coupled with an appreciation
of our significance, which is neither exaggerated nor undervalued.

This combination of humility and self affirmation is a pronounced
feature of Jesus' understanding of himself. In particular we find, in John,
the awareness that everything Jesus does emanates from the Father:

'In all truth I tell you,
by himself the Son can do nothing;
he can do only what he sees the Father doing:
And whatever the Father does the Son does too.'

(John 5:19)

Jesus' dependence on the Father is complete. In his equality he can
share his Father's fullness. But despite this overt recognition of his
Father's enablement of him, Jesus also knows his own specific value:
'Jesus knew that the Father had put everything in his hands' (John
13:3); and

'If you ask me for anything in my name,
I will do it.'

(John 14:14)

Jesus had that knowledge of his dependence on his Father, yet combined with a sense of his own immense power. Humility is not a denial

of our worth or integrity; it is not an apology for our existence. Humility, combined with awareness of one's power, is the key to service. Love of self leads to the ability to donate ourselves to others. In donating ourselves to others, we offer our goodness to them; we offer our knowledge and our skills – but above all we offer ourselves. The idea of offering ourselves in service was prominent in Jesus' teaching:

> 'You know that among the gentiles the rulers lord it over them, and great men make their authority felt. Among you this is not to happen. No; anyone who wants to become great among you must be your servant, and anyone who wants to be first among you must be your slave, just as the Son of man came not to be served but to serve and to give his life as a ransom for many.' (Matt. 20:24–8)

This combination of humility, coupled with love of self which wishes to be available in service, is a true expression of love – and we truly find it in Jesus. What impressed the crowd and the apostles was that Jesus spoke with authority – that is, there was a unity between the outer and inner man: 'Jesus had now finished what he wanted to say, and his teaching made a deep impression on the people because he taught them with authority, unlike their own scribes.' (Matt. 7:28–9). His psychological authority rested on the fact that there was no conflict between what he taught and the way he felt and believed. There was never the slightest trace of the hypocrisy which was evident in the Pharisees. That conflict between what we say, and what we do and believe, is something that casts a shadow over our whole integrity. It is difficult to love if there is a marked difference between the outer and inner person.

When we read in the Scriptures that Jesus cast out devils, we may find it difficult nowadays to visualise the meaning of devils. But we should not find it very difficult to recognise that what he was doing was helping to eliminate self rejection.

Did Jesus have a sense of self rejection or a sense of being good, that what he possessed felt good? Going back to John once more, we see in the first chapter of the gospel the sense of the goodness that Jesus had, from which we all draw:

> Indeed, from his fullness we have, all of us, received –
> one gift replacing another,

for the Law was given through Moses,
grace and truth have come through Jesus Christ.

(John 1:16)

Grace and truth are the essential goodness which resides in Jesus. Jesus himself had a sense of his own nurturing goodness in comparing himself to bread and water:

'I am the bread of life.
No one who comes to me will ever hunger;
no one who believes in me will ever thirst.'

(John 6:35)

And, more specifically, in terms of goodness Jesus says:

'I am the good shepherd:
the good shepherd lays down his life for his sheep.'

(John 10:11)

Indeed the whole gospel of John is an attestation of Jesus' inner goodness.

Loving others, the subject of the next chapter, depends on our being able to give to them a part of ourselves which feels good, and that depends on love of self. Love of self has had a bad press in Christianity, because it is linked with selfishness. There is, however, a basic distinction between love of self and selfishness. Love of self, at a deeper level, is built on self esteem – that is, an appreciation of our own worth. Ideally, the whole of our childhood was based on receiving love from our parents and relatives, which made us feel lovable, and encouraged us to link appreciation to our bodies, minds and feelings. In this way, when we try to reach out to others, we have a body, mind and feelings that feel good. When our self esteem is poor, we do not feel we have anything of value to give and we are surprised that anybody wants us. Psychiatrists repeatedly see men and women who feel unlovable and unwanted.

Love of self is crucial in loving others, because our capacity to draw near to others depends on the felt conviction that, when others make demands on our personality, there will be something positive to give them back. Indeed, it is essential to have a positive, loving image of ourselves if we are to respond to the call of others. One of the most impressive aspects of the gospels is that Jesus, sensitive to the needs

136

of others, responded positively to them. There was no call he did not register. When we have no love for ourselves, it is as if our personality is made of locked doors, and we have no keys to open them.

We frequently relate loving in ordinary life with cooking a meal and feeding friends. The meal which is offered to friend and foe is a symbol of love, but even more important than food is the availability of our selves. In Jesus' life we have seen the miracle of the multiplication of the loaves and fishes, but also the supreme act of love when he changed bread into his body and wine into his blood. Psychologically, this is the action of a person who has total confidence that what he is offering is essentially a possession of himself which is good. The Eucharist would not have been possible if Jesus had had the slightest doubt about his self esteem. One cannot conceive of such an action without the certainty of the value of what is being offered.

I mentioned above that love of self is often confused with selfishness. Selfishness is linked with what psychologists call 'narcissism'. This is defined in the Collins English Dictionary as 'an exceptional interest in or admiration for oneself'. In Freudian terms, this self admiration is considered to be usually sexual – but it is more generally considered as self aggrandisement. Narcissism is the opposite of availability to others. The preoccupation with oneself, expressed as selfishness, is a return to the childlike state of getting attention, praise, appreciation, in order to survive. It is a condition linked with receiving exclusively, calling attention to one's importance, making oneself more significant than others. Selfishness is essentially a return to childhood in which one becomes the centre of attention, without any sense of awareness of the other. It reflects an inner emptiness, a desperate need for care and attention, a state in which, as an adult, one has not outgrown the urgency of receiving. The greater the selfishness, the more wounded people are. They are psychologically lacking any sense of fulfilment, but feel and act as empty vessels whose only urgency is filling themselves up.

Love of self is possession of oneself which feels good and which is available in service to others. This is how Jesus presents himself in the gospels – and in the next chapter we shall see how love of neighbour can be examined psychologically, and how Jesus fits the picture.

19

Love of Neighbour

LOVE OF SELF IN ITS superficial sense means looking after oneself. At a deeper understanding, it means feeling recognised, wanted and appreciated, and it paves the way for doing the same for others. The most obvious way of loving our neighbours is practically, and Matthew gives us the famous Last Judgement scene when the blessed are those who fed the hungry, welcomed the strangers, clothed the naked, attended the sick, visited the prisoners (Matthew 25:34–7). But there are other ways of loving our neighbour.

At the heart of loving others is meeting their needs, whatever these are, and at the centre of this is loving availability. We can see the married man or woman being lovingly available socially, physically, sexually and emotionally to their spouse. Everyone, however, can be lovingly available in personal relationships, be they single or married. How can we be loving in personal relationships? What are the essentials of relationship? At the centre of relationships lie feelings – the capacity to listen, empathise and to be non-judgemental.

All Christian Churches have a tendency to cherish the will and the intellect. The seminaries (training colleges for Catholic priests) are concerned with developing a cognitive approach to the Scriptures. The Roman Catholic Church had a theology which was saturated with reason and law, and even now its members are expected to submit their minds and will in obedience to authority. All this has made any affinity with the spontaneity of love rather difficult. Not that love does not need reason, will, discipline and rationality – but the roots of love were planted in our childhood, when feelings were predominant, and were the main means of conveying affection to us. We are steeped in the symbols of affective feelings, and we cannot be effective lovers without a major use of feelings. The experience, registration and expression of feelings are central to loving others. Did Jesus experience feelings? We have seen in the gospel of John, in the incident of the death and resurrection of Lazarus, that, on hearing that Lazarus had died, Jesus wept (John 11:36). But beyond this demonstration of feelings, the gospels are alive with Jesus' sensitivity to his environment. In particular, he was aware of suffering – and he addressed his response to this with healing, and driving out devils from people. He sought to respond to people's inner world.

Part of an ability to love is the capacity to listen. There are those whose sole object in conversation is to wait until the other person stops talking so that they can start. This unilateral deafness has no link with love. We need to learn to listen carefully, not only to receive a rational message, but also the affective message, in order to give the other the sense of being loved. We have numerous examples in the gospels when Jesus listened carefully and responded appropriately – and, repeatedly, the crowd were amazed.

Beyond listening, we need to learn how to empathise, to put ourselves into the shoes of the other person. We do this primarily by appreciating the feeling content of what is being said to us. We get into the mood of the other. Are they worried, frightened, hurt, confused, in distress, joyful, happy? Empathy gives us the opportunity to become one with the other. It is not usually difficult to understand what they are saying rationally, but the key is the combination of rationality and feelings. Jesus was a highly empathetic person. As John says, he knew what was in others (John 2:23–5). His great love of self made it possible for him to register the needs of others with consummate skill, and not refuse their needs.

Feelings, the capacity to listen and empathy are all crucial components for loving others. Above all, we should not judge. We should try to be non-judgemental. So often people respond to others by criticism and thereby stimulate guilt. This approach of fostering guilt as a predisposition to repentance has a long history in the Christian tradition, but it had no home in Jesus. We see him being critical of the Pharisees; he rebuked Peter; but he advocated non-judgemental attitudes: ' "Be compassionate just as your Father is compassionate. Do not judge, and you will not be judged; do not condemn, and you will not be condemned" ' (Luke 6:36–7). In his approach to people, Jesus issued an invitation of love and waited for a free response of love in return; he took the opposite approach to being judgemental – he looked for the good in the other, stressed the valuable and affirmed their work. This is how he was treated by his Father and that is how he treated others. This is not a soft approach of ignoring badness, evil or sin. It is simply trying to eliminate the negative by filling its place with affirmed goodness.

In loving, we make a commitment to that person or cause. Jesus could have been tempted, in the role of Messiah, to be the leader of a rebellious group and to fight the Romans. In the end he was put to death through a combination of political suspicion from Pilate and the religious threat to the leaders of the Temple that he was the Messiah who claimed to be the Son of God. But Jesus repudiated violence: his commitment was to the kingdom of God, which was manifesting love in a variety of ways.

What are the characteristics of commitment? In everyday language, we refer to loyalty to a cause or a person. By loyalty, we mean that we neither betray nor abandon our cause. In fact, one of the essential features of commitment is continuity. We love others when they begin to experience from us the sense of continuous availability. All of us would like to feel that we can turn to those we love at any time and find them ready to respond. A call of love is a summons we cannot ignore. Jesus knew about love. He loved his friends and his disciples; above all, he loved his Father and he accepted the commitment to his Father to the end by giving his own life:

> 'The Father loves me,
> because I lay down my life
> in order to take it up again.
> No one takes it from me;
> I lay it down of my own free will.'
> (John 10:17–18)

We can, of course, offer continuity which does not answer the needs of the loved one. We can be continuously available, but not reliable. We intend to please, to satisfy, to meet the loved one's needs, but we achieve none of these things because there is a gap between what we intend and what we can achieve. The question of reliability is brought out in the parable of the ten bridesmaids:

> 'Then the kingdom of Heaven will be like this: Ten wedding attend-
> ants took their lamps and went to meet the bridegroom. Five of

them were foolish and five were sensible: the foolish ones, though they took their lamps, took no oil with them, whereas the sensible ones took flasks of oil as well as their lamps. The bridegroom was late, and they all grew drowsy and fell asleep. But at midnight there was a cry, "Look! The bridegroom! Go out and meet him." Then all those wedding attendants woke up and trimmed their lamps, and the foolish ones said to the sensible ones, "Give us some of your oil: our lamps are going out." But they replied, "There may not be enough for us and for you; you had better go to those who sell it and buy some for yourselves." They had gone off to buy it when the bridegroom arrived. Those who were ready went in with him to the wedding hall and the door was closed. The other attendants arrived later. "Lord, Lord," they said, "open the door for us." But he replied, "In truth I tell you, I do not know you." So stay awake, because you do not know either the day or the hour.' (Matt. 25:1–13)

The theological explanation of this parable is that the wedding attendants represent the Jews waiting for the Messiah, or Christianity waiting for Christ, which must be watchful, that is, keep their lamps ready – but I am using the parable as an indication of reliable and unreliable love. There is a difference between what we promise and what we deliver. When our possession of ourselves is defective, we raise expectations but we do not deliver the goods. This contrasts with Jesus' sense of reliability in the symbolism of the good shepherd:

'I am the good shepherd:
The good shepherd lays down his life for his sheep.
The hired man, since he is not the shepherd
and the sheep do not belong to him,
abandons the sheep
as soon as he sees the wolf coming, and runs away,
and then the wolf will attack and scatter the sheep.'
(John 10:11–13)

There is a picture of reliability in this scene which reflects accurately this capacity of Jesus as a loving person.

Jesus promised a great deal, but he fulfilled what he promised. This can be contrasted with people with excellent intentions, who promise so much and fulfil so little. They live a life in which excuses become second nature. This is unlike Jesus, who is fully available and continuously reliable. He can be trusted – and trust is an essential part of reliability.

To continuity and reliability, we need to add predictability. We cannot love others if we are totally unpredictable. This does not mean that pleasant surprises are not welcome. We need, however, to be able to gauge with reasonable accuracy the response of those who claim to love us. Loving needs a secure background, and that is where predictability comes into its own. Jesus had the secure basis of his Father.

If we are truly loving, we offer to our loved ones behaviour which makes sense to them. Predictable love is of vital importance to children, in particular. We expect those who love us not to let us down when we rely on their accustomed behaviour. Both personal and public life depends on being able to take certain things for granted – and predictability is an essential part of the infrastructure of loving order. If we love, we do not suddenly stop loving. If we care, we do not suddenly stop caring. Our life of love relies on predictability. Jesus created an atmosphere of predictable expectation. The crowd came to expect healing, and so they followed him around and brought the sick to him, and he did not let them down. Thus they came again to place their trust in him – and their trust was fulfilled.

One framework of loving others, then, is listening empathetically and being non-judgemental. Another framework is formed by continuity, reliability and predictability. Within this structure, there is a more intimate expression of loving in the form of sustaining, healing and growth.

One way of loving people is by sustaining them. We sustain people in demanding or adverse situations. It is emotional sustaining that makes the hardest demands on us. People turn to us for loving in a variety of situations. They may be going through a confused period in their life, such as adolescence or retirement. We are asked to sustain those who have suffered a loss through bereavement or through their spouse leaving them, those who have lost status, position and employment. In all these situations, we see the special loving of Jesus for the marginalised, the poor. Here we can place the Beatitudes:

> Seeing the crowds, he went onto the mountain. And when he was seated his disciples came to him. Then he began to speak. This is what he taught them:

'Blessed are the poor in spirit:
The kingdom of Heaven is theirs.
Blessed are the gentle:
They shall have the earth as inheritance.
Blessed are those who mourn:
they shall be comforted.
Blessed are those who hunger and thirst for uprightness:
they shall have their fill.
Blessed are the merciful:
they shall have mercy shown them.
Blessed are the poor in heart:
they shall see God.
Blessed are the peacemakers:
they shall be recognised as children of God.
Blessed are those who are persecuted in the cause of
    uprightness:
the kingdom of heaven is theirs.'

(Matt. 5:1–10)

Here, Jesus identifies people who need sustaining, who elicit love from us and from God – such as those who are depressed, sad, victims of injustice. They all create a response of love in us. In turn, blessed are they who respond to them by loving them with mercy, making peace, being an example of purity and integrity. Jesus puts together a variety of needs – which are not a reason for self hatred but for exploration of love – and justifies those who meet those needs. In this combination of meeting practical needs of hunger, thirst, nakedness, imprisonment (Matthew 25:31–46) and in meeting the spiritual and inner needs of the Beatitudes, Jesus surveys a whole range of suffering which is not seen as an unmitigated evil, but as an occasion for creating circumstances of love of neighbour. People often say, how could a loving God permit suffering? Here we find a reply. God permits suffering in order to create the occasion for loving one another. We have to care for men and women until they rediscover their way and meaning in life. We have to love the alienated – that is, the dispossessed – and this is precisely what we see Jesus doing:

Now while he was at table in the house, it happened that a number of tax collectors and sinners came to sit at the table with Jesus and his disciples. When the Pharisees saw this, they said to his disciples, 'Why does your master eat with tax collectors and sinners?' When he heard this he replied, 'It is not the healthy who need the doctor, but the sick. Go and learn the meaning of the words: Mercy is what pleases me, not sacrifice. And indeed I came to call not the upright, but sinners.' (Matt. 9:10–13)

Jesus identified with the wounded, spiritually, physically, mentally, because his nature was to love and, above all, the needy required sustaining. Sustaining the wounded means that we become the centre of loving for them. For those who are confused, we become their beacon of light. The disciples were confused most of the time, and Jesus showed them the way. We hold people's hands until they find their feet. We give them meaning from our inner world because they can not find it in their own: '"I am the way: I am the truth and life"' (John 14:6). We become a source of comfort until the loss can be integrated in the stricken one. We offer acceptance to those who have lost their dignity through no fault of their own. In order to do these things, we have to possess the strength to guide without intrusion, to comfort by sharing the grief, to accept the dignity of all men and women, independent of their social status. Such sustaining means that, for a long time, we give and we receive very little back. According to the gospels, Jesus gave much and received very little back, except the certainty that he was doing his Father's will.

We have, however an episode when the lack of gratitude went home:

As he entered one of the villages, ten men suffering from a virulent skin-disease [other translations render this as 'leprosy'] came to meet him. They stood some way off and called to him, 'Jesus! Master! Take pity on us.' When he saw them he said, 'Go and show yourselves to the priests.' Now as they were going away they were cleansed. Finding himself cured, one of them turned back praising God at the top of his voice and threw himself prostrate at the feet of Jesus and thanked him. The man was a Samaritan. This led Jesus to say, 'Were not all ten made clean? The other nine, where are they? It seems that no one has come back to give praise to God except this foreigner.' And he said to the man, 'Stand up and go on your way. Your faith has saved you.' (Luke 17:12–19)

In this story we get a glimpse of Jesus' very natural disappointment at human ingratitude. Jesus must have had his disappointments. We often are reminded of the grandeur of giving, but we cannot give unless we have the inner resources to make ourselves available, even in the absence of immediate recompense.

Who sustained Jesus? We have seen that he very likely had a most loving upbringing which gave him a plenitude of inner self love from which he could refresh himself. But his human preparedness to be loving made him a channel for his Father's love, which definitely encouraged and sustained him. The human and the divine meet, both in sustaining Jesus and also in giving him a fullness of loving availability. As we have seen, Jesus experienced disappointment at ingratitude – but he experienced even greater disappointment at the resistance he met in the people around him. This disappointment was felt particularly in his own home town of Nazareth:

> Leaving that district, he went to his home town, and his disciples accompanied him. With the coming of the Sabbath he began teaching in the synagogue, and most of them were astonished when they heard him. They said, 'Where did the man get all this? What is this wisdom that has been granted him, and these miracles that are worked through him? This is the carpenter, surely, the son of Mary, the brother of James and Joseph and Jude and Simon? His sisters, too, are they not here with us?' And they would not accept him. And Jesus said to them, 'A prophet is despised only in his own country, among his own relations and in his own house'; and he could work no miracles there, except that he cured a few sick people by laying his hands on them. He was amazed at their lack of faith. (Mark 6:1–6)

Jesus was amazed at their rejection of him, and he had to meet this doubting approach repeatedly. It was only his own singular faith which allowed him to persevere.

The essence of sustaining is to remain in relationship, and this allows love to continue to flow between people. Sustaining, however, needs to give way to healing when we love those who are wounded. The wounded in our day are those who have inherited characteristics of a painful nature, such as anxiety or depression, and those who have been brought up in a neglecting or rejecting environment. The lover becomes the person who offers a second opportunity, a second chance, to the wounded person – who thereby discovers for the first time what it feels like to be acknowledged, wanted and appreciated. In our classic understanding, the incarnate Jesus has given humanity a second chance to redeem us from original sin. Within the framework of this acceptance, the wounded acquire a new experience of themselves. They learn for the first time, in adulthood, what they missed in childhood. This new experience, which is like therapeutic healing, can be compared to spiritual rebirth:

> 'Rabbi, we know that you have come from God as a teacher; for no one could perform the signs that you do unless God were with him.' Jesus answered:
>> 'In all truth I tell you,
>> no one can see the kingdom of God
>> without being born from above.'
>
> Nicodemus said, 'How can anyone who is already old be born? Is it possible to go back into the womb again and be born?' Jesus replied:
>> 'In all truth I tell you,
>> no one can enter the kingdom of God
>> without being born through water and the Spirit;
>> What is born of human nature is human;
>> what is born of the Spirit is spirit.'
>>   (John 3:2–6)

Psychological healing is the fruit of the positive acquisition of new characteristics and the gradual extinction of undesirable ones. We can facilitate this healing by offering ourselves in loving acceptance of others, by taking the place of the original significant figures who let them down. Again, in classic Christianity, our first parents, Adam and Eve, let us down – and Jesus offers himself as a second chance.

The important point to grasp is that healing is not an intellectual conversion. We cannot heal people by telling them what to do. Emotional healing is the acquisition of loving experiences and the extinction of negative, rejecting ones. Only another human being can do this for us in the here and now. Jesus does. The gospels are full of his healing – it would be laborious to recount the healing miracles here one by one. He cures the psychologically ill (for example, the Gerasene demoniac – Luke 8:26–36) and the physically ill (for example, the crippled woman, who for 18 years was bent double and was quite unable to stand upright – Luke 13:12). In tune with the prevailing beliefs of Jesus' time, both the psychologically and the physically ill were said to be possessed by spirits. We do not have such a vision today, but we can recognise the features of their illness and the healing is no less real. For many, these cures were signs of his divine power, and they were so interpreted by Jesus' contemporaries. Nevertheless, they were not only signs of his power but also of his great love. In curing, he showed that he cared. We have the attitude of care in Mark's account of the healing of skin-disease:

> A man suffering from a virulent skin-disease came to him and pleaded on his knees saying, 'If you are willing, you can cleanse me.' Feeling sorry for him, Jesus stretched out his hand, touched him and said, 'I am willing. Be cleansed.' And at once the skin-disease left him and he was cleansed. (Mark 1:40–42)

To sustaining and healing, we can finally add growth. The first part of this book focuses on human growth and childhood – and we have seen how the baby Jesus became the person who could separate from his earthly parents and identify with his heavenly Father. Growth, however, continues throughout life and is based on our realising our potential. We love our neighbours when we facilitate their growth, in the physical, social and intellectual spheres, to convert the qualities they already possess into something better. More importantly, in the emotional sphere, our capacity to love grows deeper with time, and knows no end. The idea of growth is inherent in the life of Jesus. We see in Luke how the child Jesus 'grew to maturity, he was filled with wisdom, God's favour was with him' (Luke 2:40).

Jesus not only grew from childhood to adulthood, but became aware of his relationship with his heavenly Father (John's gospel gives us many insights into this, as we saw in Chapter 12). Jesus certainly grew in himself, but his task was to facilitate the growth of his disciples in understanding the kingdom of God. This was the kingdom where the love of God brought forth a new era. The disciples, despite being privileged members of Jesus' inner group, were slow to develop under-standing and insight: when he was arrested, they deserted him. Growth is, however, an idea of which Jesus was aware in his teaching:

> He also said, 'What can we say that the kingdom [of God] is like? What parable can we find for it? It is like a mustard seed which, at the time of its sowing, is the smallest of all the seeds on earth. Yet once it is sown it grows into the biggest shrub of them all and puts

out big branches so that the birds of the air can shelter in its shade.' (Mark 4:30–32)

In this parable, we see Jesus grasping the idea of growth. In Luke, we find a concept of the final product of the true disciple's growth of faith:

'Why do you call me, "Lord, Lord," and not do what I say? Everyone who comes to me and listens to my words and acts on them – I will show you what such a person is like. Such a person is like the man who, when he built a house, dug, and dug deep, and laid the foundations on rock; when the river was in flood it bore down on that house but could not shake it, it was so well built. But someone who listens and does nothing is like the man who built a house on soil, with no foundations; as soon as the river bore down on it, it collapsed and what a ruin that house became!' (Luke 6:46–9)

In this chapter we have seen how love of self is a prerequisite for loving availability to love our neighbour. This love of neighbour is seen in listening, empathising and being non-judgemental. This is the immediate reaction to another. Continuity, reliability and predictability are needed as the long-term infrastructure for love; within this infrastructure, love is specifically found in sustaining, healing and growth. We have also seen how Jesus demonstrated all these characteristics. In this abundant love, which was not circumscribed by these features alone, he inaugurated the kingdom of love which continues to this very day.

VI

Kingdom and Personality

20

The Kingdom of God

Having been baptised, tested in the desert and having chosen his inner group of twelve disciples, Jesus was ready to carry out his main task, which was to proclaim the kingdom of God, or heaven, which he inaugurated. There is no definition of the kingdom in the gospels. We would not expect one, as they are not scientific documents. The kingdom is the initiation of an era which is the culmination of the Old Testament and the start of the new covenant. In the new covenant, the reign of God will be supreme. This is what the Law and the prophets anticipated. It was a reign of justice, peace and, as we have seen in the last three chapters, above all of love.

Jesus claimed a close relationship between the kingdom and himself. The Pharisees wanted to know more details about the kingdom:

> Asked by the Pharisees when the kingdom of God was to come, he gave them this answer, 'The coming of the kingdom of God does not admit of observation and there will be no one to say, "Look, it is here! Look, it is there!" For look, the kingdom of God is among you.' (Luke 17:20–21)

The kingdom of God cannot be identified in any one thing; it is a presence – and Jesus is that presence. In keeping with his emphasis on the dynamic, the matters of the heart, Jesus says, '"Set your hearts on his kingdom first, and on God's saving justice, and all these other things will be given to you as well"' (Matt. 6:33). The kingdom of God was Jesus' priority in his preaching, and he talked to the crowds about it: 'But the crowds got to know and they went after him. He made them welcome and talked to them about the kingdom of God; and he cured those who were in need of healing' (Luke 9:11).

Jesus made it clear that the Pharisees whom he addressed were not fully justified, as they thought they were. Nevertheless, he reiterated that he had not come to violate the laws of the Old Testament:

'Therefore, anyone who infringes even one of the least of these commandments and teaches others to do the same will be considered the least in the kingdom of Heaven; but the person who keeps them and teaches them will be considered great in the kingdom of Heaven. For I tell you, if your uprightness does not surpass that of the scribes and the Pharisees, you will never get into the kingdom of Heaven.' (Matt. 5:19–20)

Then there follows Jesus' revision of the commandments, each of which starts with, 'You have heard . . .', and ends with, 'but I say to you . . .'. The kingdom of heaven is linked with Jesus' coming. As we have seen Jesus had the double task of affirming the old and yet proclaiming the new, the kingdom of God. This kingdom was close at hand and was closely associated with what he said and did. The old was superseded by the new. It is clear that the new kingdom of God brought the era of the old rule to an end. The last prophet of the old era was John the Baptist.

The new kingdom was not exclusive to the Jews, like the old covenant. Instead, it was open to those outside Israel, the Gentiles:

'And I tell you that many will come from east and west and sit down with Abraham and Isaac and Jacob at the feast of the kingdom of Heaven; but the children of the kingdom will be thrown into the darkness outside, where there will be weeping and grinding of teeth.' (Matt. 8:11–13)

The will of his heavenly Father was of supreme importance to Jesus, as John's gospel illustrates. Jesus also associated the kingdom with the will of his Father: '"It is not anyone who says to me, 'Lord, Lord,' who will enter the kingdom of Heaven, but the person who does the will of my Father in heaven"' (Matt. 7: 21–2).

Jesus hints strongly that the kingdom of God or heaven is not easy to enter, and he teaches some of the standards that have to be accepted:

'And if your hand should be your downfall, cut it off; it is better for you to enter into life crippled, than to have two hands and go to hell, into the fire that can never be put out. And if your foot should be your downfall, cut it off; it is better for you to enter into life lame, than have two feet and be thrown into hell. And if your eye should be your downfall, tear it out; it is better for you to enter into the kingdom of God with one eye, than to have two eyes and be thrown into hell.' (Mark 9:43–5)

Clearly, Jesus does not ask us literally to cut off hands and feet or to pluck our eyes out – but he does demand very high standards. Without self mutilation, who does Jesus think has the qualifications to enter the kingdom of God? One of the clearest answers is the poor:

Then Jesus said to his disciples, 'In truth I tell you, it is hard for someone rich to enter the kingdom of Heaven. Yes, I tell you again, it is easier for a camel to pass through the eye of a needle than for someone rich to enter the kingdom of Heaven.' (Matt. 19:23–4)

Luke stresses the point even more clearly:

Then [Jesus] said to his host, 'When you give a lunch or a dinner, do not invite your friends or your brothers or your relations or rich neighbours, in case they invite you back and so repay you. No; when you have a party, invite the poor, the crippled, the lame, the blind; then you will be blessed, for they have no means to repay you and so you will be repaid when the upright rise again.' (Luke 14:12–14)

In both these quotations the poor, who are preferred, are the materially poor – but as we have noted elsewhere, there are the materially, socially and emotionally poor. Jesus also includes these other types of poverty: '"In truth I tell you, tax collectors and prostitutes are making their way into the kingdom of God before you"' (Matt. 21:31).

In this kingdom, who is the greatest?

At this time the disciples came to Jesus and said, 'Who is the greatest in the kingdom of Heaven?' So he called a little child to him whom he set among them. Then he said, 'In truth I tell you, unless you change and become like little children you will never enter the kingdom of Heaven. And so, the one who makes himself as little as this child is the greatest in the kingdom of Heaven.' (Matt. 18:1–4)

In this reply we are expected to see the child's lack of status as the characteristic which identifies greatness in the kingdom of heaven.

153

Childhood is (ideally) a time of receptivity, openness, love – and the kingdom of God is a state of receptivity, openness and love to the word of God.

This outline of the kingdom of God was unfolded to the disciples, who had the task of proclaiming it when Jesus completed his earthly life: 'He told them, "To you is granted the secret of the kingdom of God, but to those who are outside everything comes in parables"' (Mark 4:11). Having revealed and lived the kingdom of God in their midst, Jesus, even during his own lifetime, sends the disciples into missionary activity: 'He called the Twelve together and gave them power and authority over all devils and to cure diseases, and he sent them out to proclaim the kingdom of God and to heal' (Luke 9:1–2).

This outline of the kingdom of God (or heaven) is also supplemented by parables which are associated with it. But before looking at these, it is worth summarising the main ideas again. Jesus came to inaugurate the new era, to replace the old with the new, the Old Testament with a new covenant. This new kingdom confirms the past, but sets new standards for the future – and in it, the poor and children will have priority. It was the task of the Messiah to bring this kingdom about. It was not an earthly kingdom but a spiritual one. With it, the Law and the prophets come to an end. The new kingdom was living among people in the presence of Jesus – and it was because the Pharisees did not recognise Jesus for who he was that they were not ready to receive the kingdom.

Jesus not only taught people about the kingdom of God; he also described it in parables – and I shall refer to some of these now. Jesus linked the kingdom of God with himself, and he inaugurated the new era with his life. The new covenant started with him – and so he proclaimed this with the parable of the fig tree:

> And he told them a parable, 'Look at the fig tree and indeed every tree. As soon as you see them bud, you can see for yourselves that summer is now near. So with you when you see these things happening: know that the kingdom of God is near.' (Luke 21:29–31)

The summer symbolises the new era and the budding trees are the signs found in Jesus, anticipating the summer. When the kingdom of God arrives with Jesus, it is a gift that is to be exploited, made full use of. Jesus expects his followers to develop in the kingdom, to realise the God-given gifts, just as he developed to fulfil the expectations of his heavenly Father. The kingdom is not a static entity, but a dynamic one.

In the parable of the talents we have a picture of the kingdom in terms of commercial exploitation. Money is made to grow; the spirituality of the followers of Jesus has to grow:

> 'It [the kingdom] is like a man about to go abroad who summoned his servants and entrusted his property to them. To one he gave five talents, to another two, to a third one, each in proportion to his ability. Then he set out on his journey. The man who had received the five talents promptly went and traded with them and made five more. The man who had received two made two more in the same way. But the man who had received one went off and dug a hole in the ground and hid his master's money. Now a long time afterwards, the master of these servants came back and went through his accounts with them.' (Matt. 25:14–19)

The man with the five talents reported their doubling, and so did the one with two – and both were rewarded. The last one also reported back and returned the one talent: the master was displeased with him and we have the difficult saying of Jesus, '"For to everyone who has will be given more, and he will have more than enough; but anyone who has not, will be deprived even of what he has"' (Matt. 25:29). There are many ways of interpreting this statement but, in the context of the parable as a whole, it may mean that those who are in the kingdom and work at their salvation will profit and develop, while those who remain content to wait and drift will in fact suffer. The whole point of the parable is that the spirit of the kingdom of God is a dynamic, growing enterprise and there is no room for stagnation. The language of the kingdom is growth, and the whole life of Jesus is one of growth of love, culminating in his passion, death and resurrection. (This concern with growth has been seen before in the parable of the mustard seed quoted in the last chapter.)

Jesus knows he is precious and that the era he is starting, the era of the kingdom of God, is precious too, so he compares it to a treasure or a pearl:

> 'The kingdom of Heaven is like a treasure hidden in a field which someone has found; he hides it again, goes off in his joy, sells everything he owns and buys the field.
>
> Again, the kingdom of Heaven is like a merchant looking for fine

pearls; when he finds one of great value he goes and sells everything he owns and buys it'. (Matthew 13:44–6)

The realisation of the goodness of the kingdom is not easy. It is a fight between good and evil. There are obstacles to be overcome. Jesus uses the parable of the darnel to express this tension:

He put another parable before them, 'The kingdom of Heaven may be compared to a man who sowed good seed in his field. While everybody was asleep his enemy came, sowed darnel all among the wheat, and made off. When the new wheat sprouted and ripened, then the darnel appeared as well.' (Matt. 13:24–6)

His workmen pointed out the darnel and asked him whether he wanted it uprooted:

'But he said, "No, because when you weed out the darnel you might pull up the wheat with it. Let them both grow till the harvest; and at the harvest time I shall say to the reapers: First collect the darnel and tie it into bundles to be burnt, then gather the wheat into my barn."' (Matt. 13: 29–30)

Clearly the darnel is the propensity to evil and sin. Jesus makes it repeatedly clear that those who sin will have their reward. The idea of hell-fire is not easy to grasp in our day and time. But, if God is love, we can visualise heaven and hell as proximity and distance from love. It was the same in the life of Jesus: those who understood the kingdom of God and practised its demands rejoiced in the warmth of Jesus' love; the rest were cut off.

What is the nature of the ruler of the kingdom of God? What can we expect from God? We see in the life of Jesus love, healing and compassion – but Jesus also gives an example of God's unprecedented generosity in the parable of the labourers in the vineyard. (Matthew 20:1–16). The a landowner hires labourers for his vineyard at different times of the day, from morning to evening, and at the end of the day he pays them all the same amount. Those who have worked all day naturally grumble, but the landlord persists. Without doing an injustice to anyone, he is generous to a fault.

Again, as with the darnel in the field of wheat, there are tensions – and the generosity of God must not be presumed upon. In another parable, the kingdom of God is compared to a wedding feast in which those who were invited would not come. This is usually taken as a reference to the Jews who proved unworthy – and so the king invited all and sundry to the feast. But one person came without a wedding garment, and he was rejected (Matthew 22:1–14). This parable suggests many things. The people of Israel, the chosen ones, were not really worthy to enter the kingdom of God. They had rejected Jesus, and with him the kingdom of God. So Jesus invited the outsiders. But they too must not presume on their good fortune: they had to fulfil the exacting requirements of the kingdom. Their admittance did not excuse them from fulfilling the obligations.

This chapter on the kingdom of God has reflected on the fulfilment of the old and the start of the new. The new widened the horizons – and all people are now invited to enter the kingdom, not just the people of Israel. This new era is ushered in with the life of Jesus, who heals and cures the sick, acknowledges and rehabilitates the marginalised, and proclaims a kingdom of love. In the next three chapters, we shall see in three concrete areas what this means: in relationship, sexuality and anxiety.

21

Relationship

THE INNER LIFE OF Jesus, and his relationship with his heavenly Father, are a means of throwing light on the kingdom of God which he inaugurated. In John's gospel, in the prayer of Jesus after the Last Supper, he describes his intimate relationship with the Father:

> 'May they all be one,
> just as, Father, you are in me and I am in you.'
>
> (John 17:21)

> 'All I have is yours
> And all you have is mine.'
>
> (John 17:10)

In these and other passages, Jesus' oneness with the Father is asserted. He also claims that the relationship of oneness with the Father extends to the Holy Spirit:

> 'But the Paraclete, the Holy Spirit,
> whom the Father will send in my name,
> will teach you everything
> and remind you of all I have said to you.'
>
> (John 14:26)

The Paraclete is the Spirit of truth:

> 'I shall ask the Father,
> and he will give you another Paraclete,
> to be with you for ever,
> the Spirit of truth,
> whom the world can never accept

since it neither sees nor knows him;
but you know him,
because he is with you, he is in you.'
(John 14:16–17)

Jesus, in these discourses, intimates a unique relationship of oneness between himself, the Father and the Holy Spirit:

'When the Paraclete comes,
whom I shall send to you from the Father,
the Spirit of truth who issues from the Father,
he will be my witness.'
(John 15:26)

In the relationship of Father, Son and Spirit we have the ultimate revelation of the nature of God. Just as John says in his first epistle that God is love, so we can say with equal veracity that God is relationship, a dynamic reality. Jesus was aware that his identity was embedded in relationship and the heart of this relationship is love, which he commands us to have for each other.

God's very life, which is a relationship of love, is lived out by us, by persons who love and exist together in communion. This is what we are meant to experience in the economy of creation and salvation.

If the centre of living is relationships of love which reflect the very life of God, then Jesus could be expected to proclaim principles which protect these relationships. The first principle is forgiveness: 'Then Peter went up to him and said, "Lord, how often must I forgive my brother if he wrongs me? As often as seven times?" Jesus answered, "Not seven, I tell you, but seventy-seven times."' (Matt. 18:21–2).

This basic concept of forgiveness finds a place in the Lord's Prayer:

'And forgive us our debts,
as we forgive those who are in debt to us.'
(Matt. 6:12)

'Yes, if you forgive others their failings, your heavenly Father will forgive you yours; but if you do not forgive others, your Father will not forgive your failings either.'
(Matt. 6:14–15)

Love can be defined as staying in relationship, and forgiveness is an essential component of staying in relationship.

Before the need of forgiveness comes the avoidance of conflict. Jesus proclaims a kingdom of peace, not of conflict and war. The insistence is always on an interpersonal relationship of love – in the community, between peoples and between nations. And so Jesus has a powerful inclination towards peace. In Matthew, where he is setting higher standards than those prescribed by the scribes and Pharisees, he says:

> 'You have heard how it was said to our ancestors, You shall not kill; and if anyone does kill, he must answer for it before the court. But I say this to you, anyone who is angry with a brother will answer for it before the court; anyone who calls a brother "Fool" will answer for it before the Sanhedrin; and anyone who calls him "Traitor" will answer for it in hell fire. So then, if you are bringing your offering to the altar and there remember that your brother has something against you, leave your offering before the altar, go and be reconciled with your brother first, and then come back and present your offering. Come to terms with your opponent in good time while you are still on the way to the court with him, or he may hand you over to the judge and the judge to the officer, and you will be thrown into prison. In truth I tell you, you will not get out till you have paid the last penny.' (Matt. 5:21–6)

In this passage Jesus teaches that, not only must we forgive, but we must also not provoke our neighbour. The requirements of love are extremely stringent. We also find that we not only have to forgive those close to us, but also our enemies.

This sets standards which few people find possible to maintain. And yet the sequence of thinking in this chapter is that Jesus revealed the inner identity of God to be three persons who are in the unity of love. There are no limits to that love.

Jesus knew that love himself, and testified to it by his death. He made good his promise to forgive his enemies when he forgave them at his crucifixion: 'When they reached the place called The Skull, there they crucified him and the two criminals, one on his right, the other on his left. Jesus said, "Father, forgive them; they do not know what they are doing"' (Luke 23:33–4).

Jesus Christ was the culmination of God's reign. He was the fulfilment of the kingdom of God he had proclaimed. He not only announced God's rule: he himself lived it, embodied it, and therefore was the criterion for the conclusion we draw about God's life. In his relationship of love, we find Jesus portraying the very centre of what God's life is like. He had the difficult task of persuading his apostles and the wider public that he was the Son of the Father and that he and the Father together would send the Spirit.

This harmony of love is what we Christians are expected to live out – in our relationships, friendships and marriages. Whatever breaks up relationships, alienation in all forms, is contrary to the reign of God. In some Churches a simplistic view is proclaimed that the Christian life is essentially obeying rules. It is clear, in Jesus' revelation of the inner life of God, that it is not obedience but relationship and love which should be the central ingredients. God's very life, lived out by persons who love and exist together in communion, is what we experience in the economy of creation and salvation. Entering into divine life is therefore impossible unless we also enter into a life of love and communion with others.

Jesus' revelation of the life of the Trinity reveals a life of communion among equals, not the primacy of one over another. Equality and love are the hallmarks of the reign of God inaugurated by Jesus Christ. This equality, embedded in love, is what Jesus proclaimed in John's gospel:

'You are my friends,
if you do what I command you.
I shall no longer call you servants,
because a servant does not know
his master's business;
I call you friends,
because I have made known to you,
everything I have learnt from my Father.'

(John 15:14–15)

In his revelation of the inner world of God, Jesus does not tell us about power, vengeance, punishment – but about love. In this love, he knew himself to be recognised, wanted, appreciated and unconditionally accepted by his Father. It was this acceptance that made it possible for him to persevere in the face of opposition, ridicule, rejection. All the time he knew that his Father and the Spirit of truth confirmed what he said and did – but as he proclaimed the world of loving relationships, the indifference shown to him by his own Jewish people must have hurt him a great deal.

He longed to be the vine, and to facilitate the branches to bear fruit. He did not rejoice in the rejection he received, which necessitated cutting away the branches that bore no fruit (John 15:1). He yearned to be the good shepherd, who went after the one sheep that got lost. The love, which he received in abundance from the trinitarian unity of Father and Spirit, he poured into us. What is the ultimate object of this love? The ultimate purpose of that love is peace:

'Peace I bequeath to you,
my own peace I give you,
a peace which the word cannot give, this is my gift to you.'
                                                        (John 14:27)

The world longs for peace. In all our relationships, we long for peace – and the nations spend billions on keeping the peace and trying to give it to other people. One look at the world at any time in history tells us how hard it is to obtain and maintain that peace. Breakdown of friendship, breakdown of personal relationships, conflict between parents and their children, divorce, enmity – all remind us how difficult it is to preserve peace.

In addition to relationship and love, peace is another quality of the inner life of the Godhead. Jesus revealed in his own life the necessary ingredients of avoiding conflict, forgiving friends and enemies, loving one another as the criteria for that peace. It has to be emphasised that this peace is not only external but internal. The peace that Jesus bequeaths brings harmony to the inner person in relationship to themself and to others. Peace and love of others reflect particularly the relationship we have with the opposite sex, with whom we must co-operate to establish families, have children, nurture them and carry on the work of the creator. In the next chapter we shall look at Jesus' own sexuality and his relationship with women.

22

Sexuality

It is commonly believed that all 'sexuality' comprises an erotic attraction to the opposite sex (or, in the case of homosexuality, to the same sex). This is far from the case. In the development of sexuality, three components are involved – infantile sexuality, emotional development and sexual development at puberty.

Firstly, there is the Freudian concept of infantile sexuality. As we have seen (Chapter 4) Freud postulated three zones of infantile erotic stimulation: the oral zones comprising the lips and the mouth; the anal zone, where the mucous membrane of the anus is also sensitive to touch and is associated with pleasurable sensations; and finally, there is an infantile genital arousal, in which Freud suggested that the resolution of the Oedipus complex allows the boy to withdraw from mother and identify with the father, and in a similar manner the girl with her mother. There is no reason to believe that Jesus was not subject to this infantile sexual development. The social and cultural divide of 2000 years does not change the basic psychological contours of human development.

Most people would, if they accept this infantile sexuality, jump next to puberty. This would be a mistake. We do not relate sexually solely in erotic genital encounters. Mostly we relate sexually to other persons whom we love, and so there is a second personal dimension of sexual interplay, the emotional relationship with other people.

We have seen the details of this development in Chapters 4–9. Sufficient to say here that, in order to form a loving relationship, we need to have an affective attachment – a bond of affection, tenderness and care – and to feel this for the other person. Within the context of this affective attachment (which we make through vision, sound, touch and smell), Erikson's sense of trust, established in the first year of our life, becomes vital. In order to love, we need to feel safe, to trust the other and ourselves. This first year of life, also needs a certain amount of separation, of space between 'me' and the 'other', in order to love. There has to be a separate self which donates itself to another and reciprocally receives the other back. This space between people begins with the autonomy of the child at aged two and three, but proceeds to complete separation at adolescence. It is two separate individuals who are attracted by one another, and the people in every loving relationship need to give space to each other. We find Jesus going off from time to time to pray in lonely places. He needed closeness with others, but he also required his own space for himself.

An affective attachment of care, affection, tenderness and trust leads to a relationship of love which requires intimacy and separateness. Within this bond we have seen that the opposite side of love is conflict – and the sequence of conflict, anger, forgiveness, reconciliation are part and parcel of loving encounters.

By about the age of four or five, the child – and later the grown up person – feels recognised, wanted and appreciated, which gives rise to self esteem. Feeling recognised, wanted and appreciated exclusively means feeling loved. All these components of affective attachment – trust, autonomy, intimacy and separateness, self esteem – are the elements of personal love which give us all a secure basis from which to love and to be loved. The work that is being done by thousands of therapists and counsellors all over the world is an attempt to heal the wounds inflicted in personal development in childhood, which cause adults to have difficulty in donating, registering and sustaining love. We see in the development of the human being the personal – the second dimension which goes towards sexual love.

The third aspect of sexual love occurs at puberty, when the secondary sexual characteristics appear. Now the young person separates from parents, roughly at the age of 12, and seeks relationships which are erotically grounded, with persons from outside the family. This is the sexual attraction of adults which ultimately leads to sexual bonding, marriage and the family.

We thus see that sexuality is a triple entity of infantile components, interpersonal encounters of loving attraction and erotic orientation, leading ultimately to sexual intercourse. As we have seen, there is no reason to question that Jesus possessed the components of infantile sexuality. What we have to ask is whether he had the capacity to love and be sexually aroused. We have had occasion to see that Jesus loved one of his disciples in a special way (Chapter 15). In this chapter we are looking additionally at Jesus' loving encounter with another man – Lazarus, whom Jesus raised from the dead – and with his two sisters, Mary and Martha. We are told in John's gospel that Jesus loved these two women (John 11:5–6). The same qualities that I described in Chapter 15 above, between Jesus and the beloved disciple, which pertain to love for a man, apply to women as well. We can presume that Jesus found Mary and Martha attractive personalities with whom he savoured closeness.

We can establish with some certainty that Jesus had close personal relationships with women. In extending the evidence for this beyond Mary and Martha, we can quote his intimate and personal encounter with a Samaritan woman. Their conversation veers from the personal to the spiritual:

> On the way he came to the Samaritan town called Sychar near the land that Jacob gave to his son Joseph. Jacob's well was there and Jesus, tired by the journey, sat down by the well. It was about the sixth hour [noon]. When a Samaritan woman came to draw water, Jesus said to her, 'Give me something to drink.' His disciples had gone into the town to buy food. The Samaritan woman said to him, 'You are a Jew. How is it you ask me, a Samaritan, for something to drink?' – Jews, of course, do not associate with Samaritans. Jesus replied to her:
>
> 'If you only knew what God is offering
> and who it is that is saying to you,
> "Give me something to drink,"
> you would have been the one to ask,
> and he would have given you living water.'
>
> 'You have no bucket, sir,' she answered, 'and the well is deep: how do you get this living water? Are you a greater man than our father Jacob, who gave us this well and drank from it himself with his sons and cattle?' Jesus replied:
>
> 'Whoever drinks this water
> will be thirsty again:
> but no one who drinks the water that I shall give
> will ever be thirsty again:
> the water that I shall give

will become a spring of water within, welling up for eternal
life.'

'Sir,' said the woman, 'give me some of that water, so that I may
never be thirsty or come here again to draw water.' 'Go and call
your husband,' said Jesus to her, 'and come back here.' The woman
answered, 'I have no husband.' Jesus said to her, 'You are right to
say, "I have no husband": for although you have had five, the one
you now have is not your husband. You spoke the truth there.' 'I
see you are a prophet, sir,' said the woman. 'Our fathers wor-
shipped on this mountain, though you say that Jerusalem is the
place where one ought to worship'. Jesus said:

'Believe me, woman, the hour is coming,

when you will worship the Father

neither on this mountain nor in Jerusalem.

You worship what you do not know;

We worship what we do know;

for salvation comes from the Jews.

But the hour is coming – indeed is already here –

when true worshippers will worship the Father in spirit and
truth:

that is the kind of worshipper

the Father seeks.

God is spirit,

and those who worship

must worship in spirit and truth.'

The woman said to him, 'I know that Messiah – that is, Christ – is
coming; and when he comes he will explain everything.' Jesus said,
'That is who I am, I who speak to you.' (John 4:5–26)

This was a remarkable encounter in which Jesus revealed himself to a
woman, a Samaritan at that – anticipating his revelation to the women
after the resurrection – and he showed his inner knowledge of her five
husbands. The meeting was unusual, and surprised the disciples when
they came back to find him talking to her.

We have seen that Jesus is very likely to have had the experience of
infantile sexuality, that he had the capacity to love both men and
women, to care for, and to have intimate encounters with, both. In other
words, two of my three components of sexuality were likely to have
been fulfilled in Jesus' life. The third is sexual, erotic arousal itself.

What do we know about Jesus' erotic arousal? We know nothing directly from the gospels, but it is very likely that, as part of his normal development, he was capable of appreciating female beauty and being aroused by it. While we have no record of such an occurrence, we have no reason to doubt the development of this normal human capacity.

We do have indirect evidence that he was aware of sexual arousal. In his teachings comparing the old with the new standards, he had this say: ' "You have heard how it was said, You shall not commit adultery. But I say this to you, if a man looks at a woman lustfully, he has already committed adultery with her in his heart" ' (Matt. 5:27–8). It is probable that, when Jesus taught this view of erotic arousal, he knew within himself what it implied. In keeping with the integrity of relationships described in the last chapter, Jesus forbade here the lustful look – that is, looking at a woman as an object to be desired and not as a whole person to be related to in love. Jesus further knew about prostitution and adultery, in that he dined with prostitutes and met adulterers (for example, the woman taken in adultery, described in John's gospel). Jesus was no sexual innocent. He knew about sexual reality, but he was no prude.

Nevertheless, we have no evidence that he had sexual intercourse and it is generally believed that he did not marry. It is no use speculating why he did not marry. We have already seen the unlikelihood of his being a homosexual. In my view, it would have been incompatible for a man – the Son of God, who came to make himself available to all – to confine himself to one other person. But he did not object to marriage – indeed, as we have seen, he graced the wedding at Cana with his presence and carried out there, according to John, his first miracle of transforming water into wine. He also had some stringent remarks to make about divorce. Divorce was not part of God's plan for men and women:

'It has also been said, Anyone who divorces his wife must give her a writ of dismissal. But I say this to you, everyone who divorces his wife, except for the case of an illicit marriage, makes her an adulteress; and anyone who marries a divorced woman commits adultery.' (Matt. 5:31–2)

Jesus goes back to the original status of marriage as it was from the beginning, and puts the woman on the same footing as the man. This is an example of an equal, egalitarian relationship, which stems from the equal, egalitarian relationship of the Trinity. Jesus goes further than protecting the integrity of marriage; he also has a place in the kingdom for the single state:

> But he replied, 'It is not everyone who can accept what I have said, but only those to whom it is granted. There are eunuchs born so from their mother's womb, there are eunuchs made so by human agency and there are eunuchs who have made themselves so for the kingdom of heaven. Let anyone accept this who can.' (Matt. 19:11–12)

Jesus accepted the single state, but this was not because he had no erotic feelings, or, as far we know, because he despised marriage and the family. Indeed, as a Jew, he would normally undertake both marriage and having a family in the normal course of events. Our conviction that he had no objection to intimacy with women is shown in the episode of the anointing at Bethany:

> Six days before the Passover, Jesus went to Bethany, where Lazarus was, whom he had raised from the dead. They gave a dinner for him there; Martha waited on him and Lazarus was amongst those at the table. Mary brought in a pound of very costly ointment, pure nard, and with it anointed the feet of Jesus, wiping them with her hair; the house was filled with the scent of the ointment. (John 12:1–3)

Later in the passage, Jesus defended Mary from the criticism of her action and approved of it. In the process of this anointing Jesus let himself be touched in an intimate way – he did not shrink from this. I have already presented evidence that Jesus had a comfortable familiarity with women. We also find that women, contrary to the social customs of the day, formed part of Jesus' entourage:

> Now it happened that after this he made his way through towns and villages preaching and proclaiming the good news of the kingdom of God. With him went the Twelve, as well as certain women who had been cured of evil spirits and ailments: Mary surnamed the Magdalene, from who seven demons had gone out, Joanna the wife of Herod's steward Chuza, Susanna, and many others who provided for them out of their own resources. (Luke 8:1–3)

Jesus not only allowed women to be part of his inner group of disciples, but he did not discriminate against them, as the above passage shows, in the matter of healing. In Mark, we are told of the cure of Simon's mother-in-law:

> And at once on leaving the synagogue, he went with James and John straight to the house of Simon and Andrew. Now Simon's mother-in-law was in bed and feverish, and at once they told him about her. He went in to her, took her by the hand and helped her up. And the fever left her and she began to serve them. (Mark 1: 29–31)

We see Jesus here curing a woman, not being afraid to touch her and hold her hand. There was no fear in Jesus about contact with women. Another famous cure is that of the woman with the haemorrhage, which is linked with the raising from the dead of Jairus' daughter (Mark 5:21–43). The woman suffering from a haemorrhage, a gynaecological condition, spans the centuries – for countless woman today suffer from similar symptoms. She is said to have had long and painful treatments under various doctors, and had spent a lot of money without improvement. The woman thought that if she could only touch Jesus' cloak she would be cured. She had just the sort of faith that Jesus was looking for: '"My daughter," he said, "your faith has restored you to health; go in peace and be free of your complaint"' (Mark 5:34).

It should be noted that a woman with a haemorrhage was considered ritually unclean. Jesus was not subject to these taboos. Haemorrhage or no haemorrhage, this was a woman who was suffering, and subject to his compassion. This was part of the revolution he brought about. In it, women were treated equally. All the traditional fears of menstruation, haemorrhage and other 'women's issues' were put aside in the kingdom. Other stories of healing included those of the daughter of the Syro-Phoenician woman (Mark 7:24) and the crippled woman in the synagogue who was cured on the Sabbath (Luke 13:10). Jesus not only overcame the taboos surrounding women's issues, but he also healed on the sabbath.

In this chapter we have seen that, by all criteria of sexuality, Jesus appeared normal. He did not marry and, to the astonishment of the disciples, he advocated the single state for the kingdom. Nevertheless, his relationships with women were warm, intimate and compassionate. He allowed himself to be touched by them. He had a good awareness of genitality and eroticism, and expected the latter to be integrated into relationships that were whole and loving. He healed women, overcame the taboos associated with them, and included them in his circle of disciples.

If Jesus were alive today, he would not be astonished by the interest shown in sexuality. He would know that sexuality and eroticism are among the gifts possessed by men and women created in the image of God. He would accept that both were not only good, but very good. If he had anything to criticise, it would be the trivialisation of sex and widespread marital breakdown, both of which concerned him in his own lifetime. He would welcome the emancipation of women which he initiated, and rejoice in its fulfilment in our time. Within the integrity of his humanity, he was perfectly at home in his sexuality, and sanctified it by his presence – as he sanctified the whole of creation.

23

Anxiety

Aɴxɪᴇᴛʏ ɪs ᴀ ᴜɴɪᴠᴇʀsᴀʟ experience. However, it is important to recognise from the start that the anxieties which Jesus wanted to dispel were abnormal ones. There is normal anxiety which acts as a warning system for our survival – and Jesus recommended his disciples to be as cunning as snakes (Matthew 10:16). From the moment we are born, we are subject to anxiety. Bowlby refers to the anxiety of separating from the mother. An infant is anxious when it is away from the side of its mother and is threatened by the presence of unfamiliar adults. Throughout life, we are frightened by the unfamiliar. In our relationship with our parents, we are anxious about displeasing them lest we lose their approval. We feel guilty when we have crossed them. Later on in life, when we have gained our independence and have to rely on ourselves for survival, we are anxious about material and emotional matters. Indeed, as adults we are anxious about material things, our relationships, being rejected and/or abandoned, and ultimately about spiritual things – our survival and our destiny after death.

Throughout history humankind has created gods and goddesses to be propitiated and to provide protection. Jesus refers to anxiety in the kingdom of God. In a remarkable address to his disciples, he elevates the whole anxiety of survival to a matter of trust in the Father:

> Then he said to his disciples, 'That is why I am telling you not to worry about your life and what you have to eat, nor about your body and how you are to clothe it. For life is more than food, and the body more than clothing. Think of the ravens. They do not sow or reap; they have no storehouses and no barns; yet God feeds them. And how much more you are worth than the birds! Can any of you, how ever much you worry, add a single cubit to your

span of life? If a very small thing is beyond your powers, why worry about the rest? Think how the flowers grow; they never have to spin or weave; yet I assure you, not even Solomon in all his royal robes was clothed like one of them. Now if that is how God clothes a flower which is growing wild today and is thrown into the furnace tomorrow, how much more will he look after you, who have so little faith! But you must not set your heart on things to eat and things to drink; nor must you worry. It is the gentiles of this world who set their heart on all these things. Your Father well knows you need them. No; set your hearts on his kingdom, and these others will be given to you as well, There is no need to be afraid, little flock, for it has pleased your Father to give you the kingdom.' (Luke 12:22–32)

Here is a charter for every doctor and every psychiatrist around the world. Millions of people consult their doctors about their health and their survival. Instead of the innumerable prescriptions for tranquillisers, we can listen to the words of Jesus. Note the sentence, '"Can any of you, how ever much you worry, add a single cubit to your span of life?"' Men and women are constantly worried about their survival, and both orthodox medicine and the alternative world of therapies are kept fully busy offering comfort to the worried. These worries are primarily focused on material possessions.

Security for all times, but particularly for old age, haunts Western society, and so we are concerned to amass things for the future. Jesus has a warning about this attitude in life. It is not that he does not want us to be prudent – the story of the ten bridesmaids reminds us of that need. But he warned against the attitude of thinking that material things are the answer to life:

Then he told them a parable, 'There was once a rich man who, having had a good harvest from his land, thought to himself, "What am I to do? I have not enough room to store my crops." Then he said, "This is what I will do; I will pull down my barns and make bigger ones, and store all my grain and my goods in them, and I will say to my soul: My soul, you have plenty of good things laid by for many years to come; take things easy, eat, drink, have a good time." But God said to him, "Fool! This very night the demand will be made for your soul; and this hoard of yours, whose will it be then?" So it is when someone stores up treasure for himself instead of becoming rich in the sight of God.' (Luke 12:16–21)

Jesus warned the crowd against avarice, for life does not consist in possessions (Luke 12:15). There is an intimate link between psychology and spirituality in this teaching. Jesus wanted to direct attention away from the material and from possessions towards an inner world in which his Father was the focus of attention. This is the kingdom of God, in which awareness of God forms the inner riches that we should possess. We have seen how this kingdom is compared to a precious pearl. In the same way, psychology teaches us that peace of mind really comes from a reliance on inner security, inner identity, a sense of reliance on self. There is a world of difference between the external mask, the roles that we play, and inner reliance on ourselves.

Jesus had inner reliance on himself, arising from a mature development, which protected him from anxiety and helped him in his determination to forge ahead with the requirements of the kingdom of God. These requirements challenged the scribes and the Pharisees, astonished the crowds and his disciples, and courted rejection – but Jesus persevered. This is where his inner security as a human being met the certainty of his divinity. Jesus had no home, no visible means of earning a living, no material security – but he did not feel anxious, nor did he survive by using his divine powers and working miracles for his own benefit. The crowds and the disciples were truly astonished. Accustomed as they were to their own insecurities, the calm and outward serenity of Jesus astounded. They could not believe that in Jesus, all anxiety and danger were dissolved:

> It happened that one day he got into a boat with his disciples and said to them, 'Let us cross over to the other side of the lake.' So they set out, and as they sailed he fell asleep. When a squall of wind came down on the lake the boat starting shipping water and they found themselves in danger. So they went to rouse him saying, 'Master! Master! We are lost!' Then he woke up and rebuked the wind and the rough water; and they subsided and it was calm again. He said to them, 'Where is your faith?' They were awestruck and astounded and said to one another, 'Who can this be, that gives orders even to winds and waves and they obey him?' (Luke 8:22–5)

Although the disciples were familiar with the boat, they nevertheless grew anxious – indeed, they panicked. They were under the impression that they would drown. So they woke up Jesus and sought his help, and he carried out the miracle of calming the elements. Once again, Jesus challenged the disciples regarding their faith. Despite the fact that they lived with him every day and saw all he did, at the first sign of real danger they were frightened. It is reassuring for us, 2000 years later, that the disciples were not immune to anxiety, despite the presence of Jesus in their midst. He persevered in teaching that, in the kingdom of God, anxiety was neutralised by faith – and, after the resurrection and Pentecost, the disciples were transformed to that faith.

In the mean time the disciples remained unsure. It is in John's gospel that Jesus pursues his teaching of trust. He himself trusted the Father: he placed himself physically, emotionally and spiritually totally in the hands of his Father. He invited the disciples to trust him in the same way:

> 'Do not let your hearts be troubled.
> You trust in God, trust also in me.
> In my Father's house there are many places to live in;
> Otherwise I would have told you.'
>
> (John 14:1–2)

These words are said in the context of Jesus' pending departure and death, before his passion. They illustrate, however, the triangular relationship between himself, his Father and the disciples. A new era of the kingdom of God was being instituted, in which the absence of anxiety that exists between Father and Son would also prevail.

It is very hard to get a true perspective on what Jesus is saying about anxiety. The need for anxiety about survival – physical, emotional and spiritual – disappears, if we have the faith to believe in the Trinity which Jesus revealed. It is not that Jesus removes our burden of working for our upkeep, loving our neighbour or preserving our relationships. But Jesus is giving us the assurance that, provided we do our part and leave the rest to his care, we will not be overwhelmed. Above all, with his death and resurrection, he reveals that death is not the end of our life.

So much anxiety is caused because we do not know what the future holds for us. Jesus revealed that the future is a Father who loves us.

He experienced and lived his whole life to demonstrate this. In his own life, he overcame his own anxieties with the serenity and peace of mind that came from the knowledge that he and his heavenly Father were united in being one. John's gospel reminds us that at no time did Jesus feel alone, except on the cross. He was in the constant company of his Father, who gave him sufficient meaning to negotiate his human anxieties. A particular uncertainty remained – and he had to ask the apostles who people thought he was. It was Peter who gave the decisive answer.

Jesus lived his life in a combination of human fullness and divine certainty which helped him to overcome his anxieties. He wanted to share with us these characteristics by proclaiming the kingdom. In this kingdom, the presence of God joins human endeavours to overcome anxiety in every possible way. Jesus' human integrity was lived in the harmony of the kingdom, with the certainty that this spans this life and the next. The life he inaugurated for us is an introduction to that kingdom, and anxiety in all forms is a disturbance quelled by faith.

Finally, in the kingdom we can have the assurance that the Father knows what we need, and we can have the confidence to ask for it:

> 'In your prayers do not babble as the gentiles do, for they think that by using many words they will make themselves heard. Do not be like them; your Father knows what you need before you ask him. So you should pray like this:
> Our Father in heaven,
> may your name be held holy,
> your kingdom come,
> your will be done,
> on earth as in heaven.
> Give us today our daily bread,
> and forgive us our debts,
> as we have forgiven those who are in debt to us.
> And do not put us to the test,
> but save us from the Evil One.'
> (Matt. 6:7–13)

In this classic prayer, Jesus teaches us to have the confidence to ask the Father for our basic needs – for 'bread' is more than bread. It is the totality of our requirements. It is significant that Jesus instructed the disciples to pray in the context of the kingdom. It is within the kingdom that God's power is released to allow his creativity to come into operation. Jesus contained the kingdom within himself, and with that power he overcame the anxieties of this world and ushered in a unique peace with which he wished to endow us.

24

Identity

IN AD 325 THE COUNCIL OF Nicaea solemnly defined the divinity of Jesus, and in AD 451 the council of Chalcedon solemnly defined his full humanity in everything except sin. Jesus was true God and true man, and ever since these definitions there has been a tendency to underplay one or other of his natures. The real task is to reconcile the two in a living person – and that is what I have tried to do in this book. The psychological reality must have been difficult, and yet we find no evidence in the gospels that Jesus led a schizophrenic life. He did not show a split personality. His human actions were spontaneous and not overruled by divine intervention. Indeed, Jesus was very reluctant to invoke divine powers to make his case. He wanted assent through faith, not through fear. He did not wish the disciples and the crowds to be cowed into submission by his total reality.

As we have seen, Jesus affirmed the past, but at the same time changed it, and in the process inaugurated a new era. Very early on his duality of affirmation and inauguration was shown – for instance in the episode in the Temple when he was a lad of 12. By this young age, and probably even earlier, he had realised that he had a special relationship with God – possibly he knew that he was the Son of God.

The gospel of John emphasises this Father–Son relationship and this has been spelt out in various passages I have quoted previously. He knew he was Son and yet, even with God, he developed his independence. The sense of the Trinity, which took some time to develop in Christianity, was clear within Jesus himself. He knew that he came from the Father, he had that sense of oneness with him, and yet he was a separate person. His life was his own. He was no puppet. He owned his life and he freely chose to lay it down. Within the mystery of Father and Son, there was unity and yet separateness. The unity was expressed in the kingdom he inaugurated; the separateness in the freedom he chose to express in his own actions. His actions were focused on the will of God, but they were his own. Timing, planning, execution, were his free choices.

It is difficult to express in words this unity with the Father, and simultaneously the separateness. Jesus did not do the will of God by merely repeating the divine reality. Although one with the Father and the Spirit, he nevertheless had a distinct role to play, just as the other two had their independent parts. We see the Father in the Son, but we also see the Father through the distinctiveness of the Son; and part of that distinctiveness also lay in the human features that made Jesus unique.

We do not know how extravert or introvert he was. We do not know how quickly his anger arose – all we know is that he was capable of being angry. We know that he had a loving and compassionate nature. We know that he experienced anxiety in his agony in the garden. We have no idea how much he ate, but we know he was sensitive to the hunger needs of others. We do not know whether he experienced any erotic sensations, but we do know that he was aware of them – and so on.

In other words, Jesus was not only the Son of his heavenly Father; he was also distinct as a person in the fullness of his humanity. If we just describe Jesus as an exceptional human being, we lose the intimate link with his divinity. If we concentrate on his divinity, we lose the exceptional quality of his humanity. It was the combination of the two that he sustained in his life – and the point I want to stress is that, in the gospels, he took it for granted that he had these two natures; indeed, an element of the psychological genius of his personality was that he handled both parts in such a way that both his natures were effective without one or the other dominating. When we come to consider the resurrection, I will be suggesting that Jesus was complete in that unique state because he had been at home in the unusual combination of divinity and humanity. In other words, the extraordinary became ordinary for him.

Nevertheless, the ordinary was present – and he wanted to know what people made of him. He knew within himself who he was. He needed to know how he came across, whether he had succeeded in communicating this dual message of his reality. And so he asked: '"Who do people say the Son of man is?"' (Matt. 16:14). Clearly he knew who he was, and, when he heard the correct reply from Peter – '"You are the Christ, the Son of the living God"' – he was then able to affirm Peter.

Theologians have spent a great deal of time trying to elucidate Jesus' identity from the titles found in the gospels. These titles include 'Son of man', 'Son of God', 'King of the Jews', 'Messiah', 'the Holy One of God' – and so on. This is properly the work of exegesis. In this chapter I shall confine myself to the words and actions of Jesus and enquire, psychologically, how he felt doing miracles and proclaiming new teaching. I am concerned here with his deeds and his words. Raymond E. Brown says: 'When he spoke of God's kingly rule, he spoke with originality. This was his *métier* and he brooked no opposition'.[1]

He could forgive sins. Jesus knew that the Pharisees thought he was blaspheming and yet he says, '"Which is easier: to say, 'Your sins are forgiven,' or to say, 'Get up and walk'?"' (Matt. 9:5). But to prove his point, he helped the paralytic to take up his bed and go off home. Jesus knew that he was forgiving sins, that he had control where only God ruled. As he forgave the sins of the man and proved this in the reality of his cure, he must have experienced a unique sense of power. At that moment, I suggest that he had at least two feelings: a sense of divine power and a great joy that he had released the man from the power of evil.

We know that Jesus inaugurated the kingly rule of his Father – but in addition he found the delight of the divine in restoring humanity to its pristine state. Forgiveness, as we have seen, is a condition of restoring relationships to their original state of love. In this miracle, and others, Jesus was aware that he was inaugurating the kingdom of God which was loosening humanity from the grip of evil. His joy did not lie in the extraordinariness of his power: this he took for granted. His joy was in the outcome of restoring integrity, and seeing in humans the image of God.

I am suggesting that his satisfaction lay in restoring things to how they were from the beginning. He experienced himself not as a magician, but as a restorer of integrity. And so in his battle with the Pharisees, he must have been particularly frustrated at having to answer the 'How' of his deeds: they were mainly concerned with the fact that he had no right to heal or forgive, because these were the actions of God. Jesus knew that he had that power. This was no news to him. What was exciting was to see the power of God in action, restoring integrity to humanity. He took pleasure in his miracles because his mercy, compassion, love, came into operation. These were divine qualities.

In Matthew 5, we have a lot of sayings in which Jesus altered the traditional teaching of the Law: in addition to the prohibition on killing, he insisted on the injunction not to be angry; in addition to the prohibition on adultery, he inserted the instruction to avoid lustful looks; in addition to the prohibition on breaking oaths, he insisted on not swearing at all. He recommended putting up no resistance to the wicked, but offering the other cheek. Finally, he taught that we are to love our enemies.

All this is summed up in the view that there are no bounds to love. Did Jesus know that he was love itself? These teachings would have been impossible if he had not experienced within himself a dimension of love which was absolute in its nature. It is not enough to avoid killing: love of neighbour demands that we should not be destructively angry. Jesus realised that destructive anger was highly injurious to one's neighbour. In the course of his life, Jesus must have known that, although he experienced ordinary anger, he never wished to destroy another person. At the heart of his being vibrated the love of creation, not destruction. In that energy he rejoiced, just as with the miracles, in the experience of all creative deeds. In teaching such peace, Jesus knew that he was instituting an era of mutual love – and, in the process, he must have felt the depth of that love itself. As we have seen, Jesus was aware of sexuality – but sexuality to him was more than taking pleasure, more than procreation. It was an interpersonal encounter. In the beauty of a person he saw the beauty of God, which was to be celebrated, not exploited. I have indicated that he himself enjoyed the appearance and the love of women, and he understood that appearance and love with intense integrity. He wanted to convey that sex was a precious gift of God which, combined with love, was intensely human and which belonged properly to creation.

What he taught, he experienced within himself. He rejoiced in all creation, and the man–woman relationship was the pinnacle of his Father's love for humankind. He enjoyed this pinnacle in his own life, and he transmitted that integrity to us. His teaching was not an idiosyncratic version of the truth: rather, he experienced the truth of original creation within himself, and the power of his teaching depended on the fact that he knew within himself the veracity of pre-sinful creation. He saw things as his Father did, in their original intention, before sin had distorted them.

In telling his followers to offer the other cheek, and to love their enemies, Jesus announced the supreme law of love. As with his other teachings, he experienced this love within himself, and the veracity of this instruction sprang from how he could see human beings reacting to one another. He himself was going to forgive his enemies from the cross. Love penetrated deep into his nature and, because he experienced its depth in himself, he could enunciate it for all. The kingdom was a kingdom of love.

It was this love that made him change the rule on divorce. Jesus altered the law of Moses radically, and prohibited divorce. He had such a sense of the original justice that should prevail between men and women that he safeguarded the women of his day by banning divorce. In this prohibition, Jesus reached the depth of his being and felt revulsion against such an injustice to women. He protected them, not by trivial but by radical changes. He must have felt clear, not so much about the Law, but about the radical injustice of divorce in his day which allowed the man to put his wife away. It must have taken enormous courage to change the Law of Moses. He did not hesitate – not only because he knew that an injustice was being perpetrated against women, but because, embedded within himself, was his sense of the integrity of personal relationships.

Jesus did not alter things because he was a ruler who had come to change and modify laws. He was not a new broom with an agenda of change. His alterations reflected the depths of his own being. In what he did, Jesus expressed outwardly his inner world. He introduced in his teaching the inner manifestations of his being.

In Chapter 16, we saw that, in Jesus' controversies with the Pharisees, he defined his personality. Here, I am suggesting that his inner world, as experienced by him, defined his deeds and actions. The loving way in which he cured and taught demonstrated his utter conviction that love was his nature. He saw in his miracles and what he taught the expression of his love, and his actions reassured him that the kingdom of God was safe in his hands.

He not only healed and changed the Law, but he also challenged the proprieties of the day. He broke the rules of the sabbath, the purity laws and ate with tax collectors and prostitutes. Jesus did not break these rules to attract attention to himself as an innovator. He broke

them because people are more important than rules, and love is infinitely more precious than ostracisms. He had enough confidence in
himself to break these rules in order to draw attention to the fact that,
in the kingdom, it is people that matter – and love for one another is
supreme. In this respect, he was changing the social order of his day.
The fact that he took on society was not because he wanted a social
revolution but, as in everything, he wanted to penetrate society with
the creative originality of pristine nature.

He lived within himself justice, peace, love, compassion – and his
actions did not originate in just the social or psychological dimension
of his personality. He was expressing, in his deeds and actions, the full
interiority of his being. There was no division within himself between
good and bad. His humanity experienced the fullness of intactness
and integrity, and he challenged all actions which contradicted his
interiority. He saw in his deeds and actions a profile of his inner world –
an inner world which was in touch with the creative goodness of his
Father. Jesus restored intactness. Clearly this had to be done by stages.
He healed, taught, changed all, slowly but fundamentally.

The result was that he made his listeners uncomfortable. An essential
part of Jesus' identity was his awareness that he made people
uncomfortable. They could not understand his miracles, which astonished them; some of them could see the hand of God in his actions,
but the social changes disturbed them – as all change disturbs. Even
the apostles did not always fully understand what he was doing and,
in that sense, Jesus must have felt alone. In this aloneness, he had the
comfort of his Father and the inner certainty of his personality for which
he was prepared from his childhood. Nevertheless, he had constantly to
face the tension between his inner certainty and the outward turbulence
he created.

Jesus taught as no other teacher of his time taught. He had an inner
assurance which gave him relentless drive. His identity was the product
of intimacy with his Father, and inner contact with the self that was in
touch with original creation. The creativity of love permeated his whole
being. He saw, in his deeds and words, the fruit of this love – and this
manifestation in turn reassured him that he was taking the right course.

Jesus knew that he was more than a prophet. He acted with the
strength and conviction that he reflected righteousness as the Son of
God – and this gave him the reassurance to persevere. He knew that
his perseverance was full of dangers, and we are told in the gospels

that he warned the disciples of the grievous suffering he was going to experience. In his identity, he intermingled the divine with the human, against a childhood background that had prepared him for integrity in both. He fused them in the pure essence of love. He was now ready to face his last test of suffering and death, which we will tackle in the next chapters.

VII

Endings and Beginnings

25

The Last Supper

Jesus KNEW THAT HIS hour had come. The time of supreme sacrifice and
love had arrived – and at the last meal with his disciples, he did two
things which were the pinnacle of love. First he washed their feet. Jesus
puzzled the disciples to the end: they expected a Messiah of power and
status, instead of which he washed their feet. It is not surprising that
they were taken aback. Instead of being powerful he was humble –
humble, as we know, to the point of death. John's gospel puts the
washing of the feet into perspective: 'Before the festival of the Passover,
Jesus, knowing that his hour had come to pass from this world to the
Father, having loved those who were his in the world, loved them to
the end' (John 13:1).

In this passage the emphasis is not on Jesus as a teacher, healer or
miracle worker, but as a lover. We are told that he loved those who
were his own. The disciples were animated by love, not by theology or
philosophy. They became attached to him as a secure basis in their
life. They not only wondered at the miracles. They were not persuaded
by his logic – indeed, they were even astonished by what he said and
did because they did, not expect it. The real persuasion was that they
felt loved. Love has a unique power which surpasses every other human
experience. The disciples felt that they mattered to him to an unprecedented degree, but they did not expect him to do what he did next:

> They were at supper, and the devil had already put into the mind
> of Judas Iscariot, son of Simon, to betray him. Jesus knew that the
> Father had put everything into his hands, and that he had come
> from God and was returning to God, and he got up from the table,
> removed his outer garments and, taking a towel, wrapped it round
> his waist; he then poured water into a basin and began to wash

the disciples' feet and to wipe them with the towel he was wearing. (John 13:2–5)

We can imagine the surprise of the disciples. The person who controlled the elements, healed the sick, acknowledged the marginalised, forgave sins and offered supreme examples of love was now washing their feet – a menial task which was the work of servants. My hunch is that the disciples did not know what to make of this gesture. The person whom they called 'Lord', behaving as a slave. Their world was turned topsy turvy. For us, Jesus was repeating symbolically what he had taught them repeatedly – that they were to be servants, they were to serve not to gloat in power. This is a lesson the Christian community has not always learnt. From the lowest to the highest, the temptation to turn to power instead of to love has remained. Power demands obedience. Service elicits love. Such was the surprise of the disciples that their leader manifested it in extreme terms:

> He came to Simon Peter, who said to him, 'Lord, are you going to wash my feet?' Jesus answered, 'At the moment you do not know what I am doing, but later you will understand.' 'Never!' said Peter, 'You shall never wash my feet.' Jesus replied, 'If I do not wash you, you can have no share with me.' Simon Peter said, 'Well then, Lord, not only my feet, but my hands and my head as well!' Jesus said, 'No one who has had a bath needs washing, such a person is clean all over. You too are clean, though not all of you are.' He knew who was going to betray him, and that was why he said, 'though not all of you are'. (John 13:6–11)

Peter, who is shown in the gospels to have had intense feelings, could not accept that the person he had declared to be the Christ, the Son of God (Matthew 16:17), should wash his feet. Every atom of his being revolted at such a reversal of roles. Peter lived in the world of hierarchical categories of master and servant. He had not yet grasped that Jesus was pure love and that love was defined by service. Peter may not have understood the symbolic meaning of the action but he grasped clearly the threat of rejection. So he complied. Peter was liable to these extremes of reaction. Jesus had to be very patient with him. Shortly much worse was to come: Peter would betray him. But Jesus persisted. His love would overcome Peter's ambivalence. Peter was all for triumphant gestures indicating might. Jesus was focused on humble actions which were mighty indeed, because they had the explosive power of love. It is vital for us to identify with Peter as we look for certainty in our faith through grand gestures. But the gestures we receive are hidden in the sacraments – and in the most wonderful sacrament of all, love:

> When he had washed their feet and put on his outer garments he again went back to the table. 'Do you understand,' he said, 'what I have done to you? You call me Master and Lord, and rightly; so I am. If I, then, the Lord and Master, have washed your feet, you must wash each other's feet. I have given you an example so that you may copy what I have done to you.
>
> In all truth I tell you,
>
> no servant is greater than his master,
>
> no messenger is greater than the one who sent him.
>
> Now that you know this, blessed are you if you behave accordingly.'
> (John 13:12–17)

In the Jerusalem Bible there is a footnote under the phrase 'you must wash each other's feet'. It says, 'that means, serve one another lovingly with complete humility'.[1]

It is poignant that at this Last Supper Jesus should stress loving service. His whole life was loving service. Now, while he was still with his disciples, he gave them an example which persists to our very day. The trouble with Christianity is that Christians find loving service so hard that they concentrate instead on liturgy and prayer. Not that liturgy and prayer are not crucial – they certainly are. But, if we are not careful, they give us the false security that in them we have done all that is required of us. And loving service is arduous, unceasing, demanding and it penetrates to the roots of our personality. If we are not careful, we can escape to prayer instead of undertaking loving service for our children, spouse, friend – which is infinitely more demanding. Jesus did not escape from the demands of loving service, notwithstanding that he prayed.

We naturally focus on Jesus' physical suffering, but his mental pain was worse. For a being who was love itself to be betrayed by someone he had loved throughout his public ministry was indeed a trial. In the betrayal by Judas, humanity can identify all betrayal that men and women suffer in their lives – parents let down by their children or vice versa, spouses by each other, friends estranged, nations at war. All that human beings undergo, Jesus also experienced – and he too suffered the poignancy of love returned by hatred:

> Jesus was deeply disturbed and declared, 'In all truth I tell you, one of you is going to betray me.' The disciples looked at each other, wondering whom he meant. The disciple Jesus loved was reclining next to Jesus; Simon Peter signed to him and said, 'Ask who it is he means,' so leaning back close to Jesus' chest he said, 'Who is it, Lord?' Jesus answered, 'It is the one to whom I give the piece of bread that I dip in the dish.' And when he had dipped the piece of bread he gave it to Judas son of Simon Iscariot. At that instant, after Judas had taken the bread, Satan entered him. (John 13:21–7)

Even though Jesus knew he was going to be betrayed, his awareness did not remove the pain of the event. The Son of God was deeply disturbed. We can speculate that the reason for the deep disturbance was the depth of his sensitivity. This was not a person accustomed to letting other people down. On the contrary, his nature, which was love, was to understand, empathise, meet the needs of others, heal, complete, forgive, be compassionate. Betrayal was not part of his human repertoire – and yet he had to experience it from one on whom he had bestowed liberally all these positive characteristics. Betrayal was to his humanity what sin was to his divinity – it was foreign and alien. Judas left the room quickly. He could not stand the contradiction within himself. To betray someone who loves you is a contradiction. Judas felt this tension within himself and, in the graphic words of John's gospel, he went out into the night. Night stands for darkness – the opposite of light, life and truth. The night was a suitable place for him to hide himself. Jesus was life, and Judas, who undertook to extinguish that light, was in turn extinguished by the tremendous notoriety of his action. It could be well understood that he was engulfed by despair. Judas experienced total negativity and was opposed by the positiveness of the love of Jesus. It is not surprising that John's gospel says that Satan entered his being. Satan is the apotheosis of negativity, and Judas was saturated by it.

Despite this betrayal, Jesus persisted in his farewell discourse – telling his disciples that love is the supreme criterion of the life of a Christian:

'I give you a new commandment:
love one another;
you must love one another
just as I have loved you.
It is by your love for one another,
that everyone will recognise you
as my disciples.'
(John 13:34–5)

Can Christians really claim that they are recognised by their love for each other? Can they really claim to have spent as much energy in understanding love as they have expended in pursuing obedience or chastity? I have emphasised that Jesus' inner world revolved round love and his relationship with his heavenly Father, which was pure love. It is my contention that the Christian Church has a long way to go to understand the inner world of Jesus, which is a world of love; nor can it do so until it puts love on the map.

Jesus put love on the map by his suffering and death, but before that he did something of uttermost significance at the Last Supper:

Now as they were eating, Jesus took bread, and when he had said the blessing he broke it and gave it to the disciples. 'Take it and eat,' he said, 'this is my body.' Then he took a cup, and when he had given thanks, he handed it to them saying, 'Drink from this, all of you, for this is my blood, the blood of the covenant, poured out for many for the forgiveness of sins.' (Matt. 26:26–8)

This is a crucial event of love which anticipates his suffering and death. The changing of bread into his body and wine into his blood is a transformation of his total personality. No one would dare to do a thing like this unless he had immense trust in his inner world. The Eucharist is a total self donation which reflected Jesus' whole being. It is significant that the event took place in the setting of a meal, which is traditionally an invitation of love to others.

Jesus offers himself and, in the transformation of the bread and wine, we are the recipients of his total maturity, security, love, certainty of his self esteem – the total recognition of himself as a loving person. To this very day the Eucharist, in all Christian communities, tends to be submerged in the liturgical setting of the event – and we miss the depth of loving outpouring.

191

In a previous period, in the Roman Catholic Church in particular, this love was lost in the dual psychological experience of compulsory duty and the fear of missing Mass and committing a sin. Even to this day, many people find this sacrament a ritual which loses its power to portray the outpouring of love it contains. Jesus was pouring himself in the transformation of bread and wine – and all his life, from his birth to his ascension, was condensed in the event. More than that, he lives on now in the Eucharist and he bestows his loving care through it. All that is captured in a few lines of the gospels.

It is possible that the disciples did not appreciate what was happening at the Eucharistic transformation. Jesus' blood is poured out as a covenant, a new covenant, which will hold the people of earth together and cement them in love. And so, in the Last Supper, Jesus brings together a new entity of love – love expressed in service, love expressed in self giving. Jesus wanted to love so much that, before he suffered and died, he wanted to leave a living memorial of himself for all time. This memorial is not a symbol; it is the reality of himself, totally and completely. Psychologically, it is fascinating that the availability of each one of us is constrained by our physical, emotional, social and spiritual limitations. In the Eucharist, Jesus overcomes these limitations, offering himself totally and in his entirety. It is a moment of limitless love – which he expresses in the suffering that is to follow and in the death on the cross. The Eucharist is total availability – and total availability is love without boundaries. With loving service and total availability of love, Jesus has concluded his preparation for being the centre of love. Now he is ready for the physical and mental suffering of his agony – the subject of the next chapter.

26

The Agony in the Garden

AFTER JESUS HAD CHANGED bread and wine into his body and blood, he took his disciples and went to the Mount of Olives:

> Then Jesus said to them, 'You will all fall away from me tonight, for the scripture says: I shall strike the shepherd and the sheep of the flock will be scattered, but after my resurrection I shall go ahead of you to Galilee.' At this, Peter said to him, 'Even if all fall away from you, I will never fall away.' Jesus answered him, 'In truth I tell you, this very night, before the cock crows, you will have disowned me three times.' Peter said to him, 'Even if I have to die with you, I will never disown you.' And all the disciples said the same. (Matt. 26:31–5)

In this passage we see Jesus' awareness of the future. He knew the disciples would be scattered. This foresight did not make it any easier. The divine insight which allowed Jesus to read the future did not lessen the implications of the events that were to follow. On the Mount of Olives Jesus, although surrounded by his disciples, in fact stood alone. Here, the security of his inner world provided him with the strength to face the ordeal that was to come. He wanted support, reassurance and comfort – but, as we shall see, he did not get any of these from his disciples. Indeed, he had to endure the typical compulsive protestation from Peter, who as usual exaggerated. His words, '"I will never fall away"', expressed Peter's conviction that he would persist to the end.

At this moment, we have a contrast between Peter and Jesus: the former, well-meaning, inclined to showmanship, but as yet not having the inner resources to match his aspiration with deeds; the latter, having been prepared from childhood, from the handling of his mother and father, to have a secure base, was facing the future with apprehension but inner certainty:

> Then Jesus came with them to a plot of land called Gethsemane; and he said to his disciples, 'Stay here while I go over there to pray.' He took Peter and the two sons of Zebedee with him. And he began to feel sadness and anguish. (Matt. 26:36–7)

Jesus began to feel sadness and anguish. In the garden of Gethsemane he came face to face with his impending suffering and death. He was alone with his Father. The fact that he was God did not diminish one iota the dread of what was going to happen. Given his acute sensitivity, he anticipated fully the horrors that he was going to face. The words 'sadness and anguish' describe accurately his state. He was sad because he was going to die. Death is the ultimate loss. We lose what we hold most precious – our life. Our life defines our meaning. We are what we are because we live. Jesus was no exception. His life was precious to him: he knew that he was living his last moments, and he was acutely sad. The sadness of the moment led to pain, to anguish. Jesus had a personality that fully relished life.

There are many people who question the meaning and purpose of life, who find consolation in being pragmatic, in making money, in seizing power, in having control over others, in pursuing pleasure. Jesus did not substitute pragmatism for life. Life was synonymous with love. He lived it fully in expressing love fully. Now he was on the fringe of losing it, and he grieved over this loss. In fact, he agonised. In the gospel of Luke we are told that 'his sweat fell to the ground like great drops of blood' (Luke 22:44). The agony which Jesus experienced was both physical and mental. It is at this moment, we realise, that his divine nature and his relationship with his heavenly Father did not spare him from human tribulation. Sweating is a symptom of the autonomic involvement which appears under stress. Jesus, as he anticipated his suffering and death, was under great stress. His whole being revolted at what was to come. His divinity did not remove his pain, and so naturally he looked towards an escape:

> Then he said to them, 'My soul is sorrowful to the point of death. Wait here and stay awake with me.' And going a little further he fell on his face and prayed. 'My Father,' he said, 'If it is possible,

let this cup pass me by. Nevertheless, let it be as you, not I, would
have it.' (Matt. 26:38–9)

The intensity of mental pain which Jesus experienced is dramatically
portrayed in this passage. Such was its intensity that he was prepared
to face the repudiation of his whole purpose by asking that the cup be
taken away. Jesus knew that his mission was to reconcile humankind
to his Father. The price he had to pay was his suffering and death. And
yet the contemplation of this was so excruciating that he was asking
his Father to take it away. For me, this is a moment of profound psychological ambivalence. The Father, whose love was the basis of his life,
was being asked to take away from him his mission. Love and denial
came together at this moment and, psychologically, it is the high-point
of Jesus' vulnerability. His whole life was dedicated to the mission of
salvation – and yet, for a moment, he could not face it.

There was no guilt or recrimination at this point of vulnerability.
Human beings are crucified by remorse at their weakness. This was not
the case with Jesus. He accepted this moment of fragility and, by this
step, he elevated fragility to spiritual respectability. It is perfectly alright
to be weak and fragile. The suffering of this weakness is raised to
an acceptance of ambivalence. In the face of sacrifice, we are often
ambivalent. We want suffering and we do not want it at the same time.
Jesus wanted to please his Father and accept his suffering – and yet at
the same time he wanted to avoid it. In this way he bestowed approval
on uncertainty.

However, Jesus' inner resources of determination and perseverance
allowed him to return to the Father and say, 'Nevertheless, let it be as
you, not I, would have it'. Those who love to portray the significance
of obedience, often infantile obedience, would claim that these words
showed the obedience of Jesus to his Father. I, having fought against
infantile obedience, would rather claim that it is love which is motiv-
ating Jesus to accept the will of his Father. Love is his nature, and it is
love which shapes his behaviour. At this central moment of his life, it
is love which inspires in him the desire to do the will of the Father. So
the ambivalence is resolved in favour of accepting the suffering and the
cross.

He came back to the disciples and he found them sleeping, and he
said to Peter, 'So you had not the strength to stay awake with me

for one hour? Stay awake, and pray not to be put to the test. The spirit is willing enough, but human nature is weak.' (Matt. 26:40–41)

It is important to note that, at this crucial time of his mental agony, the disciples and Peter went to sleep. Peter had recently made the grand gesture of offering to die with Jesus. In fact, he could not even stay awake for an hour. The sleep of Peter and the disciples showed how isolated and lonely Jesus was. He warned that human nature is weak – but we see at this moment how strong he was: 'Again, a second time, he went away and prayed: "My Father," he said, "if this cup cannot pass by, but I must drink it, your will be done."' (Matt. 26:42).

We have here another interval of prayer in which we must assume that Jesus went through, a second time, the ambivalence of acceptance and refusal. Once again, this conflict must have seared his inner being – for what was at stake all the time was his love for his Father. We should remember that his decision was devoid of blind obedience, fear or simply duty. It is clear that he was making a singularly free choice. In this choice, there was no proclivity towards sin or its avoidance, but the energetic pull of love, and love won hands down. It is really the answer to the suffering of the passion and death of Jesus. Suffering there was in plenty. What made it bearable was not some superhuman strength, but the full measure of love. Love for the Father was Jesus' sole strength and, armed with this, he could anticipate what was coming. For human beings, suffering is a severe obstacle. We can face it with stoicism, and, when we cannot endure it, we choose the short cut of ending our life. The age in which we live, which prefers to embrace death rather than life, does not know what to do with suffering. For the Christian, suffering can only have meaning if embraced with love, as Jesus did. Jesus loved life; he was not going to death with any particular joy. The whole episode of Gethsemane shows us how reluctant he was to embrace death. Love for his Father was the only reason he did it:

And he came back again and found them sleeping, their eyes were so heavy. Leaving them there, he went again and prayed again for the third time, repeating the same words. Then he came back to his disciples and said to them, 'You can sleep on now and have your rest. Look, the hour has come when the Son of man is to be betrayed into the hands of sinners. Get up! Let us go! Look, my betrayer is not far away.' (Matt. 26:43–6)

It is my contention that, by the time Jesus told his disciples to get up, he had come to terms within himself, with his agony of suffering. His main battle was not with those who inflicted physical suffering on him. His test was within himself, to accept or reject the suffering, to love or not to love his Father. Once that tension was resolved he was ready for the rest:

> And suddenly while he was speaking, Judas, one of the Twelve, appeared, and with him a large number of men armed with swords and clubs, sent by the chief priests and elders of the people. Now the traitor had arranged a sign with them saying, 'The one I kiss, he is the man. Arrest him.' So he went up to Jesus at once and said, 'Greetings, Rabbi,' and kissed him. (Matt. 26: 47–50)

As Jesus goes on to say, it is interesting that the authorities sent a large number of men armed with swords and clubs to arrest him, although he had spent a long time with the people preaching, teaching and curing. There is a contrast here between the disclosed apprehension of the authorities that Jesus and his disciples would resist arrest, and the calm way in which Jesus accepted it. Indeed, calmness was a strong feature in Jesus' behaviour in face of provocation. He was not taken by surprise. He had known for a long time that this would be the outcome. He had rehearsed the scene in his mind. Nothing took place which surprised him. He was in command of the situation.

Moving on to Judas: clearly the 30 pieces of silver were influential in his act of betrayal – but that is not, psychologically, the important point. What had alienated Judas? He had access to Jesus throughout his whole ministry. It is interesting to speculate that Judas felt challenged by the goodness of Jesus. His master preached peace, love, accepted people unconditionally. It would seem that all this loving behaviour made Judas uncomfortable. It showed him the kind of humanity which he could not match. Instead of admiring it, as the other disciples did, he envied it. He felt that his own emptiness, in comparison, was a staggering criticism of himself.

The religious authorities found Jesus uncomfortable because he was claiming to be the Christ, the Son of God. Judas felt uncomfortable because Jesus, as the Son of God, impinged on him and made him feel inept. This contrast between the challenge of Jesus' goodness and the discomfort felt by Judas is expressed in the act of betrayal. The betrayal was carried out with a kiss, customarily a social greeting – but it is ironic that the sign of friendship was distorted by Judas into a moment of betrayal. Judas was using his intimate relationship with Jesus to identify him but, in the interpersonal exchange, Judas was also transforming the signal of affection into one of hatred. Jesus must have felt betrayed. He was accustomed to betrayal. He was let down by the disciples who could not keep awake. He was soon to be let down by Peter. The difference between Peter and Judas was that Peter betrayed Jesus through human weakness, whereas Judas was (according to my theory) betraying a sacred trust of friendship in the process of revenge. Judas felt that, if he was not good enough to match Jesus' aspirations, he would destroy him and thus eliminate the source of goodness: 'Then they came forward, seized Jesus and arrested him' (Matt. 26:50).

It is interesting to speculate that, at the moment when Jesus was arrested, he was treated as a criminal. Theologians treat the incarnation as the act of atonement for humankind's sins. At the moment of his arrest, the innocence of the man, his reality, was replaced by criminality. It is an aspect of the incarnation in which badness, defect, sin, are reversed by innocence. Jesus was innocent, and yet he submitted to being arrested. He was seized as a criminal and, totally innocent as he was, he accepted the guilt of humankind through the humiliation of his seizure:

> And suddenly, one of the followers of Jesus grasped his sword and drew it; he struck the high priest's servant and cut off his ear. Jesus then said, 'Put your sword back, for all who draw the sword will die by the sword. Or do you think that I cannot appeal to my Father, who would promptly send more than twelve legions of angels to my defence?' (Matt. 26: 51–3)

Jesus had taught the love of enemies. Here, at the moment of his arrest, he had the option to fight – indeed, one of his followers drew his sword. Nevertheless, Jesus resisted this. He put into practice what he preached. He was not going to fight. His resistance was moral. After 2000 years, what remains is not the epic of a battle between Jesus and his opponents, but Jesus' integrity in the face of betrayal and rejection. It is this integrity that endures through the ages. Jesus however makes his point: '"Am I a bandit, that you had to set out to capture me with swords and clubs? I sat teaching in the Temple day after day and you never laid a hand on me"' (Matt. 26:55).

Just as with Judas, the hidden battle with the religious authorities was not that they felt his claim to be the Son of God was unacceptable. The real issue was that his goodness threatened them intensely. He stood for something which they dimly comprehended was divine, and which they could not match – so the way to deal with it was to smother it, to annihilate it. They hoped that, with his death, they would eliminate the moral threat they experienced. He stood for pure love – they felt overwhelmed by it. Against that, they have brought swords and clubs. This is a battle that has raged ever since. Pure goodness is either embraced or attempts are made to annihilate it. It is like dazzling light: it blinds the person.

'Then all the disciples deserted him and ran away' (Matt. 26:56). This a moment of marked emotional distress for Jesus. The disciples, whom he had tenderly nurtured throughout his public ministry, dispersed through fear. All his efforts to engender courage and strength were of no avail at that moment. He understood their weakness – and yet he must have been sad. He stood all alone, with his heavenly Father as his only friend. But the mystery of the incarnation is that, though his Father was a real presence who influenced his total personality, he did not allow that presence to mitigate his pain. Jesus felt deserted. He was alone in a hostile setting.

27

The Trial

> The men who had arrested Jesus led him off to the house of
> Caiaphas the high priest, where the scribes and the elders were
> assembled. Peter followed him at a distance right to the high
> priest's palace, and he went in and sat down with the attendants
> to see what the end would be. (Matt. 26:57–8)

PETER REMAINED CLOSE to Jesus. Matthew portrays Peter's attendance
as a quest of curiosity. Certainly, Peter wanted to know what would
happen to Jesus – but he was also held there by emotional bonds. He
was not only curious, he also cared about Jesus. It is true that shortly
his fear would override his care, but nevertheless he persisted as far
as he could go.

'The chief priests and the whole Sanhedrin were looking for evidence
against Jesus, however false, on which they might have him executed'
(Matt. 26:59–60) – it is clear that the chief priests and the whole
Sanhedrin felt threatened by Jesus. It is interesting that the whole
Jewish race was awaiting the Messiah – and here Jesus claimed to be
the one, backed by unique teaching and miracles, all immersed in the
manifestation of love. The reason that the Jews were blind was not that
they did not welcome the arrival of the Messiah – this they did. But a
Messiah who was pure love made them so uncomfortable that, instead
of embracing him, they wanted to eliminate him. They wanted to
execute him. That was their whole aim. Such a Messiah challenged their
way of life to its very foundations.

The chief priests brought witnesses to confront him, and they asked
him to respond to their accusations. Matthew says that Jesus was silent
(Matthew 26:63). Jesus had said all he needed to say in his daily
teaching. Here, in this trial, he knew that there was going to be no

justice. No one intended there to be a fair hearing, and so Jesus was silent. There is dignity in this silence.

> And the high priest said to him, 'I put you on oath by the living God to tell us if you are the Christ, the Son of God.' Jesus answered him, 'It is you who say it. But, I tell you that from this time onward you will see the Son of man seated at the right hand of the Power and coming on the clouds of heaven.' (Matt. 26:63–4)

The high priest was intent on getting Jesus to admit that he was the Christ. His purpose was to get evidence to execute him. Instead of embracing Jesus' messianic reality with joy, the high priest found that the credentials of Jesus were threatening to the utmost, and the religious authorities wanted him eliminated.

Jesus, when confronted with his very identity, was not silent: ' "It is you who say it" '. With these words, he did not deny that he was the Christ. In Luke, to the question as to whether he was the Christ, he replied, ' "If I tell you, you will not believe, and if I question you, you will not answer" ' (Luke 22:68). Jesus had manifested his identity by his preaching and his deeds. In this quotation from Luke he portrays the uselessness of the proceedings. This was not a fair trial. His judges were deaf to the truth, and Jesus knew this. He knew that whatever he did, he was bound to lose:

> Then the high priest tore his clothes and said, 'He has blasphemed. What need of witnesses have we now? There! You have heard the blasphemy. What is your opinion?' They answered, 'He deserves to die.' (Matt. 26:65–6)

It is not clear what the blasphemy was – but the high priest and the members of the Sanhedrin were not fussy about details: all they wanted was to find an excuse to put him to death.

We should consider here Jesus' state of mind. He knew that his trial was a charade. The man for whom truth was of profound significance – who, indeed, was truth – had to endure a farce. It must have been highly repellent to him. He had to participate in something that was a mockery. He could not withdraw from the proceedings: he could only be silent – except when he had to defend his identity. He knew that the process was false and the conclusion was foregone. His pain was to witness falsehood.

'Then they spat in his face and hit him with their fists; others said as they struck him, "Prophesy to us, Christ! Who hit you then?"' (Matt. 26:67–8). Here we have the first painful evidence of physical maltreatment of Jesus. The physical pain that Jesus suffered was real enough – but the mental trauma was his greatest suffering. His sensitivity was assaulted – and the sense of injustice, knowing who he was and being denied his identity, must have been a nightmare. He came to embrace humanity with his love, and the price he paid for his magnanimity was torture and assault. The supreme quality of his personality was demonstrated in the fact that he knew he was being repudiated unjustly but he did not give up his task.

It would have been easy for him, even at this late stage, to make a public denial of his position. He could have saved himself – not by divine intervention, which would have contravened his humanity, but by being fully human and recognising that he was not accepted. To do this, however, would have meant repudiating all he stood for – and he could not do it. He who had prophesised so much was now being asked to prophesy who had hit him. This was the gap between his reality and their grasp of it.

In the mean time Peter was waiting in the background. 'Meanwhile Peter was sitting outside in the courtyard, and a servant-girl came up to him saying, "You, too, were with Jesus the Galilean." But he denied it in front of them all' (Matt. 26:69–70). Peter denied that he was a disciple of Jesus three times:

> Then he started cursing and swearing, 'I do not know the man.' And at once the cock crowed, and Peter remembered what Jesus said, 'Before the cock crows you will have disowned me three times.' And he went outside and wept bitterly. (Matt. 26:74–5).

Peter recognised that he had betrayed his beloved master. His inner world was intact. This intactness was remorse. There is integrity in genuine remorse, feeling sorry for what we have done. We cannot undo the betrayal – but it can be repudiated psychologically if there remains within ourself a desire for integrity. Forgiveness of others is really a way of giving them a chance to repair the damage they have done. We allow them to resume the relationship of love with us. Forgiveness of ourselves is the resumption of a relationship of love with ourself. Peter wept, and he wept bitterly. He was truly sorry for what he had done, and the relationship would be restored after the resurrection.

Peter's behaviour is to be contrasted with that of Judas:

When he found that Jesus had been condemned, then Judas, his betrayer, was filled with remorse and took the thirty silver pieces back to the priests and the elders saying, 'I have sinned. I have betrayed innocent blood.' They replied, 'What is that to us? That is your concern.' And flinging down the silver pieces in the sanctuary he made off, and went and hanged himself. (Matt. 27:3–5)

Judas also felt remorse. Both Peter and Judas had betrayed Jesus. Why did one reconcile himself to the fact, weep and be ready to pick up the relationship of love again, while the other hanged himself? This is a psychological question. Peter had within himself the remnants of genuine love, not exhausted by his betrayal. His emotional attachment to Jesus stood fast, and so there was a lifeline between them which was not erased by the betrayal. The personality is made up of several layers, and deep inside him Peter had an honest love for Jesus which, although it was temporarily subdued by fear, was not extinguished. The attachment of affection remained.

Judas also felt remorse – but the next layer of his being revealed the enmity, the emptiness, the antipathy, that he felt towards Jesus. It was this antipathy that motivated his betrayal – unlike Peter's betrayal, which was based on fear. Judas could not tolerate Jesus' invocation of love. It was foreign to him. When he recognised his betrayal he had, unlike Peter, nothing to fall back on. The next layer of his being was emptiness. He had nothing to cherish and so his life had no meaning.

Suicide is contemplated when life has no meaning and, above all, when there is no relationship of love to sustain it. Peter, despite his betrayal, still had a relationship of love with Jesus. Judas really had nothing but an inner, meaningless void which overwhelmed him. The void was saturated with guilt, without access to forgiveness of self. In order to extinguish the guilt, he had to extinguish himself. Extinguishing himself seemed to be a positive action. Most suicide victims kill themselves because they see death as a salvific act. The person who kills themself finds it an act of release from the meaninglessness of their life. They have nothing to live for, so death is a logical solution to desolation. Many people who seriously attempt suicide, claim, when their attempt is unsuccessful, that they wanted to die to put an end to their meaninglessness. They could no longer carry the burden of belonging to no one.

Judas had no one to belong to. He had betrayed Jesus. In this betrayal, he perhaps hoped that Jesus would be punished, cut down to size – but he did not expect that they would want to execute him. He had badly miscalculated the consequences of his action. Now he had no one to turn to, and the void within himself overwhelmed him.

Judas and Peter are important prototypes for all of us. Both betrayed Jesus after extended intimacy with him. We too betray Jesus in a variety of ways. Judas felt that there was no way back. For him, the only possible outcome was despair. For Peter, there was a retracing of his steps, remorse and personal reconciliation. That is the way that we have to follow. No matter how often we betray Jesus by not loving, there is always a chance to return to loving him.

The Jews were determined to put Jesus to death. They believed that in this way they would eliminate the problem. So they insisted that Pilate, who had the power to crucify, handled the matter:

> So Pilate came outside to them and said, 'What charge do you bring against this man?' They replied, 'If he were not a criminal, we should not have handed him over to you.' Pilate said, 'Take him yourselves and try him by your own Law.' The Jews answered, 'We are not allowed to put a man to death.'
>
> So Pilate went back into the Praetorium and called Jesus to him and asked him, 'Are you the king of the Jews?' Jesus replied, 'Do you ask this of your own accord, or have others said it to you about me?' Pilate answered, 'Am I a Jew? It is your own people and the chief priests who have handed you over to me: What have you done?' (John 18:29–31, 33–5)

It is interesting that Pilate should seek to find out whether Jesus was king of the Jews. This was a dialogue between a Gentile and a Jew, and the common thread was kingship. The spiritual dimension of the drama being enacted was missed by Pilate:

> Jesus replied, 'Mine is not a kingdom of this world; if my kingdom were of this world, my men would have fought to prevent my being surrendered to the Jews. As it is, my kingdom does not belong here.' (John 18:36–7)

Jesus brought Pilate back to his reality: that his kingdom is not of this world. For the second time, Jesus insisted that, if he had wanted, he could have mustered resources which would have defended him. Be it angels or soldiers, Jesus could have resisted arrest. His destiny, however, was to die – and in this way reconcile humanity to God:

> Pilate said, 'So, then you are a king?' Jesus answered, 'It is you who say that I am a king. I was born for this, I came into this world for this, to bear witness to the truth; and all who are on the side of truth listen to my voice.' (John 18:37)

Jesus' reply was spiritual: he attempted to familiarise Pilate with his mission. Jesus summarised his vocation as a witness to the truth, as a witness to his Father. His extraordinary teaching, his miracles, his rehabilitation of the oppressed, can all be summarised as being the witness to the truth. They are all condensed in one word – love. Just as the Jews could not comprehend the love demonstrated by Jesus, so Pilate finds the word 'truth' incomprehensible – and so he utters the question that has reverberated ever since: '"Truth?" said Pilate. "What is that?"'

The Jewish authorities could not face the religious truth surrounding Jesus; Pilate found in the word a language he did not comprehend. Between them, Jesus stood no chance. And so to our very day, both within the Christian community and outside it, what Jesus stands for is not always clear – and substitutes are imposed. To his credit, Pilate was puzzled but not conned by the Jewish authorities:

> 'I find no case against him. But according to a custom of yours, I should release one prisoner at the Passover; would you like me, then, to release for you the king of the Jews?' At this they shouted, 'Not this man,' they said, 'but Barabbas.' Barabbas was a bandit. (John 18:39–40)

Pilate tried to release Jesus. Such was the enmity of the Jewish authorities – which, in my terms, means their anxiety, their inability to face the truth – that they preferred a bandit. Pilate did not give up. He had Jesus taken away and scourged. Jesus' physical pain continued. The person who had taken pain away from so many, now endured it himself. This was physical pain, and we have to explore, psychologically, what it meant to him.

There is no evidence that Jesus was a masochist. He did not enjoy pain. It was just as unpleasant for him as it had been since the world began to every child, man and woman. Did he accept it with stoical submission? Stoicism has a human point of reference. We have seen

Jesus as someone whose inner psychological world was built on a childhood of security which gave him the utmost tenacity against suffering. Jesus, however, had another point of reference: his Father in heaven. He knew that, in his suffering, he was loving his Father – who accepted it as the means of reconciliation between himself and the world. God the Father was moved by his Son's suffering and Jesus knew that, within this suffering, lay the key to atonement. In no way did Jesus enjoy his suffering – but he made it an offering of love to his Father. Christians can offer their suffering to God as an expression of love. Since the suffering of Jesus, we can ally our suffering with his and in this way endow it with special meaning. Without Jesus, without the Father–Son love relationship, suffering has no ultimate meaning. The world accepts suffering as a warning of something to be eliminated – as in the case of pain, which gives a clue to disease. Pain in itself has no survival value; the secular world has no understanding of what to do with it except to eliminate it – and so there is an ever-increasing demand for euthanasia. Alliance with Jesus gives meaning to suffering as it becomes an offering of love to God the Father.

And so Pilate scourged Jesus and brought him out wearing a crown of thorns and a purple robe. In addition to physical pain, Jesus was humiliated: 'Pilate said, "Here is the man." When they saw him, the chief priests and the guards shouted, "Crucify him! Crucify him!"' (John 19:6). The sight of Jesus must have indeed been pitiful. But nothing moved the hearts of the chief priests.

'When Pilate heard this his fears increased. Re-entering the Praetorium, he said to Jesus, "Where do you come from? But Jesus refused to answer' (John 19:8–9). Jesus' words were few and measured. He did not want to enter into an exchange with Pilate. Neither physical pain nor humiliation were going to make him lose his dignity:

> Pilate then said to him, 'Are you refusing to speak to me? Surely you know I have power to release you and I have power to crucify you?' Jesus replied, 'You would have no power over me at all if it had not been given to you from above; that is why the one who handed me over to you has the greater guilt.' (John 19:10–11)

It is interesting that Jesus returned to the dialogue when he had a chance to reveal his identity. Previously he had acknowledged that he was king; here he made a reference to a power given from above, which was his heavenly Father. In this way Jesus acknowledged that it was only because his Father had given permission that he was in this situation. The world by itself had no power over Jesus. All that he underwent, he did willingly because it was the will of his Father – and the spirit of obedience is love.

Pilate was becoming more and more anxious. It is interesting to speculate that the personality of Jesus must have made a powerful impact on Pilate. His exchanges with Jesus elicited stunning replies. Pilate could see that this was no ordinary criminal. He was familiar with criminals, and Jesus did not fit into the type. So he wanted to release him. His instincts were correct but – like the two other leading characters, Judas and Peter – he was a weak man. When the Jewish authorities threatened him with being an enemy of Caesar if Jesus was freed, he capitulated, and handed him over to be crucified. Pilate must be given full marks for trying. Jesus' destiny was sealed, not by Pilate, not by the Jews, but by the history of salvation and sin. Sin is a denial of love, and perfect love was needed to repair the damage. Jesus was condemned to be crucified, and he was led away.

28

The Crucifixion

When they had reached a place called Golgotha, that is, the place of the skull, they gave him wine to drink mixed with gall, which he tasted but refused to drink. When they had finished crucifying him, they shared out his clothes by casting lots, and then sat down and stayed there keeping guard over him. (Matt. 27:33–6)

JESUS WAS CRUCIFIED as a common criminal. What were his thoughts as he was crucified? Jesus was not puzzled as to how he found himself in this predicament. He knew that the Son of God had to die. Sin is death, death of the soul – and he had to penetrate the very depths of sin to come to terms with it. It was not given to him actually to sin. This he could not do – but he could die. In this way, he could embrace sin without actually sinning. Most people reflect on the physical pain of his crucifixion, which was indeed dreadful. But he had by now come to terms with physical pain: he had been scourged, he had worn a crown of thorns, he had to carry the cross. All this had prepared him for the cruelty of the nails. But the crucifixion was a reality which he had to endure, even though he was totally innocent. This contradiction between innocence and the pain of guilt must have weighed on Jesus' mind. Like everything else, Jesus reconciled the two by accepting them totally with love. This love is shown by his forgiveness of those who accused him and crucified him: 'Jesus said, "Father, forgive them; they do not know what they are doing"' (Luke 23:34).

To the very end, Jesus had the good of others to the forefront. He knew that if those who had done these terrible things to him were confronted with the meaning of their actions, they would have been overwhelmed. So he asked his Father to forgive them in their ignorance. It could be said that all evil acts are done in ignorance because, if people knew the goodness and love of God, they would not commit sin – but God gives us freedom. We may not know the full depth of the meaning of our actions, but we have sufficient freedom to be responsible for them. This responsibility Jesus took on himself. He took our responsibility on the cross, and forgave both our ignorance and our culpability. The balance of the two in each human action is only for God to decide – but the cross makes full reparation, whatever the mixture.

We now have an interesting interlude in the crucifixion narrative. Two criminals were crucified with Jesus:

> One of the criminals hanging there abused him: 'Are you not the Christ? Save yourself and us as well.' But the other spoke up and rebuked him. 'Have you no fear of God at all?' he said. 'You got the same sentence as he did, but in our case we deserved it: we are paying for what we did but this man has done nothing wrong.' Then he said, 'Jesus, remember me when you come into your kingdom.' He answered him, 'In truth I tell you, today you will be with me in paradise.' (Luke 23:39–43)

This incident is interesting for several reasons. One thief recognised Jesus as the Christ and approached him in an opportunistic way. He was asking Jesus to save all three of them. Jesus must have been sorely tempted to come down from the cross. It would have been a terrific miracle. But Jesus knew that, whatever he did, the Jewish authorities would not believe. Only death and resurrection would give the convincing answer. Nevertheless, the temptation to come down from the cross must have been there. The other criminal was also opportunistic – but in a different way. He too knew who Jesus was, and also recognised his innocence. He did not expect to have his life saved miraculously, but he did request his ultimate salvation. Jesus responded positively and movingly to this recognition.

As Jesus hung on the cross the passers-by jeered at him:

> The passers-by jeered at him; they shook their heads and said. 'So you would destroy the Temple and in three days rebuild it! Then save yourself if you are God's son and come down from the cross!' The chief priests with the scribes and the elders mocked him in the same way, with the words, 'He saved others; he cannot save himself. He is the king of Israel; let him come down from the cross now, and we will believe in him. He has put his trust in God; now

let God rescue him if he wants him. For he did say, "I am God's son".' (Matt. 27:39–44)

This was a moment of triumph for the Jewish authorities. The chief priests had achieved what they wanted: they had Jesus on the cross. Throughout his public ministry, Jesus had had the better of them. During this time, all their challenges had been of no avail. He had refuted them all. Now, at last they had pinned him down. He was at their mercy, nailed to the cross, and so they mocked him. This is a common human response, to degrade those who are at your mercy. The chief priests, the scribes and the elders hated Jesus because he was a threat to what they stood for. They stood for a tradition which had placed them in positions of authority, which they felt he wanted to take away. Now they saw their chance to eliminate this danger. It was a moment of triumph to savour.

Jesus knew this. He had voluntarily submitted to the crucifixion. It was his way of pleasing his Father. He knew that, even if he had come down from the cross, it would not have made any difference to the hearts of his accusers, for they were closed to the truth. His main concern, however, was to please his Father whom he loved – and so he endured the mocking. It was an endurance of great tenacity. He knew that he could have come down from the cross, but that would have been a betrayal of love.

Jesus' thoughts on the cross were those of love, as they had been through his life – and so they turned towards his mother. In his public ministry, Jesus seemed to distance himself from his family. His concern was the kingdom of God, the kingdom of his Father. He was concerned with the loving relationships that he wanted everyone to have with his Father. This does not mean that he did not love his mother. So here, at the end of his life, he showed his concern for her:

> Near the cross of Jesus stood his mother and his mother's sister, Mary the wife of Clopas and Mary of Magdala. Seeing his mother and the disciple whom he loved standing near her, Jesus said to his mother, 'Woman, this is your son.' Then to the disciple he said, 'This is your mother.' And from that hour the disciple took her into his home. (John 19:25–7)

This scene reminds us what an important role women played in the life of Jesus, particularly his mother. She, who was his principal nurturer and who had made it possible for him to bear his divinity in his humanity, who had given him the tenacity to endure what he was suffering on the cross, had herself to endure the agony of seeing him suffer. It is not likely that Mary was privy to his resurrection. All that she knew was that she was about to lose her son whom she deeply loved. She probably found it very difficult to make sense of it all. Nevertheless, she remained by his side to the end. Mary is someone with whom we can identify – not in the exaggerated apotheosis that is sometimes given to her, but in the psychological disposition that we too believe but are not sure, we too cannot fully understand where our belief is leading us to. We too hope that our death will be followed by a meaningful after-life, but we are not certain. Mary knew in her heart of hearts that her son's life had profound meaning, but seeing him on the cross must have put doubts in her mind. Was this the tragic end of all his endeavours?

And this must also have been the experience of the beloved disciple. There was genuine love between him and Jesus. Their relationship was more than the devotion of disciple to master. They were dear friends, and the beloved disciple must have been agonising at the foot of the cross. What is so devastating is that we have no evidence of the presence of any of the other disciples. They were truly scattered. Fear was all-pervasive. They were loaded with feelings of fear and despair. Their master was on the cross. Defeat stared them in the face. They had given up everything to follow him, and now he was going to die and desert them. Meaninglessness must have overcome them. For the moment, however, they were too busy hiding in order to survive.

So Jesus, hanging on the cross, was left all alone. He was alone, with the relationship with his Father standing between him and despair – but even this link was tenuous:

> From the sixth hour there was darkness over all the land until the ninth hour. [That is from noon until three o'clock.] At about the ninth hour, Jesus cried out in a loud voice, 'Eli, Eli, lama sabachthani!' That is, 'My God, my God, why have you forsaken me?' (Matt. 27:45–6)

Exegetes have tried to soften these words of despair. I want to treat them at their face value. This is the second time that we have, in the gospels, a threat to the relationship between Father and Son. The first was in the garden of Gethesemane, where Jesus experienced ambivalence in his love. The second was on the cross, where the human side of Jesus faced a total eclipse. It was a moment of profound psychological significance. Jesus did not suffer and experience the crucifixion with his divine nature encouraging him to feel that all this suffering was temporary and was going to be followed by the resurrection. I do not believe that Jesus was thus spared the acute suffering of the cross. His knowledge of the resurrection was there, but it did not mitigate his sacrifice. There was a price to be paid, and Jesus paid it fully. He would have cheated if, at any time, he had allowed himself to be comforted by his divine nature. And so on the cross, it would have been most natural for Jesus to have felt let down. Here, he was tasting his full humanity. He had loved his Father totally, and here he was, hanging as a common criminal, suffering excruciating agonies. He would have been less than human if he had not felt that he deserved better. Jesus died on the cross in a mood of despair. But by this despair, he opened the gates of hope for all of us who come after him. The way in which we die is a mixture of the despair of giving up life, the most precious thing we have, and the hope of gaining eternal life, the most precious aspiration that we possess.

John's gospel tells a different story from the despair of Matthew:

> After this [that is, placing his mother into the care of his beloved disciple], Jesus knew that everything had been completed and, so that the scripture should be completely fulfilled, he said: 'I am thirsty.'
>
> A jar full of sour wine stood there; so, putting a sponge soaked in the wine on a hyssop stick, they held it up to his mouth. After Jesus had taken the wine he said, 'It is fulfilled'; and bowing his head he gave up his spirit. (John 19:28–30)

John's gospel does not portray the despair of Jesus shown by Matthew and Mark. For John, Jesus dies with his work fulfilled. The three gospels have to be taken together. The despair is the human side of Jesus, as he expressed his dread of death; John shows the divine side of Jesus, which tells us of the fulfilment and completion. These two aspects stand side by side and argue, on the one hand, the complete involvement of Jesus in suffering and, on the other, the certainty of the divine plan of the incarnation.

After Jesus' death, John's gospel tells us that Jesus' limbs remained intact – the customary breaking of the legs did not happen. Instead, one of the soldiers pierced his side with a lance – and blood and water poured out. The gospel goes on to say: 'This is the evidence of one who saw it – true evidence, and he knows what he says is true – and he gives it so that you may believe as well.' (John 19:35). This piece of writing strongly reinforces the view that the evangelist was present at the crucifixion.

> They took the body of Jesus and bound it in linen cloths with the spices, following the Jewish burial custom. At the place where he had been crucified there was a garden, and in this garden a new tomb in which no one had yet been buried. Since it was the Jewish Day of Preparation and the tomb was nearby, they laid Jesus there. (John 19:40–42)

Jesus came to this world to reconcile humankind to his Father. The rift was large: sin had torn apart the original unity of God and creation. The remedy needed to be radical. Life, as it was, had to be extinguished, and new, redeemed life had to take its place.

29

The Resurrection

THE DEATH OF JESUS was the return of his being to the Father. He had consummated his existence and, in his death, he gave back to his Father what had been given to him in his life. His death was a thanksgiving – but it was not the end. There was going to be resurrection, the completion of his life. The evidence for the resurrection consists of the empty tomb and the appearances of Jesus to the women and to the disciples:

> After the Sabbath, and towards dawn on the first day of the week, Mary of Magdala and the other Mary went to visit the sepulchre. And suddenly there was a violent earthquake, for an angel of the Lord, descending from heaven, came and rolled away the stone and sat on it. His face was like lightning, his robe white as snow. The guards were so shaken by fear of him that they were like dead men. But the angel spoke; and he said to the women, 'There is no need for you to be afraid. I know you are looking for Jesus, who was crucified. He is not here, for he has risen, as he said he would. Come and see the place where he lay, then go quickly and tell his disciples, "He has risen from the dead and now he is going ahead of you to Galilee; that is where you will see him." Look! I have told you.' Filled with awe and great joy the women came quickly away from the tomb and ran to tell his disciples. (Matt. 28:1–8)

It is interesting that it is women who were privileged to witness the first evidence of Jesus' resurrection, just as Mary and Elizabeth were witnesses to his arrival in the world. In the history of 2000 years of patriarchal ascendancy, with women being in second place, it is good to be reminded that Jesus had no such predilection for the subordination of women. For him, the sexes were of equal value in love, and so women were the first to herald the great event of the resurrection. They were also the first group to whom Jesus appeared:

> And suddenly, coming to meet them, was Jesus. 'Greetings,' he said. And the women came up to him, and clasping his feet, they did him homage. Then Jesus said to them, 'Do not be afraid; go and tell my brothers that they must leave for Galilee; there they will see me.' (Matt. 28:9–10)

In the mean time, the Jewish authorities had the problem of an empty tomb:

> Now while they were on their way, some of the guards went off into the city to tell the chief priests all that had happened. These held a meeting with the elders and, after some discussion, handed a considerable sum of money to the soldiers with these instructions. 'This is what you must say, "His disciples came during the night and stole him away while we were asleep." And should the governor come to hear of this, we undertake to put things right with him ourselves and to see that you do not get into trouble.' So they took the money and carried out their instructions, and to this day that is the story among the Jews. (Matt. 28:11–15)

The story perpetrated by the chief priests does not stand up to examination. If the disciples had stolen the body of Jesus and had known that he had not risen from the dead, it would have been impossible, psychologically, for them to have had the motivation, stamina and endurance to go on and propagate faith in Jesus – and, in some cases, give their life for a cause that had no foundation.

And now we turn to John's gospel:

> Mary was standing outside near the tomb, weeping. Then, as she wept, she stooped to look inside, and saw the two angels in white sitting where the body of Jesus had been, one at the head, the other at the feet. They said, 'Woman, why are you weeping?' 'They have taken my Lord away,' she replied, 'and I do not know where they have put him.' As she said this, she turned round and saw Jesus standing there, though she did not realise that it was Jesus. (John 20:11–15)

It is interesting that, just like the disciples on the road to Emmaus, Mary did not recognise Jesus at first. This speaks of the transformation (described below, pp. 218–19). Jesus was changed in his resurrected body, in a way which made him unrecognisable until he revealed himself. The goodness of his being was now transfixed in his flesh, which bore the imprint of completion.

The orthodox position on Jesus' life, death and resurrection is that he paid the price of Adam's original sin and thus reconciled humankind to God. Another way of describing this sin is to see Adam manifesting in his being a sense of incompletion. Such a view would be in keeping with the Darwinian theory of evolution. In this way, the incarnation could be seen as an act of completion. Jesus finished what God had started in creation. Adam's failure was thus not one of disobedience but one of incompletion. Adam's incompleteness did not give him enough freedom for him to know what he was doing – thus his sin came from his lack of freedom. Jesus lived out, in his incarnation, the perfection of humankind, and he had the freedom to respond to his Father with that perfection. In the resurrected Jesus, human beings had to have the perfection revealed to them – because of themselves, they could not recognise it:

> Jesus said to her, 'Woman, why are you weeping? Who are you looking for?' Supposing him to be the gardener, she said, 'Sir, if you have taken him away, tell me where you have put him, and I will go and remove him.' Jesus said, 'Mary!' She turned round then and said to him in Hebrew, 'Rabbuni!' – which means Master. Jesus said to her, 'Do not cling to me, because I have not yet ascended to the Father. But go and find my brothers, and tell them: I am ascending to my Father and your Father, to my God and your God.' So Mary of Magdala told the disciples, 'I have seen the Lord,' and that he had said these things to her. (John 20:15–18)

Once again Jesus reveals himself to a woman, and it is important to note that she recognised him in an exchange of tender love. Mary was seeking someone she loved and whom she had lost. She was heartbroken. She thought the gardener had shifted the body. Even though Jesus was dead, she wanted to find him and she was weeping. Jesus had to say only her name and she recognised him. In this exchange we see the depth of the personal encounter that Jesus could generate. In one word, he could signify a world of love, because in that one word was contained his whole personality of love.

Jesus told her not to cling to him. The person he must cling to is his Father. It is in the relationship with his Father that Jesus finds his complete identity and, in his moment of triumph, it is to him that he must go.

Now we move to the fascinating incident on the road to Emmaus:

> Now that very same day, two of them were on their way to a village called Emmaus, seven miles from Jerusalem, and they were talking together about all that had happened. And it happened that as they were talking together and discussing it, Jesus himself came up and walked by their side; but their eyes were prevented from recognising him. (Luke 24:13–17)

It is not only the disciples who fail to recognise Jesus. The inability to see him is a question of faith. These two, like the rest of his disciples, were depressed. They had had great hopes in him – but the crucifixion put an end to these. None of the disciples had the faith to believe and expect his resurrection. So they did not recognise him.

> He said to them, 'What are all these things that you are discussing as you walk along?' They stopped, their faces downcast. Then one of them, called Cleopas, answered him, 'You must be the only person staying in Jerusalem who does not know the things that have been happening there these last few days.' He asked, 'What things?' They answered, 'All about Jesus of Nazareth, who showed himself a prophet powerful in action and speech before God and the whole people; and how our chief priests and our leaders handed him over to be sentenced to death, and had him crucified. Our own hope had been that he would be the one to set Israel free. And this is not all: two whole days have now gone by since it all happened; and some women from our group have astounded us: they went to the tomb in the early morning, and when they could not find the body, they came back to tell us they had seen a vision of angels who declared he was alive. Some of our friends went to the tomb and found everything exactly as the women had reported, but of him they saw nothing.' (Luke 24:17–24)

I have quoted this account at length because it reflects the beliefs of those who followed Jesus. They had been impressed by a prophet who was powerful in action and speech. They were mourning the passing of someone who had altered their lives. At the same time, they were puzzled by the report of the women who had found the tomb empty.

They wanted to believe them, but they were not sure. Their hopes were rising but the news was too good. Jesus said to them: '"You foolish men! So slow to believe all that the prophets have said! Was it not necessary that the Christ should suffer before entering into his glory?"' (Luke 24:25–6).

Then he explained to them the passages of the Scriptures about himself. Jesus had to contend continuously with the expectation of his disciples, and indeed, those of the crowds, of a Messiah who would manifest his glory in salvific deeds on behalf of Israel. They did not expect a suffering Messiah, and so they could not believe. Jesus was patient – patient to the point of death, and now patient in his resurrection. He had to explain the Scriptures to them. The infinite patience of Jesus is undoubtedly one of his human characteristics that expressed his divinity:

> When they drew near the village to which they were going, he made as if to go on; but they pressed him to stay with them saying, 'It is nearly evening, and the day is almost over.' So he went in to stay with them. Now while he was with them at table, he took the bread and said the blessing; then he broke it and handed it to them. And their eyes were opened and they recognised him; but he had vanished from their sight. Then they said to each other, 'Did not our hearts burn within us as he talked to us on the road and explained the scriptures to us?' (Luke 24:28–32)

There are two points to be made about this passage. First, this was evening and presumably dusk had set in. Despite the darkness, the scene is one of expectation. Unlike the Last Supper, when Judas went out into the darkness, this darkness is full of hope because the resurrected Jesus is present. The second point is that Jesus says nothing explicitly about himself. The passages of Scripture were indirect. He took the bread, said the blessing, broke it and handed it to them. It is clear that, from the New Testament times, Jesus revealed and gave himself in the Eucharist, as he does to this very day.

And then he vanished from their sight. In the resurrected Jesus, we have to come to terms with a transformed person. The limitations of time and space do not pertain. One moment he was there and the next he was gone. How did Jesus cope with a resurrected being? It seems to me that it came to him very naturally. He had expected the resurrection. He had anticipated the freedom and extension it would give him. As always, he did not use his new powers to melodramatic effect. He took it for granted that he could disappear. He had complete control over nature, and he did not hesitate to use it. He was at home with transcendence, as we all will be at our resurrection. The Emmaus disciples recognised that their hearts had burned within them as they had listened to him. This experience is vital to our understanding of our own experience of having our lives animated by the presence of Jesus, invisible though he might be. He communicates to us through our feelings. We embrace him in our emotions.

John continues in his gospel with the appearance to the disciples: 'In the evening of the same day, the first day of the week, the doors were closed in the room where the disciples were, for fear of the Jews' (John 20:19). The disciples were assembled together behind closed doors because they were frightened. It is remarkable to see how disintegrated the disciples had become through fear. Here is a scene which shows the gap between fallen human nature, or (as I have suggested above) incomplete human nature, and the perfection of the resurrection:

> Jesus came and stood among them. He said to them, 'Peace be with you,' and, after saying this, he showed them his hands and his side. The disciples were filled with joy at seeing the Lord, and he said to them again, 'Peace be with you.' (John 20:19–21)

Jesus clearly demonstrated the reality of his resurrection. He showed them his pierced hands and his side to show that he was the same, real Jesus who had been crucified. As in all his other appearances, Jesus defied the obstacles of ordinariness: the doors were closed, and yet he stood among them. Solidity was no problem to him. But it is important to note that he does not say to them, 'See how clever I am to come in through closed doors'. He took his powers for granted. This was the sign of the resurrected Christ. He took his transformation as given.

Nevertheless it is not the physical that mattered. What he bestowed on them was psychological in nature. It was peace. His peace had the ability to calm all their fears. The disciples were filled with joy. One moment they were in the grip of fear and the next they were overwhelmed with joy:

> After saying this he breathed on them and said:
> 'Receive the Holy Spirit.

219

> If you forgive anyone's sins,
> they are forgiven;
> if you retain anyone's sins,
> they are retained.'
>
> (John 20:22-3)

Then we come to one of the most significant episodes in the history of Jesus' resurrection:

> Thomas, called the Twin, who was one of the Twelve, was not with them when Jesus came. So the other disciples said to him, 'We have seen the Lord,' but he answered, 'Unless I can see the holes that the nails made in his hands and can put my finger into the holes they made and unless I can put my hand into his side, I refuse to believe.' (John 20:24-5)

We all owe Thomas an immense debt because he put into words the eternal doubt of humankind. Thomas was told by his brothers that they had seen the Lord. This, however, did not convince him. He wanted concrete evidence:

> Eight days later the disciples were in the house again and Thomas was with them. The doors were closed, but Jesus came in and stood among them. 'Peace be with you,' he said. Then he spoke to Thomas, 'Put your finger here; look, here are my hands. Give me your hand; put it into my side. Do not be unbelieving anymore but believe.' Thomas replied, 'My Lord and my God!' Jesus said to him:
> 'You believe because you can see me.
> Blessed are those who have not seen and yet believe.'
>
> (John 20:26-9)

Thomas' doubt is our permanent gain. Many Christians would like the certainty of putting their finger in the side of Jesus and into his hands. Thomas replied with that answer that rings through history – 'My Lord and my God' – and we have to believe without seeing; but the authenticity of John's gospel rings true through the centuries. In addition to the empty tomb, the appearances helped the disciples to re-establish their emotional bonds with Jesus. This attachment helped them to internalise his reality, and in this internalisation were the psychological foundations of their faith.

John says that there were many other signs that Jesus worked in the sight of the disciples, although they are not recorded in the gospel. But we are told about one other appearance – Jesus' appearance on the shores of Tiberias.

'Simon Peter said, "I am going fishing." They replied, "We'll come with you". They went out and got into the boat but caught nothing that night' (John 21:3). The emptiness of the catch is going to be contrasted with the fullness that follows when Jesus is present – the fullness of the resurrection. 'When it was already light, there stood Jesus on the shore, though the disciples did not realise that it was Jesus' (John 21:4). Once again the disciples did not recognise Jesus. It is a feature of many of the resurrection appearances that Jesus was not recognised. It is an indication that he was somewhat transformed until he chose to reveal himself:

> Jesus called out, 'Haven't you caught anything, friends?' And when they answered, 'No,' he said, 'Throw the net out to starboard and you'll find something.' So they threw the net out and could not haul it in because of the quantity of fish. (John 21:5–7)

This generous catch reminds us of other miracles in which Jesus offered plenitude, because plenitude was his nature and it is the mark of love: 'The disciple whom Jesus loved, said to Peter, "It is the Lord"' (John 21:7). It takes love to recognise love. The beloved disciple at once recognised the Lord as if there were hidden, unconscious signals of love that were exchanged between them. 'Simon Peter tied his outer garment round him (for he had nothing on) and jumped into the water' (John 21:8).

It is interesting to contrast the love of the beloved apostle and that of Peter. For the beloved disciple, love was intuitive, spontaneous; for Peter, it was a spirit of exuberance. Peter did not so much feel his love as act it out by throwing himself into the water. He yearned to love, but it was somehow out of his reach. He had to work for it – and he did this with an enormous exuberance. His behaviour was exaggerated. The beloved disciple felt his love, but did not have to reach out to grasp it:

> As soon as they came ashore, they saw that there was some bread there and a charcoal fire with fish cooking on it. Jesus said, 'Bring some of the fish you have just caught.' Simon Peter went aboard and dragged the net ashore, full of big fish, one hundred and fifty-three of them; and in spite of there being so many, the net was not

broken. Jesus said to them, 'Come and have breakfast.' None of the disciples were bold enough to ask, 'Who are you?'. They knew quite well it was the Lord. Jesus then stepped forward, took the bread, and gave it to them, and the same with the fish. (John 20:9–14)

This passage is full of details which can only have come from someone who was an eye-witness. It describes accurately the strange relationship of the disciples with the resurrected Jesus. Such was his appearance that they did not dare to question his identity overtly, and yet they knew who he was. This distant recognition appears to me to be a heralding of the sacraments, in which we know that Jesus is present, and yet there is a veil. He is hidden.

When they had eaten, Jesus said to Simon Peter, 'Simon, son of John, do you love me more than these others do?' He answered, 'Yes, Lord, you know I love you.' Jesus said to him, 'Feed my lambs.' (John 21:15–16)

Jesus did not ask Peter whether he believed in him, rather whether he loved him. This is the crucial hallmark of Christianity – the presence of love. And Jesus makes the connection between love and nurture. The Christians who were to emerge after his ascension would be nurturing – that is, loving – and Jesus makes this explicit in this connection between love and nurture. It is not quantities of belief that are central to Christian life, but a life of love and, in this final exchange between Jesus and Peter, it is love that is underlined:

A second time he said to him, 'Simon son of John, do you love me?' He replied, 'Yes, Lord, you know I love you.' Jesus said to him, 'Look after my sheep.' Then he said to him a third time, 'Simon son of John, do you love me?' Peter was hurt that he asked him a third time, 'Do you love me?' and said, 'Lord, you know everything; you know I love you.' Jesus said to him, 'Feed my sheep.' (John 21:16–18)

This triple question reminds us of Peter's triple denial. It is also a reminder of Peter's leadership of the disciples, and of the future flock of the emerging Christians. But the emphasis is not on faith and authority, but on love and care. The principal mark of the institution of the Church is not an emphasis on authority but on love. Jesus makes this amply clear in his whole life, and particularly in this last dialogue between himself and Peter.

'There was much else that Jesus did; if it were written down in detail, I do not suppose the world itself would hold all the books that would be written' (John 21:25). Thus ends this remarkable gospel of John, which has all the marks of being the work of an eye-witness who penetrated to the heart of the mystery of the incarnation.

And so finally to Jesus' last act, the ascension:

> And so the Lord Jesus, after he had spoken to them, was taken up in to heaven; there at the right hand of God he took his place, while they [the disciples], going out, preached everywhere, the Lord working with them and confirming the word by the signs that accompanied it. (Mark 16:19–20)

And so the life of Jesus on earth concluded. But he lives on and, through the pages of the gospels, remains fully alive. In the next and final chapter we will look at the meaning of the incarnation for us today.

30

The Incarnation

THE INCARNATION, the Word taking flesh, is the most important event in human history. It is God taking human form and, in that person, we see the nature of God. That is why understanding the person of Jesus is so important. In the minutiae of his personality, we discover what God is like, and what we have to be to participate in the life of God. Hence the renewed interest in the historical Jesus. At the beginning of this book a warning was given that these historical accounts are heavily laden with the projections of the writers, who in turn reflect their own social, cultural and psychological background – and the results tell us more about them than Jesus. This warning cannot be ignored: C. J. den Heyer, who reviewed many historical accounts of Jesus, ends his book with an unembellished account, which I quote at length to show what a neutral statement about Jesus can be like:

> In the first half of the first century there lived in Galilee a Jew who made history. He answered to the name of Jeshua, but later became known all over the world as Jesus Christ. He came from Nazareth, which at that time was a small unimportant town without traditions or pretensions. Virtually nothing can be said for certain about Jeshua's youth. He grew up as the oldest son of the carpenter Joseph and his wife Miriam/Mary. The family consisted of five sons and an unknown number of daughters. Presumably both parents were sympathetic to the ideal of the Pharisees and brought up their children to be familiar with the Scriptures and to respect the commandments of the Torah.
>
> Joseph practised the trade of a carpenter and, as was usual at that time, Jeshua, as the oldest son, followed in his father's footsteps. He learned the trade of a carpenter from Joseph.

Marriage and a family were held in high regard in the early Jewish tradition. By present-day standards, the age of marriage was particularly low: for girls around their thirteenth or fourteenth year, for young men a few years later. Anyone who was not married by the age of twenty was regarded as rather odd. Parents on both sides played an important role in the arrangement of a marriage. Joseph and Mary, too, will have looked in and around Nazareth for a bride for their oldest son. We do not know whether a marriage ever took place. But something different did happen. At a given moment the life of Jeshua changed decisively. It is not clear precisely when this change took place. Probably it happened somewhere between his twentieth and thirtieth birthday. Then Jeshua left Nazareth and began to lead an itinerant existence. However, he remained in the north of Jewish territory. He preferred to limit himself to the area round the Sea of Galilee. He was regularly seen in some small towns set attractively on the shores of this sea, Magdala and above all Capernaum, and he seems to have had friends and acquaintances who offered him hospitality.

Jeshua very soon attracted public attention. The former carpenter from Nazareth gathered a group of disciples around him, men and women who had come under his spell and were fascinated by his words and the things that he did. Quite often his interpretation of the commandments was surprisingly creative. Moreover he had special powers. He healed the sick and cleansed lepers, and after his intervention evil spirits left their victims in peace. Jeshua was an inspired man, a real charismatic. He also seems to have been a mystic. For him the God of Israel was not far away. He experienced this God as a reality in his own life. Jeshua felt a deep spiritual bond with the God who had made himself known to the people of Israel in scripture and tradition and was also now revealing himself to him. Jeshua lived an exemplary life. But he did not just spread joy and happiness. He also caused offence. His piety and loyalty to the commandments of the Torah did not prevent him from seeking the society of people with a less scrupulous lifestyle. He entered into friendships with sinners and publicans. He even ate with them. When asked for an explanation of what in the eyes of the pious was offensive behaviour he said that he had come to seek the lost. Just as a shepherd makes an effort to restore to the flock a sheep that has gone astray, so he was drawn by the lot of people who risked the same fate.

Jeshua's conduct aroused curiosity. Who was he? What could be expected of him? Almost a century earlier, Judea had become part of the Roman empire. This situation left deep marks on society and divided the Jewish population into parties which threatened, hated, and even fought with one another. There was considerable conflict and there were those who even encouraged their supporters to engage in armed resistance to the Romans. They were firmly convinced that God was their ally and would not leave them in the lurch. Others were afraid that rebellion would end in a blood-bath and thought it better to renounce weapons and wait for divine intervention. There were also Jews who collaborated with the Roman forces of occupation. The fanatics regarded them as collaborators, and when they gained the upper hand they took their revenge on them. Jeshua lived in this sharply divided Jewish society. Which side did he take? It is not easy to give a clear answer to this question. He does not seem to have been a hothead, far less a fanatic. Jeshua made it quite clear that he opposed the use of force. He refused to write people off or to vilify them because they adopted different standpoints. He even seems to have been notably forgiving towards tax collectors, who became rich as a result of the unfair Roman system of taxation. In the view of the fanatical Zealots, Jeshua was far too gentle. He was attracted by people's fate, showed little or no interest in political questions.

Jeshua was cautious and restrained. He seldom if ever used big words. He usually rejected the term Messiah. Sometimes he spoke about the coming of the Son of Man, but what he meant by this was vague: himself or someone else? On numerous occasions he pointed to the nearness of the kingdom of God. But even then, his view has an ambiguous character. In general he gives the impression that the kingdom still lies hidden in the (imminent) future. However, on one occasion he seems to suggest that in principle the kingdom of God is already present in this world.

In accord with the commandments, when the annual Passover approached he went to Jerusalem as a pilgrim. When he arrived in the city, the situation became dangerous for him. Remarkably, though a gentle and peaceable man, he now no longer avoided conflict. On the contrary, he deliberately created tensions. He organised an entry into the city, with the result that he invited suspicions of having pretensions to be king. In the Temple he perplexed friend and foe by his unexpected action against the traders present there. His criticism of how things were done recalls some Old Testament prophets. What did Jesus of Nazareth want? On one point at any rate the authorities were clear: he was dangerous and so had to be done away with as quickly as possible. His strange behaviour could inspire others to take action and therefore formed a serious threat in a situation which at best can be described as an armed peace. Jewish leaders and Roman occupation authorities soon got together and entered into a monstrous alliance. In the darkness of night they arrested Jesus, and condemned him to death in a mock trial. The execution took place the very next day and Jeshua died on the cross. Was that the tragic end of a good man? A short time later the mood of his followers changed dramatically. Despite the death of their teacher, their spiritual leader and source of inspiration, they took new courage. They told an amazing story. Some of them had seen Jeshua again alive. They believed that God had raised him from the dead. His followers reported this with so much conviction and joy that others also began to believe. Jeshua is not dead, but alive![1]

This concludes the unembellished account of the life of Jesus. This summary, however, cannot be a sufficient basis to inspire millions of people all over the world. There is a hunger for more, to understand what made this man function – hence the repeated attempts to add flesh to the bones.

In my view, the repeated attempts to reconstruct the historical Jesus have to be taken seriously. Admittedly, there is in part projection from the standpoint of the writer, but increasingly there is also an accumulation of objective, universal truth which stands the scrutiny of time. In this book I have taken dynamic psychology as my background. In the above account, we are told that we know next to nothing about the childhood of Jesus. By contrast, in my account, based on theories of universal validity, I have reconstructed a Jesus whose childhood was a time of interpersonal growth between himself and his parents, which provided the foundation for trust, security, self esteem, and a basis for the growth of love which became the underlying principle of his whole life.

This has enormous implications for us as a community. Childhood is the basis of the maturity of the adult person. Childhood depends, in turn, on family life. The childhood of Jesus should inspire us to help parents and children to grow in the best possible way in order to develop love. It should make us ask whether we Christians have our priorities right, and whether we are focusing correctly in putting our resources primarily into our schools. Perhaps we should be shifting our energies to place our attention on the first dozen years of life, and to helping parents bring up their children in an atmosphere of love.

I have no doubt that the family in which Jesus grew at Nazareth was the foundation for his adult maturity and his capacity to love. It is this maturity and capacity to love which made him what he was. We see in his adult life a plenitude of being – and this plenitude, based on maturity and love, became the foundation on which his divinity rested. He had no problems living as God and man because his humanity had the structure to bear his divinity – and that humanity is something to which we can all aspire, so that we too can be the recipients of the divine image.

There is a danger of creating a historical figure who is so perfect that he is beyond us. In this book, I have stressed both Jesus' maturity and his capacity to love. His capacity to love was the combination of a divine love that penetrated, and was responded to by, human love. This love gave him an immensity of compassion and fullness that allowed him to make room for the integration of the poor, the marginalised, the sick, the possessed. What was lacking in them was brought to wholeness by his abundance of love.

Jesus' love is not, however, so immense that it is beyond us. We too can love to the limits of our capacity, and go on growing in that capacity to love. We have clear instructions that, if we are to remain in Jesus' presence and share his life, we have to love one another. That is the mark of his life and our mark too. In other words, he came to earth to inaugurate the kingdom of God – which is a community of love. In this community of love, the key to life is communion, relationship and love. This love is expressed by care for each other, in which the poor have priority and relationships are egalitarian. Relationship, equality and love are the life of the Trinity, which Jesus came into this world to reveal.

Psychologically, Jesus was able to put into operation this pattern of relational love because of the fullness of his being. We are incomplete and only partially full. That is what sin is – the partial, the incomplete – and love helps to restore us to the pristine pattern of creativity. In the community of love set up in Jesus' image, there would be no inequality due to race, colour, sex or status. We are all persons equally loved by God, and that must be the pattern of our love for each other. That is why, whenever we move in the direction of egalitarian relationships of love, we move towards the goal set up by Jesus.

When we look at the fruit of the incarnation today, what do we see? How has the Church managed to retain the pristine object of Jesus, the community of love? Not very well. From the time of Constantine, when Christianity amalgamated with the world, we compromised Jesus' model of equality and love with a model based on hierarchy or order, where inequality because of race, colour and sex, and priesthood has taken its place. Women, half of humankind, have suffered at the hands of patriarchy. Children have been abused by their elders. All forms of slavery have existed. The community of love set up by Jesus has been supplanted by a community based on law and hierarchy.

In theology, the intellect has supplanted love as a means of understanding God, and institution has taken over the life of the people of God in the Church. People crave love and compassion and are given law, order and subordination. We have gone severely wrong – far from that ideal community of love set up by Jesus. We have to retrace our steps.

The incarnation came about because Jesus took on our humanity to complete it in love. He did so in his life, death and resurrection – and we have to go on attempting to maintain the model he set up. We can do this in two ways. As far as society is concerned, we have to return to the principles of a community of love – that is, the trinitarian relationship of love which Jesus came to reveal. In this community, egalitarian relationships between men and women, children and parents, persons and persons, have to be restored. All forms of oligarchy and despotism have to give way to egalitarianism.

Within the Church, rules and regulations have to give way to mercy, compassion, care, justice and love. The present model of the Church does not stem from Jesus' community of love but from the worldly pattern of power. Love has to replace power; compassion has to replace fear. There is a need for change in the structure of the Church so that it embodies relationships of love not a hierarchy of power. In its thought, love and compassion have to dictate its conclusions, not logic and reason derived from the Hellenic world.

In the personal life of the Christian, the relationship of love between the child and its parents, husband and wife, and persons within the community, are the key exchanges of love, and these have to be shored up by what we are learning through psychology. We have to return to Jesus' community of love – and only when Christians return to a model which causes people to say, 'Look how they love each other', will they want to embrace us again.

In this book I have attempted to bring out Jesus' life of love – not romantic love, but love as a donation of self to each other. Jesus' upbringing and maturation made him full, and he combined his human fullness with his divine fullness to become unique, really to show us the image of God in himself. We too have to translate this fullness of love in our community, the Church, the people of God – and in our private lives. Jesus revealed that love and communion among persons are the truth of existence, the meaning of our salvation, the overcoming of sin, and the means by which God is praised. That is what incarnation is.

References

PART I: A BACKGROUND

1 The Historical Jesus

1 R. W. Funk, R. W. Hoover and the Jesus Seminar, *The Five Gospels: The Search for the Authentic Words of Jesus*, New York, Macmillan, 1993.
2 M. J. Borg, *Jesus in Contemporary Scholarship*, Pennsylvania, Trinity Press, 1994.
3 G. Vermes, *The Religion of Jesus the Jew*, London, SCM, 1993.
4 A. Schweitzer, *The Quest of the Historical Jesus: A Critical Study of its Progress from Reimorous to Bede*, Introduction by James M. Robinson, New York, Macmillan, 1968 (first published 1906).
5 R. Bultmann, *The History of the Synoptic Tradition*, Oxford, Oxford University Press, 1963 (originally published 1921).
6 Vermes, *The Religion of Jesus the Jew*.
7 Borg, *Jesus in Contemporary Scholarship*.
8 E. P. Sanders, *Jesus and Judaism*, Philadelphia, Fortress Press, 1985.
9 B. Mack, *A Myth of Innocence: Mark and Christian Origins*, Philadelphia, Fortress Press, 1988.
10 E. Schüssler Fiorenza, *In Memory of Her: A Feminist Theological Reconstruction of Christian Origins*, New York, Crossroad, 1983.
11 M. J. Borg, *Conflict, Holiness and Politics in the Teachings of Jesus*, New York/Toronto, Edwin Miller, 1984.
12 R. Horsley, *Sociology and the Jesus Movement*, New York, Crossroad, 1989.
13 J. D. Crossan, *The Historical Jesus*, Edinburgh, T. & T. Clark, 1991.

2 The Gospels

1 C. F. D. Moule, *The Birth of the New Testament*, London, Adam & Charles Black, 1981.

3 Psychiatry and Psychology

1 H. J. Eysenck, *The Biological Basis of Personality*, Illinois, Springfield, 1967.

PART II: PSYCHOLOGICAL THEORIES

5 Melanie Klein (1882–1960)
1 M. Klein and J. Riviere, *Love, Hate and Reparation*, London, The Hogarth Press and The Institute of Psychoanalysis, 1967.

7 John Bowlby (1907–90)
1 J. Bowlby, *Attachment and Loss*, Vol. 1, *Attachment* (1969); Vol. 2 *Separation, Anxiety and Anger* (1973); Vol. 3, *Loss, Sadness and Depression* (1980); London, Hogarth Press and The Institute of Psychoanalysis.
2 J. Bowlby, *The Making and Breaking of Affectional Bonds*, London, Tavistock Publications, 1979.

8 Erik H. Erikson (1902–94)
1 E. H. Erikson, *Identity, Youth and Crisis*, London, Faber & Faber, 1968.
2 ibid.

PART III: FAMILY RELATIONSHIPS

11 Jesus and his Father
1 F. Dreyfus, *Did Jesus Know he was God?* Cork, Mercier Press, 1991.

12 Jesus and his Heavenly Father
1 F. Dreyfus, *Did Jesus Know he was God?*, Cork, Mercier Press, 1991.
2 R. E. Brown, *An Introduction to New Testament Christology*, London, Geoffrey Chapman, 1994.

PART IV: SIGNIFICANT PEOPLE AND EVENTS

13 John the Baptist and the Baptism of Jesus
1 The New Jerusalem Bible, London, Darton, Longman & Todd, 1985.
2 ibid.

14 The Temptation in the Desert
1 R. E. Brown *et al* (eds), *The New Jerome Biblical Commentary*, London, Geoffrey Chapman, 1990.

PART V: LOVE

17 The Centrality of Love
1 C. H. Dodd, *The Founder of Christianity*, London, Fontana, 1973.
2 ibid.

References

3 V. P. Furnish, *The Love Command in the New Testament*, London, SCM, 1973.
4 The New Jerusalem Bible, London, Darton, Longman & Todd, 1985.

PART VI: KINGDOM AND PERSONALITY

24 Identity
1 R. E. Brown, *An Introduction to New Testament Christology*, London, Geoffrey Chapman, 1994.

PART VII: ENDINGS AND BEGINNINGS

25 The Last Supper
1 The New Jerusalem Bible, London, Darton, Longman & Todd, 1985.

30 The Incarnation
1 C. J. den Heyer, *Jesus Matters*, London, SCM Press, 1996.

Index